Boundaries of Love

Interracial Marriage and the Meaning of Race

Chinyere K. Osuji

NEW YORK UNIVERSITY PRESS

New York

NEW YORK UNIVERSITY PRESS
New York
www.nyupress.org

References to Internet websites (URLs) were accurate at the time of writing. Neither the author nor New York University Press is responsible for URLs that may have expired or changed since the manuscript was prepared.

Library of Congress Cataloging-in-Publication Data
Names: Osuji, Chinyere K., author.
Title: Boundaries of love : interracial marriage and the meaning of race / Chinyere K. Osuji.
Description: New York : New York University Press, [2019] |
Includes bibliographical references and index.
Identifiers: LCCN 2018026990| ISBN 9781479878611 (cl : alk. paper) |
ISBN 9781479831456 (pb : alk. paper)
Subjects: LCSH: Interracial marriage—United States—Case studies. | Interracial marriage—Brazil—Case studies. | Racially mixed families—United States—Case studies. | Racially mixed families—Brazil—Case studies.
Classification: LCC HQ1031 .O79 2019 | DDC 306.84/50973—dc23
LC record available at https://lccn.loc.gov/2018026990

New York University Press books are printed on acid-free paper, and their binding materials are chosen for strength and durability. We strive to use environmentally responsible suppliers and materials to the greatest extent possible in publishing our books.

Manufactured in the United States of America

10 9 8 7 6 5 4 3 2 1

Also available as an ebook

To Ndidi and Kemdi Joshua Osuji,
I love and cherish you both

CONTENTS

PREFACE

Amid the swirl of lawsuits challenging affirmative action policy in universities in the United States in the early 2000s, Brazilian universities had decided to implement a quota system for Brazilians who were poor or who were Afro-Brazilian. Why was the United States dismantling policies to increase diversity in higher education at the same time that Brazil was creating them?

I had never been to Brazil. I spoke Spanish fluently and knew a smidgen of French and Catalan but no Portuguese. Many questioned why I wanted to look south instead of eastward to study black people since my parents emigrated from Nigeria. However, I was interested in the African diaspora. Since Brazil received thirteen times more enslaved Africans than the United States, it became the obvious site for developing this research interest. A year later, I moved to Los Angeles to work under Edward Telles at UCLA. Moving from Chicago, I was surprised by the number of interracial couples that I saw in West Los Angeles. I noticed a gender imbalance with many black men who seemed to exclusively date nonblack women and several white men doing the same with Asian women. My black girlfriends and I commented on how rare it was to see black–black couples or black women paired off with anyone in Los Angeles. We joked that Los Angeles was a city where if you were a black woman, it was BYOM: Bring Your Own Man. A friend who was originally from Los Angeles mentioned that to see couples involving both black men and women, I had to go to South Los Angeles or other neighborhoods far from the west side, where UCLA was located.

I did an exchange with the US-Brazil Consortium in which I spent two months in Brazil doing an internship with the Geledés Institute of the Black Woman (*Instituto da Mulher Negra*), a black feminist NGO (nongovernmental organization). Coming from Los Angeles, I was struck by the homogeneity of the couples in São Paulo. Given Brazil's status as a society where race mixture was prevalent, I had expected a more random color assortment of couples. However, I had seen more interracial couples in affluent Westwood, next to wealthy Bel Air, than I did in Jardins, a well-to-do neighborhood in São Paulo! There, couples largely shared the same skin tone, from the darkest to the lightest. I saw far more cross-color or interracial couples in Los Angeles than I had in São Paulo!

Living in Jardins, most people looked like they were solely descendants of Italian and Portuguese immigrants. Those who had my dark-brown skin were often domestics, chauffeurs, garbage collectors, and security guards. I stood out less in predominantly white West Los Angeles than in Jardins. In addition, notwithstanding the large proportion of Asians in São Paulo, I rarely saw them interracially partnered off, if I saw them at all in Jardins. Despite moving to a country where whites only made up half of the population, and in a city where Afro-Brazilians were approximately 35 percent of the population, in São Paulo, I lived in a predominantly white world. With most Afro-Brazilians relegated to the lowest rungs of the socioeconomic ladder, class segregation aided the racial segregation that I experienced firsthand.

But this was not supposed to happen. Brazil is a country that has celebrated its history of race mixture and characterized itself as a racial democracy. In this ideology, popularized by Gilberto Freyre, color is not supposed to be an impediment to interpersonal relations.[1] By contrast, preventing relations between black men and white women was part of the justification for de jure racial segregation in the United States. Yet I had seen far more interracial couples in Los Angeles than I had in São Paulo. Something was amiss, and I was determined to find out what it was.

Upon my return to Los Angeles, I decided to do a comparative study of black-white couples in Brazil and the United States, with Rio de Janeiro and Los Angeles as my research sites. Both my dissertation advisor, Edward Telles, and I had many friends and contacts in Rio de Janeiro that could facilitate my research. However, this project has ballooned into something much bigger than the "Search for the Missing Interracial Couples." It is now one of many firsts: It is one of the first studies to compare how both black and white people in Brazil and the United States make meaning of race, ethnicity, and color in their lives. It is also one of the first to take an intersectional approach to understanding these dynamics across societies. It is one of the first cross-national studies of interracial couples and multiracial families. Furthermore, it offers a new approach to understanding the well-known adage that race is a social construction.

Introduction

Race Mixing and Ethnoracial Boundaries

Edward's Story

Edward had never expected to marry a white woman. A dark-skinned black man in his late twenties, Edward said that while he had dated a few white women in the past, his last long-term, serious relationship was with a black woman named Melissa. They had dated in high school back in Washington, DC, where he had grown up and also when he went away to college. When it came to looking at white women romantically, he said, "I saw white women, and to be honest with you, I didn't even look at them in a romantic sense." While there were some "extraordinary" white women who stood out and that Edward would notice, he largely did not think of them that way: "I never said to myself, 'I don't want to date a white woman,' but I just didn't. I was too busy looking for the next black woman, you know?"

Edward saw himself as a bit of a reformed playboy. After Melissa, he dated several women, some at the same time, often without their knowledge. If they found out about it, Edward said that he would "flat-out lie": "So obviously, if you do those sorts of things, you're going to piss some people off. And so, yeah, I had women call me everything, every four-letter word under the sun. . . . I've had a car keyed." Looking back, Edward attributes this behavior to his immaturity at the time. These women included a few whites, with whom, he said, "there was no long-term potential." Edward told me, "I would say this: if you had told me years ago that someday I would be married to a white woman, I would have laughed at you."

But then Edward met Stella. They were both in graduate school and were friendly toward one another. He had always been attracted to her smile: "I thought she was a very warm person. I thought she was a very sort of welcoming person, and I love that about her." One night, they ended up talking for a long time and barely noticed when it started to rain.

He preferred women with Stella's tall, slim physique, although Melissa had not been like that. Yet there was one thing that Stella and Melissa had in common. He said that he knows that he is a tough person to deal with, however: "When I met Stella, she was just, her personality just kind of matched mine." While other women had been "really confrontational, in the sense of . . . calling you out on things," Stella was one of the few women who did not do that. Instead, she "just recognizes my BS for what it is, and it's just BS, and [she] can just sort of bottle it up somewhere and just say, 'That's just Edward.'" Edward said that Melissa, his first serious girlfriend, and Stella, his wife, are the only two women who have ever had that ability in their interactions with him.

Unfortunately, Stella's family did not approve of her relationship with Edward. They refused to speak to her because of her decision to move with him to Los Angeles. Their reaction took a negative toll on Edward. He said, "It was the first significant time in my life where I felt sort of dehumanized." Although Edward had not really thought about interracial relationships until he was in one, his (now) in-laws' reaction showed him "the animosity that a lot of people have towards these sorts of relationships."

Tatiana's Story

I conducted an interview in Rio de Janeiro with Tatiana months after I spoke with Edward. A self-described black woman (*negra*), with dark-brown skin, natural hair, and in her late twenties, Tatiana's first husband, the father of her daughter, was also black (*negro*). Her second husband, Gaspar, is a white man (*branco*). I asked Tatiana if there was a time when she decided to date only white men (*brancos*). She laughed and said, "Yeah, when I separated from [my first husband], me and some friends started a movement." Laughing, she said, "We laugh, but we ourselves don't know if the movement is serious. It's the 'BMANG' movement."

"What's that?" I asked.

"It stands for 'Black Men Are No Good' [*Homem Preto Não Presta*]." In BMANG, Tatiana said, she and some girlfriends at work decided not only to only date whites but to prefer men who were "blond [*loiro*], *gringo*—someone really foreign!" For Tatiana, as for many Latin Americans, the term *gringo* refers to any foreigner, regardless of race, and does not always carry a pejorative connotation. She explained, "I went out for a while with a German guy, so I came to the store [where we worked] and said, 'Look, a German! The movement is strong!'"

Tatiana said that the women's bitter experiences with black men had prompted the "movement." Her ex-husband, Alexandre, would come to the store where she worked and force her and her coworkers to wait on him and his new love interest. Her friend Rosa enjoyed a night of lovemaking with her boyfriend, followed by breakfast in bed in the morning, only to have him break up with her right afterward. Yet another contracted hepatitis from her boyfriend.

Tatiana and Gaspar had been in a band many years ago and had lost touch. They had each married and had other relationships. They ran into each other after a concert and spent the rest of the evening talking, spending the night together. They dated for a month before deciding to move in together. He was not satisfied with cohabitation, so they became official and got married (*casado de papel*).

However, Tatiana said that the "movement" was "a joke" and did not really determine her romantic life. She had dated a black man in the middle of the "movement": "It was one of those things where he arrived, we fell in love, and that was the end of it," she said. However, the other women kicked her out of BMANG until she broke up with him for reasons unrelated to race. Tatiana acknowledges that all the women in BMANG are now married to white men. While Tatiana described the "BMANG movement" as a joke, their "collective action" may have had some effect.

* * *

Like other social boundaries,[1] ethnic and racial boundaries divide "us" from "them" and are a way of creating distinction and order in diverse social spaces. The boundaries are both internally and externally determined, with actors signaling their identification to members and nonmembers of their respective categories.[2] As actors define others in a particular way, conflicts can arise when the imposition of an ethnoracial boundary negatively affects another's social experiences. This was the case for Edward, who saw his in-laws drawing a racial boundary in terms of who their daughter should marry, leaving him feeling othered and, as he said, "dehumanized."

Interacting in close proximity to members of another population does not in and of itself lead to a demise of ethnoracial boundaries.[3] In fact, ethnic and racial distinctions can become heightened *because* of cross-boundary interactions, including interracial marriage. For some couples, ethnic and racial distinctions may be part of the foundation of their relationships.[4] For instance, in Tatiana's BMANG movement, she and her fellow black female coworkers pursued relationships with white men because of racial difference. Since ethnoracial boundaries and categories are both internally and externally determined, analyzing the perceptions of black-white couples shows how they negotiate them in their lives. Rather than being "love's revolution," interracial marriage can serve to reproduce race in unintended yet important ways. They may structure their romantic lives in terms of ethnoracial distinctions; apply ethnoracial meanings to themselves, their partners, and their children; structure their lives around its boundaries, as well as create new meanings and distinctions.

Anthropologist Fredrik Barth theorized on the nature of ethnoracial boundaries. Rather than focusing on the cultural material of different groups, such as the types of foods they eat or rituals in which they participate, Barth emphasized a "constructionist" approach that focused on the ways that people engage in the social construction and reproduction of ethnoracial boundaries.[5] Constructionism addresses the relations between peoples and emphasizes that as social actors, they determine the markers of difference that are salient. They also decide the social norms for how to negotiate those differences. For example, in the United States, language, skin color, and eye shape are a few of the important markers of whether people are on the same or different sides of an ethnoracial boundary. Whether those same characteristics matter to the same extent in a different society like Brazil is a question that *Boundaries of Love* seeks to unpack.

Scholars of ethnicity and nationalism have challenged the essentialization of ethnicity and race by examining the social construction of boundaries between religious, ethnic, and minority groups around the world. They have examined "groupness," the sentiment that members of a social category belong together, even if there is little or no interaction among them.[6] More than just a sense of commonality, groupness reveals how individuals understand their level of connection to other members of an ethnoracial category. It is a characteristic that varies across time and space and cannot be taken for granted in all settings, especially since people who seem to share a category can give different meanings to it and manifest their membership in different ways. Scholars like Livio Sansone and Stanley Bailey have emphasized the lack of groupness among Brazilians within color categories.[7]

In addition, scholars of ethnicity and nationalism have examined how the state creates and counts its populations[8] and the role of public policy on classification.[9] They have also illuminated how and when ethnicity and race matter for relationships in spaces as diverse as social media networks[10] and neighborhoods.[11] There is substantial literature on the fluidity of ethnoracial boundaries in Brazil and Latin America, more broadly, which exposes how factors like class, region, and gender can influence how an individual is classified.[12]

However, these scholars have been overwhelmingly focused on how elites interact with the state on behalf of their ethnoracial constituents. Particularly in post–Atlantic slave trade societies, they have often neglected how nonelites produce and reproduce ethnoracial and national boundaries through social interaction. This includes how everyday people make sense of belonging to ethnoracial categories, interactions with members of other categories, experiencing discrimination, de facto segregation, and family formation—all processes that largely happen away from the purview of the state.

On the other hand, race and ethnicity scholars have largely taken ethnoracial boundaries for granted. One likely reason is the rigidity of ethnoracial boundaries in the United States. Law and public policy have played a major role both historically and in the present era in fortifying ethnoracial boundaries. Both have maintained white supremacy through residential segregation[13] and the denial of citizenship, voting, and marriage rights[14] to prevent people from interacting as equals across ethnoracial categories. While social psychologists have conducted many studies to understand interracial contact,[15] other social scientists have overlooked how nonelite social actors on different sides of an ethnoracial boundary negotiate it through social interaction. As a result, much scholarship on race and ethnicity focuses on the lives of members *within* ethnoracial categories, rather than their interactions with those across them.

Some sociologists have shown how social actors negotiate ethnoracial boundaries in everyday life. This can include reproducing residential segregation through steering potential black homebuyers toward predominantly black neighborhoods.[16] Ethnoracial boundary negotiation has also included less nefarious forms such as: black parents steering their children into elite black social organizations while living in predominantly white neighborhoods,[17] students sanctioning peers when they date ethnoracial others or adopt cultural mannerisms and symbols that do not pertain to their own category,[18] and family formation in which mothers socialize their children into their partners' cultural practices instead of their own.[19] However, discussion of the social construction of ethnoracial categories has largely been absent, and analyses of its boundaries have often been subtle.

When explicitly understanding the construction of ethnoracial boundaries, US scholars of race and ethnicity have focused overwhelmingly on multiracial/biracial[20] or Latinx[21] classifications;[22] the social construction of "mono-racial" categories such as "black" or "white" have been underexamined. In other fields, anthropologists and ethnic-studies scholars have largely focused on the performative elements of blackness and whiteness, especially seen in controversial educational discussions of US black children "acting white."[23]

The ways that race and ethnicity "work" in the United States are not the same the world over. As immigrants bring different meanings attached to race and ethnicity to the United States,[24] a growing number of scholars have shown how immigrants understand US ethnoracial categories and transmit them as "racial remittances"[25] to people in their homelands or make sense of them upon their return.[26] In addition, burgeoning international scholarship by sociologists has compared the meanings of race and nationality for migrants and nonmigrants across Latin America and the Caribbean. Yet how people construct ethnoracial boundaries, often assessed as fluid in the case of Latin America and the Caribbean, is often not a part of their analyses.

Critical Constructionism

Boundaries of Love: Interracial Marriage and the Meaning of Race is novel in placing the ethnoracial boundary at the center of understanding how ethnicity and race operate for black-white couples in the United States and Brazil. However, it goes beyond aforementioned constructionist approaches by drawing on tools from critical race theory (CRT)[27] to explicitly examine how different social categories can work with one another to produce differences in outcomes. CRT grew out of 1980s critical theory in legal scholarship and challenges essentialism by demonstrating how race is made and remade through the law. It also employs "intersectionality," showing how social categories, such as gender and race, can mutually constitute, reinforce, and naturalize one another.[28] This goes beyond a criminal-justice focus and is more than just a critical perspective of race and ethnicity.[29] Critical constructionism stresses the symbolic interactionist elements of ethnoracial boundaries to unpack the meanings that nonelite social actors give to them. *Boundaries of Love* improves on typical US scholarship of race and ethnicity by revealing the intersectionality of race, gender, and education level on people's understandings of an ethnoracial "us" versus "them." It clarifies how, often unwittingly, people recreate ethnoracial boundaries, even as they challenge them.

I employ this critical constructionist approach through examining the boundary negotiation of people in black-white couples in two post–Atlantic slavery societies: the United States and Brazil. *Boundaries of Love* examines how people in two large, diverse, multicultural cities—Los Angeles and Rio de Janeiro—understand and navigate being married to a person with membership in a different category. By adopting a critical constructionist perspective, this book does not take blackness, whiteness, or race mixture for granted. It examines the labels of "black" and "white" for the partners identified as being a black-white couple. It also assesses how nonelites make sense of being a black-white couple in terms of constructing, negotiating, bridging, redrawing, and pushing against ethnoracial boundaries. Rather than focusing on the state or the law, the family is centered as an important site for understanding the social construction of race and ethnicity.

Boundaries of Love compares how people in "black-white" couples negotiate ethnoracial boundaries as they (1) understand their ethnoracial romantic trajectories, (2) classify black spouses, (3) classify white spouses, (4) classify their children, (5) become integrated into white extended families, and (6) spend time as a couple in public. This approach examines the family as a site for interpreting, representing, and explaining racial dynamics as both an antiracist and racist "racial project."[30] *Boundaries of Love* reveals the meaning of race mixture between blacks and whites in discursive practice and how couples' everyday experiences as well as the institutions around them are organized according to contemporary meanings of race mixture in their respective societies. I compare and contrast these meanings in these two societies, revealing that race mixture can reproduce white supremacy in unintended and covert ways.

This book is not about how interracial couples and their families are racist. Instead, *Boundaries of Love* shows how in societies structured by racial hierarchies and inequality, white supremacy can coexist with loving relationships across color. *Boundaries of Love* challenges the naïveté that interracial couples and their children provide an antidote to racism. Rather, it traces the contours of how marriage and the family are central institutions for reproducing race. Nevertheless, *Boundaries of Love* also reveals how these couples challenge notions of black inferiority and white superiority through everyday realities of loving and forming families across ethnoracial boundaries.

Why (Exclusively) Black-White Couples?

Both the United States and Brazil have large populations of people who do not neatly fit into a black-white binary. As a multiracial society, the United States has significant populations of Latinxs, Asians, indigenous peoples, and even multiracials who do not fit neatly into any one racial or ethnic category. Latinxs are the largest minority group in the United States, outnumbering the black population. While the term *Latinx* refers to people with origins in Latin America and the Spanish-speaking Caribbean, it includes people from a variety of national origins, ethnoracial identifications, and communities. As Brazil is the largest country in Latin America, presumably all Brazilians are Latinx.[31] For this reason, including a US-based notion of Latinx intermarriage in this study, such as those involving "non-Hispanic" whites and Latinxs, has no Brazilian equivalent and would be problematic.

Since it was a British colony, black-white relations have been central to US ideologies of race and race mixture; black-white intermarriage has been the most heavily policed in the United States, with every single antimiscegenation law including a stipulation specifically prohibiting them.[32] This is different from Brazil, where race mixture between blacks, whites, and indigenous peoples—whether involving marriage, concubinage, sexual liaisons, or rape—is central to national ideologies of what it means to be Brazilian.[33] This is despite Brazil's significant (yet regionally specific) Japanese, Jewish, and Syrian-Lebanese populations.[34] A substantial proportion of Brazilians understand themselves as *mestiça* or mixed, yet unlike the United States, this does not preclude also having a black or white identity.[35] Despite these differing approaches, in both societies, race relations between blacks and whites were central to ideologies of race and race mixture. *Boundaries of Love* does not purport to examine all the varieties that race mixture can take in the two societies. Nevertheless, focusing specifically on black-white intermarriage illuminates contemporary meanings of one of the most influential forms of race mixture in the two societies.

There is also an implied heteronormativity in discourses of race mixture in the two societies; namely, heterosexual relations are the engine behind race mixture. For this reason, this study focuses exclusively on heterosexual black-white couples in the two settings. However, there is a burgeoning scholarship on how same-sex interracial couples navigate race in their relationships.[36] While these concerns are beyond the scope of *Boundaries of Love*, more studies are necessary to complicate heteronormative discourses of race mixture in the two societies and the social construction of race in everyday life more broadly.

Black-White Race Mixture in the United States and Brazil

The meanings that people attach to ethnoracial boundaries can vary with the cultural repertoires and structural resources of different societies.[37] For this reason, it is important to understand the histories of race mixture in the United States and Brazil as well as its current meanings that circulate in these two societies. Black-white couples may draw on or challenge these meanings as they make sense of their lives, relationships, and children.

Race Mixture in the United States

For much of US history, the policing of racial boundaries was institutionalized through antimiscegenation laws. Between the 1660s and the 1960s, forty-one states or colonies enacted laws regulating sex or marriage between blacks and whites.[38] While some laws also prohibited marriage between whites and, variously, Native Americans, Asians, and Pacific Islanders, blacks were included in every antimiscegenation law across the United States. These laws did not always embrace hypodescent or the "one-drop" rule as the definition of blackness, in which any known black ancestry renders a person black. However, those that did encouraged the notion that such a rule was enforceable.[39]

When white settlers came to what is now the United States, interracial liaisons and marriages occurred between white indentured servants and enslaved Africans. However, the ethnoracial boundary between blacks and whites hardened by the mid-eighteenth century as the demand for slavery increased. Romantic relationships between whites and blacks violated a variety of social norms surrounding white racial dominance.[40] For example, in 1787, Thomas Jefferson wrote that blacks do not feel love, which whites were capable of, only erotic desire.[41] Master-slave sex was popular in the social circles of the Jeffersonian Virginia elite, with "black dances" where white men would consort with black women. Jefferson's comments are particularly ironic given his own decades-long relationship with his slave Sally Hemings. His relationship with her may have been possible for him because he saw mixed-race individuals, such as Sally Hemings, as taking on white capacities for love.

Sexuality is central to ethnoracial boundaries and has often been used to assimilate ethnoracial "others" into a dominant culture (as seen with indigenous peoples); it has also been used to reinforce power relations[42]—for example, with whites over blacks. The use of sexuality to cross ethnoracial boundaries between whites and these "others" titillated whites with the sense that blacks and other nonwhites represented "forbidden frontiers" over which they had power. This was readily enacted in white men's sexual abuse of black women.

Political elites reformulated British slave laws to make slaves out of the children of the sexual violation of female slaves. As a result, white slave owners not only could satisfy their desires through the sexual abuse of their black female slaves but also received economic benefits through an increase in their slaveholdings. After the Civil War and abolition, the sexual abuse of black women continued into the Jim Crow era. In addition, illicit long-term relationships were common, again, often involving white men with black women. It was widely known that many white men, including political leaders, had black mistresses and formed second families alongside their legitimate white wives and families.[43] This was particularly a common occurrence in the South, where ethnoracial boundaries were the most rigid and formalized through Jim Crow segregation. However, this was also a common occurrence in the North, where warding off the sexual advances of white men was common for black women and was open knowledge in black communities.[44]

The children of these relationships continued to violate norms surrounding inheritance, threatening the wealth of white relatives. For example, the legal historian Randall Kennedy highlights several cases in which the free children of white fathers and black mothers fought white relatives for inheritance, often unsuccessfully.[45] Unlike during slavery, these free children could petition the courts for their rights as heirs. Such interactions between blacks and whites hardened racial boundaries and maintained a sociolegal context that made interracial relationships taboo.

On the other hand, sexual relations between black men and white women, whether real or imagined, were used as an excuse to lynch black men.[46] This practice was a form of social control that simultaneously created fear in black communities and maintained white patriarchy over white women. It continued for almost one hundred years following the Civil War and further stigmatized intermarriage. In addition, white fears surrounding black men having sex with white women dominated prosegregation arguments during Jim Crow.[47]

While the North lacked Jim Crow laws, they also feared race mixture. Black-white couples were forced to live in predominantly black communities. A 1944 study by Swedish sociologist Gunnar Myrdal found no regional difference in responses to his survey asking whites and blacks to rank the importance of different forms of integration. At the very top of whites' list was interracial marriage and sex, with political disenfranchisement, legal discrimination, and economic discrimination at the bottom of their list.[48] For African Americans, this was reversed, with economic and legal discrimination as the most important. At the same time, warding off the sexual assault of white men, including recent Italian immigrants, was common for black women and was open knowledge in black communities.[49]

The US civil rights movement led to a dismantling of de jure segregation, including the 1967 *Loving v. Virginia* Supreme Court decision that invalidated state antimiscegenation laws across the country. However, recent decades have seen an increase in replacing overt bigotry with a more laissez-faire[50] or color-blind[51] racism in which institutional and subtle means reproduce racial inequality. It understands racial inequality as due to nonracial dynamics such as individual choice, market dynamics, naturally occurring phenomena, and the supposed cultural limitations of nonwhites. Although overt bigotry still exists, color-blind racism is more prevalent and aids in maintaining racial boundaries between blacks and whites. This contemporary racism justifies disapproval for race-based policies targeting racial inequalities by avoiding the language of race. It also absolves most Americans from being responsible for the reproduction of race despite its socially constructed nature.

Nevertheless, over the last several decades, the United States has seen increases in interracial marriage and cohabitation: 8 percent of formal marriages (up from 4 percent in the last decade) and 14 percent of cohabiting couples are interracial.[52] These increases have led some to argue that racial boundaries are declining in the United States. However, this rosy picture ignores the patterns of gendered racial exclusion among these couples. For example, Asian-white couples, one of the most common types of interracial marriage, largely involve Asian women and white men. Black-white couples disproportionately involve black men with white women. These patterns suggest that both race and gender influence the dynamics of interracial marriage. What this means for our understandings of interracial marriage is one of the questions that *Boundaries of Love* will address.

Several studies have shown that interracial couples and multiracial families are not immune from dealing with race in the United States.[53] In fact, they can be central to challenging social norms involving race.

For example, white women who have had children by black men played a crucial role in changing the US census to accommodate their rejection of the "one-drop rule."[54] While the campaign for a multiracial category on the census was not successful, their actions led to a "mark one or more" (MOOM) option for the first time on the 2000 census, with close to seven million people identifying as "more than one race" that year.[55] In 2010, this increased by 32 percent, with nine million people identifying as more than one race.[56] One of the most common combinations was "white and black," with 1.8 million individuals identified as such. Nevertheless, one concession was that to prevent a decrease in "monoracials" such as black populations, multiracials would still be counted as part of their numbers.

In addition to these changes in racial identification, increased immigration from Asia, Latin America, and the Caribbean since the 1960s has complicated dichotomous understandings of race in the United States. Some have argued that US understandings of race increasingly resemble those common in Latin America.[57] However, whites are less likely to marry blacks than any other major ethnic or racial minority group, suggesting a continued stigmatization rooted in the earliest antimiscegenation laws.[58] In addition, today's interracial marriages are less common in the South, where laws against interracial marriage were codified longer than in other parts of the country.[59] They are also more common in the West than in the East, where race mixture was historically more stigmatized.[60] This suggests that racial boundaries between blacks and whites remain rigid and that the legacy of antimiscegenation laws continues to this day.

Early Race Mixing in Brazil

In the late fifteenth century, the goal of the Portuguese was conquest and trade, rather than creating a settler society as in the United States. Unlike the United States, where entire families migrated to the New World, migrants to Brazil were largely Portuguese men, resulting in a scarcity of Portuguese women in colonial Brazil.[61] Brazil was also the largest recipient of enslaved Africans in the New World, receiving close to thirteen times more than the United States.[62] Far from their families of origin (and the wives many left behind), Portuguese men often mated with indigenous and Afro-descendant women, producing Brazil's initial racially mixed populations.

There were never US-style antimiscegenation laws in Brazil. However, during the Portuguese colonization of Brazil, the Catholic Church brought its Inquisition-era concerns over the purity of bloodlines.[63] The church encouraged marriage between social equals, and the custom of women's dowries and other policies were tactics to promote endogamy between whites. Most relationships between white men and women of color were unequal relations between white slave owners and the women that they owned or concubinage between poor whites and women of color. With the lack of white women, especially outside of city centers; the large populations of slaves; and growing numbers of free people of color, the crown and the church's attempts to stigmatize interracial sexual relations and marital unions were often ineffective.[64]

Brazil had higher rates of manumission than the United States; while they were mostly self-manumissions, blacks also organized as families and members of fraternal orders to free family members, usually women and children.[65] Many who were freed were also the illegitimate children of slave owners; for women of color (especially the enslaved), engaging in race mixing increased possibilities of upward mobility for their offspring. This dynamic, alongside Brazil's large *mulato* elite population, influenced racial ideologies of understanding intermarriage as a way to increase social status.

Race Mixing and the Nation

After abolition in 1888, elites viewed nonwhite descendants of former slaves as a hindrance to Brazilian development and evolution into a first-world nation. They cited demographic evidence of Afro-Brazilians' lower fertility levels and higher rates of disease, malnutrition, and infant mortality to argue that they were dying out and that over several generations, whites would outnumber them.[66] Basing their ideas on scientific racism, whites supposedly had stronger genes and would thrive. To speed up this "whitening" of the nation, the Brazilian government subsidized migration to Brazil for thousands of European immigrants while prohibiting black immigration.[67]

Even W. E. B. Du Bois, the noted US black scholar and activist, was aware of this pervasive ideology. On his initial voyage to Brazil, he praised their race relations, holding them up as a benchmark for US treatment of blacks. However, after later experiences there, Du Bois critiqued Brazilian ideologies of race mixture in which many "have grown used to being told the settlement of the Negro problem in Brazil is merely a matter of time and absorption: that if we shut our eyes long enough, a white Brazil . . . will emerge and Africa in South America disappear."[68] Later, black activists such as Abdias do Nascimento levied a similar critique of race mixing as a form of genocide.[69] This was before his own interracial marriage to US-born Elisa Larkin, a white woman and noted scholar-activist for the rights of Afro-Brazilians. This perspective of interracial relations forming a part of black genocide, while extreme, still exists on the margins of black communities.

In the 1930s, Gilberto Freyre, a Brazilian sociologist and public intellectual, popularized the concept of Brazil as a nation with harmonious race relations, integration, and large amounts of interracial mating.[70] Unlike his peers, Freyre valued the African cultural heritage of Brazil and saw race mixture as the foundation of Brazilian culture. In his seminal works *Masters and the Slaves* and *The Mansions and the Shanties*,[71] Freyre praised the large amount of interracial mating that occurred among Brazilians, interpreting it as evidence of a lack of conflict in race relations, especially compared with the United States. In fact, with nostalgic longing, he referenced his own sexual relations with *mulata* domestics who worked for him and his family, ignoring its suggestions of sexual coercion and rape.

Although he never used the term himself,[72] the concept of Brazil as a "racial democracy" has often been attributed to Freyre. While it is unclear whether he referred to sexual liaisons, concubinage, or formal marriage,[73] the ideology of "racial democracy" influenced future race scholars of Brazil and became part of the Brazilian national creed. For example, a Brazilian "mulatto escape hatch" supposedly allowed individuals of racially mixed ancestry to enjoy freedom from the stigma of blackness and engage in upward mobility.[74]

Whereas the United States used segregation to assuage whites' fears of race mixture with blacks, in Brazil and other Latin American countries, race mixture was viewed as evidence of the social inclusion of blacks and indigenous peoples.[75] In this "racial democracy," racial boundaries did not exist not because everyone was white, as in whitening ideology, but because color was supposedly not an impediment to interpersonal relations, and racism was not a feature of Brazilian society. Yet racial democracy still encouraged race mixture as an ideal. In the 1950s, a study of "elites of color" showed that people gained prestige through marrying whites and had the expectation that their children would have a whiter appearance.[76] A different study found that whitening was "a 'universal' aspiration" of all nonwhites as well as a way of increasing social status. No longer solely an elite ideology, whitening was a strategy that nonwhites used to move up the status and racial hierarchy. This ideology is exemplified today by the popular adage that "money whitens." As this idea suggests, racial boundaries have not disappeared; instead, nonwhites have purposefully negotiated them to receive the benefits associated with whiteness and to approximate whiteness over generations.

For decades, elites used the ideology of Brazil as a racial democracy to obscure racial inequality as well as prevent black and indigenous mobilization.[77] However, the end of the twentieth century ushered in an increased prominence of black consciousness-raising. Black movement activists mobilized, though unsuccessfully, for a black (*negro*) category on the Brazilian census.[78] In 2000, over forty thousand people participated in a historic march in Brasilia emphasizing the continuing existence of racial inequality.[79] Activists attended the 2001 UN World Conference against Racism in Durban, South Africa, publicly challenging the notion of Brazil as a racial democracy. Since then, over fifty state and federal universities have created racial quotas for the poor and for Afro-Brazilian students.[80] Former president Luiz Inácio "Lula" da Silva ("Lula") created the Ministry for the Promotion of Racial Equality (SEPPIR) in 2003. More Brazilians have embraced a *negro* racial identity[81] and are using the color terms brown (*pardo*) or black (*preto*) on the census to identify themselves.[82] In addition, mounting scholarly evidence of racial disparities has problematized the notion of Brazil being a racial democracy.[83]

Despite the mythologizing of race mixture in Brazil, actual romantic relationships involving blacks and whites are still taboo, with white Brazilians still stigmatizing marriage with blacks.[84] In addition, race mixing is not as common as often thought; although nonwhites are the majority of Brazil, cohabitation and formal marital unions across racial categories compose only 30 percent of all marriages.[85] This is low given Brazilian ideologies of racial democracy suggesting interracial marriage is widely prevalent. In addition, demographers have argued that marriages between whites and nonwhites are often characterized by status exchange in which nonwhite spouses make up for their lower racial status by having higher levels of education than their white partners.[86] Thus ethnoracial boundaries still appear to be a factor in interpersonal relations, including marriage and family formation.

Methodology

Boundaries of Love is part of the move to use social scientific and empirical methods in critical race theory.[87] It is based on 103 qualitative interviews that I conducted between 2008 and 2012 in Los Angeles and Rio de Janeiro. These include ninety-three individual qualitative interviews with each member of forty-seven black-white couples as well as ten preliminary couple interviews (see tables I.1 and I.2). (For one of the Brazilian couples, I was only able to interview the wife, a black woman.) Fifty-five individual interviews took place in Rio de Janeiro and thirty-eight in Los Angeles. In all, I interviewed twenty-seven couples in Rio de Janeiro and nineteen couples in Los Angeles. Respondents ranged in age from twenty-one to sixty-five (see appendices A and B). Rather than testing a hypothesis, I "take talk seriously"[88] by analyzing these qualitative interviews to understand how black-white couples construct meaning in their social lives and what this means for how race is lived in the two societies. As Jessie Bernard famously articulated, in every (heterosexual) marriage, there are two relationships: "his" and "hers."[89] To capture this difference in perspectives, I interviewed all the spouses separately. This also prevented one partner from dominating or steering the interview. Since I am fluent in Portuguese, I conducted all the interviews in Rio de Janeiro myself.

TABLE I.1. Individual Interviews

	Rio de Janeiro	Los Angeles	Total
Black men with white women	34	20	54
Black women with white men	21*	18	39
Total	55	38	93

* For one of the Brazilian couples, I was only able to interview the wife, a black woman.

TABLE I.2. Couple Interviews

	Rio de Janeiro	Los Angeles	Total
Black men with white women	1	5	6
Black women with white men	2	2	4
Total	3	7	10

Research Sites

As important urban areas, with large populations of blacks and whites, both cities represent their respective countries in the international mindscape: Los Angeles through its Hollywood industry and Rio de Janeiro with its yearly *Carnaval* and, more recently, hosting both the 2014 World Cup and the 2016 Olympics. In both Brazil and the United States,[90] interracial couples tend to congregate in urban areas, making these sites amenable to finding black-white couples. In addition, after controlling for racial composition, Los Angeles has the highest rates of black out-marriage of any major US city.[91] Nevertheless, it is also the site of many black uprisings, whether in Watts in 1965 or after the 1992 acquittal of the police officers who beat Rodney King. While neither city is representative of their respective societies, they provide important insight into the variations in experiences of black-white couples in the two countries.

Recruitment and Dilemmas of Racial Identification

Since race is a social construct, what constitutes a black-white couple can differ in the two societies. In the United States, whiteness is understood as more exclusive and is based on perceived (albeit not actual) "racial purity" in one's ancestry.[92] Race in Brazil has historically been characterized by a color continuum with more fluid categories. In Brazil, whiteness does not prohibit acknowledging black ancestry because blackness is determined more by phenotype than strictly ancestry.[93] In addition, similar to many nations in Latin America, Brazil understands itself to be a nation where everyone is reputedly of mixed-race ancestry.[94] Due to these differences in classification, people in my sample who are black by US standards might not be considered black in Brazil.

Although Brazil is characterized by a continuum, the census categorizes residents into one of five color categories: white (*branca*), brown (*parda*), black (*preta*), indigenous (*indígena*), and yellow/Asian (*amarela*). The term *parda* literally refers to a grayish-brown color that is rarely used in common parlance and is mostly an official categorization. The indigenous and Asian categories together make up about 2 percent of the population.[95] The Brazilian government and the black social movement often collapse the *preta* and *parda* categories into one encompassing black (*negra*) category. In Portuguese, *preta* refers to the color of an item, such as black shoes (*sapatos pretos*), while *negra* is about having dark skin as well as having primarily African ancestry. Increasingly, *negra* is becoming a term used by Afro-descendants outside of the Brazilian black movement.[96]

I asked a variety of native Brazilians—including friends, professors, street vendors, and housekeepers—if they knew any couples involving "a black person married to a white person," using that exact phrase (*negro casado com branco*). Using this phrase, Brazilian informants often mentioned the couples that they knew involving black men with white women in Rio de Janeiro. To be inclusive of both types of pairings, I was careful to use specific gendered terms when asking for contacts, saying I was looking for a black man married to a white woman (*negro casado com branca*) or a black woman married to a white man (*negra casada com branco*).

This tactic initially prioritized the perspective of Brazilian outsiders in identifying black-white couples over individuals' self-identification. Yet to reflect how Brazil operates on a color continuum, I also interviewed spouses who self-identified using intermediate terms like *mixed* (*mestiça*) or *brown* (*moreno, parda*) despite being classified as black or white by the Brazilian informant. Within these parameters, only three Brazilian respondents self-identified differently from outsiders. This is similar to Brazilian nationally representative studies showing that self-identification overwhelmingly corresponds to outsider racial identification.[97] None of the couples overlapped in racial identification. I explain black and white identities among Brazilian respondents in greater depth in chapters 2 and 3.

In Los Angeles, I relied on referrals from friends and colleagues and scouted for couples in public spaces, including grocery stores and shopping malls, using my outsider identification as an aspect of sample selection. I found that white friends and colleagues were more likely than friends and colleagues of color to refer couples in which the nonwhite member identified as multiracial. This dynamic revealed the tenacity of the one-drop rule, especially for white Americans.[98] However, unlike Brazil, the majority of US blacks and whites do not see themselves as multiracial, despite actual different-race ancestry. For this reason, in Los Angeles, I excluded people who self-identified as biracial or multiracial from this analysis.

In both sites, I also used snowball sampling, a technique ideal for finding hard-to-reach individuals.[99] Since black-white couples are the minority of married couples in both countries, this technique was useful for finding black-white couples. Using this technique, I asked the couples that I interviewed for referrals of other black-white couples. There was never a snowball of respondents; couples that I interviewed usually knew one other couple. I frequently resorted back to searching for couples through my personal contacts and, in Los Angeles, public spaces. Still, I found more potential interviewees using this method than if I had not done so.

Again, these combinations do not reflect the plethora of intermarrying possibilities in the Brazilian context. Nevertheless, this selection process allowed me to stay true to local understandings of race and color. It also provided more homogeneity in how outsiders identify and treat black-white couples in both sites.

Sampling by Race-Gender Combinations and Education

To capture variation by race-gender combination and education, I also used purposive sampling techniques. Overall, twenty couples involved a black woman with a white man, and twenty-seven couples involved a black man with a white woman (see appendices A and B). To stay true to the status exchange prevalent in Brazilian intermarriage, I sampled for couples involving three different educational-attainment groupings when they married: neither partner having college experience, one partner having college experience, and both spouses having some college experience. There is substantial diversity in the educational statuses of these black-white couples, including those involving status exchange (see appendix table 1). In the United States, interracial marriages are concentrated among college-educated populations. This likely reflects college as an important site for students to encounter people from backgrounds for the first time. It is also likely related to the overall US growth in educational assortative mating over the last several decades, in which spouses increasingly have the same educational level.[100] As a consequence, almost the entire Los Angeles sample has at least some college experience (appendix table 2). Throughout the book, I discuss the implications of race-gender combinations and education levels on the meanings that these couples give to negotiating ethnoracial boundaries.

Casado, *Cohabitation, and Marriage*

Brazilians and people in the United States have different understandings of what it means for couples to live together outside of formal marriage. "Stable unions" (*uniões estaveis*) have always been common in Brazil, where these cohabiting relationships were only recently formalized by the state.[101] Today, stable unions make up close to a third of all marital unions in Brazil and are often long-term, with levels of commitment similar to formal marriage.[102] The 1988 Brazilian constitution recognized stable unions as families, with inheritance and community property rights similar to those of formal marriage.[103] Brazilians in stable unions often use the term for married (*casada* or *casado*) to describe their status, implying that they share a home, or *casa*, regardless of being officially married (*casado de papel*).

In the United States, cohabitation is a recent phenomenon; most people who cohabit move into a formal marriage state or separate within a few years.[104] Marriage remains more common among upper-middle-class people, like my Los Angeles respondents, than long-term cohabitation. However, there is variation by race; cohabitation is often a precursor to marriage for whites but is more of an alternative to marriage for blacks and Latinxs.[105] For these reasons, the meaning of cohabitation is unclear for interracial couples in the United States.

In consideration of these issues, I interviewed people in both cohabiting and formally married unions in both societies. My only requisite was that the couples saw themselves as being in a marriage-like union. This decision allowed for greater comparability between the two research sites.

Black Woman in the Field

Conducting research on black-white couples as a black woman meant that there were two stereotypes that I had to navigate. First, many respondents assumed that I was in an interracial relationship. I was not. It was only when I met them in person to conduct the interviews that a few respondents, having seen my (Igbo) last name, asked about my Japanese husband. This assumption meant that a few interracial couples likely saw a camaraderie with me, making them more open to participating.

On the other side of the spectrum was the "angry black woman" stereotype that all black women are against interracial marriage, especially those involving black men with white women.[106] To combat this stereotype, I purposefully smiled even more than I normally do to cultivate a nonthreatening, cheery persona that would make couples comfortable. In addition, I started interviews by asking respondents about their childhoods, their experiences in school, and their neighborhoods when they were growing up. This enabled me to build a rapport before asking difficult questions. I discuss these dynamics further in appendix B.

Overview of the Book

In chapter 1, I discuss the "romantic career," the ways that people draw on prior romantic and dating experiences to understand their ethnoracial preferences or (lack thereof) for romantic partnership and marriage. This chapter reveals how preferences for "big black men," or *negão*, are very explicit in Rio de Janeiro. This is different from Los Angeles, where there is a great deal of silence surrounding ethnoracial preferences despite life histories that suggest them. Overall, I illustrate the ways that partners construct boundaries and hierarchies of preference based on ethnoracial characteristics.

Chapter 2 shows how black spouses in Los Angeles and Rio de Janeiro understand their position within the boundaries of black racial categorization. I analyze how and why they consider themselves black and examine ethnoracial congruency between this and their white partners' assessment of their blackness. Contrary to many scholars of Brazil, I find that black spouses have a sense of groupness[107] in which they understand blacks as part of their "imagined community";[108] this, along with ancestry, physical appearance, and official documentation, make up their black identity. In Los Angeles, black respondents articulated a stronger sense of groupness and perceived history and resistance to oppression as elements tying them to other blacks. However, they saw class distinctions, immigrant ancestry, and less fluency in black culture as putting them on the margins of blackness. White husbands and wives understood their black husbands and wives as existing at the margins of blackness in both sites yet did not recognize the importance of groupness. I find more ethnoracial congruency between black-white couples in Los Angeles than in Rio de Janeiro.

Chapter 3 examines how white spouses understand their whiteness as well as congruency with their black partners. In both sites, there were whites who identified with blackness, but this was more prevalent among white Carioca (people from Rio de Janeiro) wives. In Rio de Janeiro, white spouses redrew, pushed against, and bridged over ethnoracial boundaries. In Los Angeles, whites had less flexibility in navigating ethnoracial boundaries yet bridged over class differences within whiteness. They also changed the meaning of the boundary by converting it from a racial one to one full of many "ethnic options."[109] Black partners in both places largely considered their white spouses unquestionably white. Overall, ethnoracial boundaries were more flexible and permeable for white spouses than black spouses in both societies.

Chapter 4 compares the ways that parents in the sample racially identify their children in these two societies. I find that Carioca parents often expected their child to be black, yet once they were born, the child's phenotype dictated how the parents categorized them, whether white, black, or a middle category. No one used the term *mulato/a* to refer to their child, despite its prevalence in popular and historical discourse. I found that black was the most common category that Carioca parents used to identify their children; it was also the category with the greatest congruence between parents. In Los Angeles, parents identify their child as "biracial," complicating the one-drop rule. This term also had a great deal of congruence. This chapter demonstrates the involvement of parents in the construction of new racial boundaries as well as the strengthening of preexisting ones due to new forms of racial categorization. This chapter also discusses the implications of these categorization processes for affirmative action policy in both sites. It shows how white parents understand the material benefits of affirmative action for their offspring and adjust understandings of racial categorization accordingly.

Chapter 5 compares how black spouses in both sites negotiate and challenge racial boundaries as they marry into white extended families. I find that white Brazilian families express overt displeasure about their white daughters dating black men. In what I call the *irony of opposition*, a history of race mixture in white Brazilian families is not correlated with black acceptance. In the United States, couples describe their family members as expressing disapproval of relationships with black men. These findings are counterintuitive given the long-standing narrative that unlike in the United States, Brazilians do not practice overt interpersonal racism. I also find that higher rates of domestic migration among US couples result in less integration of black spouses into white families than among Brazilian couples, whose tight-knit family relationships lead to more incorporation of black spouses. The experiences of black spouses as they integrate into their white partners' families demonstrate the continuing salience of white supremacy and antiblackness despite intermarriage.

In chapter 6, I discuss the ways that interracial couples negotiate racial boundaries in public spaces. I show the different tactics of avoidance that they employ to navigate outsiders' potential stigmatization, including avoiding predominantly black settings in the United States and predominantly white, wealthy ones in Brazil. I also describe their experiences of stigma, which includes what I term *racial boundary-policing* to refer to the ways outsiders react to people who challenge racial boundaries. While other scholars have discussed "policing the color line,"[110] I use the critical constructionist approach to place ethnoracial boundaries—understandings of "us" versus "them"—at the center of analysis. This illustrates how social actors—whether in interracial marriages or outsiders who harass them—reproduce these boundaries through their social interactions.

I find that black women in Rio de Janeiro describe being treated as prostitutes when with their white husbands in wealthy, white, touristy areas of Rio. In the United States, white women describe hostility from black women in public in incidents that their husbands describe with less animosity. This chapter shows how couples perceive and reconstruct racial boundaries in their understandings of interactions with outsiders.

Within each chapter, I deviate from the writings of many comparative sociologists by having separate sections on Rio de Janeiro and Los Angeles. I do this for ease of reading as well as to highlight important distinctions in the two sites. Nevertheless, each section within the chapters includes comparisons with the other site as a reminder of both the similarities and the differences.

I conclude with a discussion of how racial hierarchies privileging whiteness remain unchallenged by bonds of love across racial boundaries in both Brazil and the United States. Specifically, white spouses in both places experience more flexibility and porosity in racial boundaries than their black spouses. I discuss how, similar to racial integration in other institutions, such as schools and housing, multiracial families do not automatically eliminate racial boundaries. Instead of assuming that interracial marriage fosters the creation of a racial paradise, interracial couples reveal how ethnoracial boundaries and white supremacy continue to exist in family life. They also demonstrate that love is no substitute for public policy or social movements addressing racial inequality.

A Book of Firsts

There is a long tradition of cultural exchange in which US scholars like E. Franklin Frazier and W. E. B. Du Bois went to Brazil and initially praised the easy relations between blacks and whites.[111] Similarly, Brazilian scholars such as Gilberto Freyre spent significant amounts of time studying and traveling in the United States, bemoaning the lack of integration in a society plagued by Jim Crow, both formal (in the South) and informal (in the North and West). These scholars often made comparisons between the two societies that relied on their impressions, not on systematic evidence.

Recently, comparative approaches abound on understanding race in the two societies that are indeed based on evidence. These have included comparative historical approaches to the role of race in state formation and policy[112] as well as large-scale quantitative studies providing nationally representative comparisons of racial categorization, segregation, intermarriage, and racial attitudes in the two countries.[113] Qualitative scholars have examined the effect of migration to the United States on how Brazilians understand race both while abroad[114] and when they return home. The most ambitious qualitative study to date has compared how members of marginalized ethnoracial populations, including Afro-Brazilians, negotiate their stigmatization in the United States, Brazil, and Israel.[115]

However, *Boundaries of Love* offers one of the first systematic comparisons of how nonelite Americans and Brazilians, both black and white, make sense of and give meaning to race and ethnicity in their lives. Through using a critical constructionist perspective, this book uncovers the implications of Brazil's flexible versus the US's rigid boundaries in the lives of people who take them for granted. At the same time, it reveals how people negotiate those boundaries, whether by employing cultural repertoires that reproduce, push against, bridge over, blur, or dismantle them. Furthermore, this is the first comparative study to take an intersectional approach to comparing race across different societies. As a book of many firsts, hopefully *Boundaries of Love* offers a new way of understanding race for scholars and nonscholars alike.

There have been many qualitative studies examining the lives of interracial couples in the United States across a variety of ethnoracial categories, including blacks, whites, Latinxs, and Asians.[116] This has also been true in Brazil, although to a lesser extent.[117] *Boundaries of Love* is one of the first studies to compare the experiences of interracial couples across societies. It is unique in drawing on the experiences of interracial couples to not just understand these relationships but provide a microcosm of societal dynamics, looking at the meanings of interactions between members of both stigmatized and dominant groups across ethnoracial boundaries. *Boundaries of Love* is also the first book to inter-rogate how both race and gender as well as other social categories can combine to produce particular meanings of race mixing.

Boundaries of Love is not a love story. Those seeking a romance novel should look elsewhere. Instead, I ask the reader to suspend ideas that "love conquers all" as they engage the next several pages.

Onward and upward!

1

Preferences and the Romantic Career

Charlotte is a black woman who lives with her husband, Vincent, in a black working-class neighborhood in Los Angeles. During her individual interview, she shared how her husband was not the first white man whom she had ever dated. She recalled her first relationship, when she studied at an Ivy League college on the East Coast. Vladimir was from Russia and had a cute accent. Although he did not understand American cultural references or her need for connection with other black people, they got along well, writing bad poetry together and sharing their mutual homesickness.

However, Charlotte's father was angry about her relationship with Vladimir. She laughed about it as she said, "It was like something coming out of a movie, like an after-school special. 'Blacks should stay with blacks, and whites should stay with whites.'" Charlotte offered his being born and raised in the South as the main reason for his animosity toward her boyfriend. Her father's reaction was similar to previous research showing that black men found black men–white women couples more palatable than the reverse.[1] While Charlotte's father took no issue with black men being involved with white women, he was from Alabama, where he thought it was common for white men to see black women solely as sexual objects—a common occurrence in Southern history.

Charlotte learned many things from her relationship with Vladimir, including that she liked men who were artistic, did not have big tempers, and were informed about the world. In addition, she said, "Dating white men wouldn't give me the heebie-jeebies, like you weren't going to drop dead." Charlotte's recognition that there were no serious casualties from her dating a white man led her to date other white men, including her now-husband, Vincent. Charlotte's father passed away before she got married to her husband, but her friends and family were happy that she had met someone in Los Angeles, so far from home, to keep her from being lonely. For Charlotte, her first experience crossing racial boundaries informed her later experiences with dating and eventually led to her marriage to a white man.

Similar to breaking other social norms, crossing racial lines in marriage does not usually occur in one fell swoop. Prior interracial dating often leads to interracial marriage.[2] In addition, there are a number of predictors for interracial dating, including living in multiracial neighborhoods, attending schools with a large variety of racial and ethnic communities,[3] and being a member of a small population within a school or geographic area.[4]

People who intermarry can undergo a process of understanding their romantic desires for people who do not share their phenotype, cultural background, or experiences of racialization. Deviance scholars have examined the process of how people conceptualize breaking social norms. For example, Howard Becker wrote a classic account of the process by which a person becomes a marijuana user.[5] Before becoming marijuana users, people have to learn how to smoke a joint, learn how to understand the feelings of the effect of the marijuana on their bodies, and decide whether it is worth their while to do so again in the future. Becker's work shows that there are processes by which people not only learn how to break social norms but also come to understand their nonconformity. As seen in Charlotte's case earlier, breaking the social norm of intraracial dating was a process that included learning that although dating a white man was taboo (as seen in her father's reaction), it was certainly still possible.

People draw on prior romantic and dating experiences to understand their preferences for romantic partnership and marriage. In an "identity career," a person has critical moments in their life that lead to transformations in their self, the way they understand their social world, and their behavior.[6] Applying this perspective to dating and family formation, I call this process the *romantic career*. This includes how people come to understand their individual personality traits, physical characteristics, and ethnoracial preferences. In the romantic careers of people who interracially marry, interracial dating is often a precursor, and many spouses have had "practice" negotiating ethnic and racial boundaries in romantic relationships. This chapter goes beyond previous studies of interracial couples that describe the ethnoracial preferences for dating and marriage by examining the ways that respondents arrive at using these distinctions, if they do at all.

In this chapter, I examine the romantic careers of black-white couples in the two research sites. I discuss the narratives and accounts that respondents use to make sense of the trajectory toward marrying a person of a different color. I draw on responses to questions about their first and last serious relationships, dating experiences, and "hookups."

What Is a Relationship? Intersections of Gender and Race

When interviewing spouses about their prior serious relationships, I asked, "Tell me about your first/last serious relationship: Who was this person? How did you meet?" A gendered pattern emerged in which many of the men whom I interviewed in both sites first wanted me to define a "serious relationship." Given the types of questions men asked afterwards, it seemed that they were often thinking about their prior "sexual experiences" or crushes that they had in the past. None of the women that I interviewed asked me to clarify this term. My working definition during those interviews was that a relationship involved a reciprocation of emotional or romantic attachment with another person. After clarifying the question, male respondents proceeded to discuss their prior girlfriends and wives, with many having their first romantic relationships in high school. It was not uncommon for male respondents with prior dating experience to tell me that their first serious relationship was their current one with their wives. Strikingly, several black husbands, but not white husbands, revealed that they had been involved as teenagers with much older women, often women who were not black. While it was a badge of honor for many of them, the racial differences among these husbands suggested a hypersexualization of black male youth by older women.

Overall, I found that Carioca spouses were overt about placing boundaries front and center in their desires for an ethnoracial other for romantic partnership. In Los Angeles, there was more silence surrounding ethnoracial preferences across the boundary. However, in both sites, whites enjoyed a "privilege of preference" that their black partners did not.

Ethnoracial Preferences in Rio de Janeiro

Of Blondes and Black Men

While looking for couples to interview in Rio de Janeiro, the phrase that I heard over and over was: *Toda loirinha gosta de um negão* (Every [little] white woman loves a [big] black man). In Portuguese, the term *loira* literally means blonde but is often a generic term for white people, especially those with light-colored hair. By US standards, a person with light skin who is a natural blonde, is a redhead, or even has light-brown hair would be collapsed into a *loira* or *loiro category*, although it is most often used in the feminine form directed at women. *Loirinha* is a diminutive of *loira* and can be a more affectionate term for *loira*, denote smallness, or involve both connotations.

The term *negão* can refer to the supposed large penis size of black men. (This stereotype is not specific to Cariocas. On a trip to Salvador, the third largest city in Brazil, a white taxi driver told me about his *mulata* wife. He then explained, "Many people think that *negros* are like this." He took both of his hands off of the steering wheel and placed his palms parallel to one another, about a foot apart.) This stereotype is similar to how black men are often reduced to their body parts, including penis size, in the United States.[7] In the United States, white women who date blacks[8] and Latinxs[9] can suffer the stigma of being labeled a slut. However, in Colombia, romantic partnering with black men was a sign of sexual liberation for white women.[10] It was unclear to me whether the white women who had preferences for black men suffered the same stigma of being labeled as sluts. While white wives in Rio de Janeiro were often proud of their desire for black men, it was never clear whether it was due to sexual liberation, appreciation for blackness, some combination of the two, or another factor altogether.

The racialized nature of these white wives' desire was reminiscent of white sex tourists, both male and female, who pursue ethnoracial preferences for experiences abroad with "exotic" nonwhites.[11] However, unlike white female sex tourists, these white wives did not commodify these preferences or understand their relationships with *negão* as a form of leisure, nor did they discuss being in systems of exchange with their black partners, past or present. White wives saw their relationships with black men as integral parts of their lives and as sources for potential long-term companionship, unlike white sex tourists. As will be seen in chapter 4, these relationships were a part of their racial project of pushing against their own white identity.

Several white wives that I interviewed admitted that many people, including other blacks, joked with them about their love for black men. Although this specific saying was not uttered by the white wives whom I interviewed, the sentiment behind the words was alive and well among them. For example, Brígida is a white woman married to Caetano, a black man. They are both in their sixties, and of their three children, two of them, a son and a daughter, are blacks married to whites. When I asked Brígida if there were a type of man that she liked the most, she said, "I have always liked the brown color [da *cor morena*]! My first hookup back when I was in school . . . he was a ticketer. He was brown [*moreninho*], very dark [*escurinho*]. [*laughs*] And then I ended up marrying a black man too."

Brígida saw her first experience with a black man as coloring her romantic career. In her interview, Brígida also spontaneously mentioned how white women understand dating and having relationships with black men.

BRÍGIDA: [White women] even boast about it, about whites being with blacks [*morenos*]. They boast about it.

ME: Really? Why?

BRÍGIDA: I don't know why! It's something that attracts, you know? It's an innate attraction, really, that we do not understand. Every time you see a white woman [*loira*], you ask her which color she likes the most, and it is the dark color [*cor escura*] of the really black man [*preto mesmo*]! [*laughs*]

Brígida associates blackness with desirability that draws in white women in general. This was similar of other white wives in Rio de Janeiro who often said that they were unable to resist the magnetism and sensuality of black men, repeating age-old stereotypes of black hypersexuality and their irresistibility to other Brazilians, particularly whites.[12] In their understanding, black maleness had essential characteristics that were magnetic for white women. This was not the case for any of the Los Angeles white wives whom I interviewed. None of them revealed uncontrollable desires for black men. In fact, most of the white Angelino wives had only dated white men before they married their black husbands.

This was not the case for Ana María, a white woman who lives with her husband, César, a black activist, in a working-class shantytown near the center of Rio de Janeiro. Ana María grew up poor in a large city in the predominantly white south of Brazil. The first man that Ana María had a serious relationship with was Gonçalo, a taxi driver whom she described as being very dark, almost black (*muito moreno, quase negro*). Ana María overlooked Gonçalo's sexual overtures, which she found too eager; his unappealing manner of speaking; and his laughing too much—as well as the fact that he was married. He increasingly treated her with more respect, divorced his wife, and moved in with her and her child from a white man. Eight years later, they married formally, but their relationship ended when he became involved with another woman and started to abuse drugs.

After Gonçalo, Ana María dated several black men, which she described as only flings (*flertes*). Another casual encounter, with a white man, led to the conception of a son. Before the birth of her second child, she began to date another man. She said that this man was brown but, like Gonçalo, "closer to black." Ana María described her romantic career as one in which her preference for black men was not necessarily apparent in the colors of her partners:

"[There was] always that attraction, you know, for the black man: knowing about his life, about his culture. I also wanted to become involved with black men because of this. . . . I was raised like this: 'The black man is different; he has different ways of acting, of religion, of everything.' Despite having lived with it all and already knowing this, I still wanted to know more."

Ana María met César, her current husband, at a dance. She recalled, "Suddenly, I saw everything that I wanted in a man, in a black man, you know?" They began dating and moved together to Rio de Janeiro. Although they were not legally married, when I spoke with them, they had been living together for ten years.

Many white Carioca wives that I interviewed were like Brígida and Ana María, who experienced critical junctures that led to racial and color preferences in their romantic careers. Although scholars have uncovered racial preferences among Asian-white couples[13] and same-sex couples[14] in the United States, these white Brazilian wives were different in key ways: the women experienced affiliative ethnicities[15] in which they felt close to and sought out relationships and cultural practices of Afro-Brazilian men. Many of them referred to themselves as having a black soul (*alma de preto*), in addition to referring to how much they adored *negão*. For these white women, dating and marrying black men was a form of self-actualization in which they became more of who they really were. Like Ana María, these white women placed "difference" at the center and drew on essential characteristics to understand a preference for black men throughout their romantic careers. They reproduced ethnoracial boundaries by seeing these men as racially distinct and pursuing them because of those distinctions. At the risk of fetishizing blackness, these women inverted norms of black inferiority in their pursuit of blackness. This was not a pattern among any of the black-white couples whom I interviewed in Los Angeles.

Accepting the Chase

Sérgio is a black postal worker who lives in a racially mixed, working-class suburb of Rio de Janeiro with his white wife, Hilda. When I asked him about his experiences with people teasing him about liking white women, he said that he himself jokes like that. Using the term *loira*, he explained, "I have a lot of luck with blondes. It's why I have more experiences with white women than with black women. But it's not because of me, OK?" Sérgio claimed that when he was single, he flirted with ladies of all colors, but that blondes were more open to his advances, making it "easier to win them over." This sentiment was similar to US stereotypes that white women are easier to date than black women.[16]

Sérgio also said that he prefers *morenas*. *Morena* is an ambiguous term that, depending on the context, can refer to Afro-Brazilians, people with dark skin, white men or women with dark-colored eyes and hair, or people with a tan. Although it is a very popular term, mainly because of its ambiguity, it has not been used on the Brazilian census.[17] In his interview, Sérgio uses the interpretation of *morenas* being "white women with dark hair" and describes *morenas* and *loiras* as two different types of white women. He also described *morenas* as people who were his own medium to light shade of brown but specified that he prefers white women with dark hair. This suggests the ambiguity of the term in his own narrative.

Sérgio discussed how despite his own ethnoracial color preferences, he "started giving in" to the pressure from *loiras*:

> But the only ones who appear are blondes, blondes, blondes! So I started giving in, you know? Not everything is the way we want it. It's like this: if I like Jane Doe, but Jane doesn't like me, but Mary likes me, you know? So then, come on, it doesn't make sense for me to want to run after the person who is running away from me. I have to run towards whatever is running towards me. Because if [do] not, I will not be able to date anyone. Imagine if you were to think like this: "I want to date a guy who is just like Brad Pitt." . . . [But] only Denzel Washington appears before you? You go, "Well, now that there is no Brad Pitt, I'm going to date Denzel Washington," right? Otherwise you end up not dating anyone. So that's what happens. We have our preferences, but . . . if our preference is not interested in having a relationship with us, are we going to keep running after them? No, right? . . . We have to like whomever likes us.

Like Sérgio, several black Brazilian men said that white women, especially blondes, expressed the most receptivity to their flirtation and interest in them. For black men in Rio, dating white women was a rational choice and a path of least resistance. Black husbands like Sérgio suggest they have no control over the race of the women they date, unless they are content to be alone rather than have a relationship with a white woman. In comparison, none of the black husbands in Los Angeles discussed being pursued by white women or women of any other ethnoracial category.

Several black Carioca husbands were like Sérgio and felt that interracial romance had found them, not the other way around. The statements that many white Carioca women made about pursuing relationships with *negão* seem to support this interpretation. For example, in Hilda's interview, she revealed that she made the first move with Sérgio by initiating a winking game with him in the college-exam (*vestibular*) preparatory class where they initially met. For these husbands, they did not act based on ethnoracial boundary-drawing but were the targets of it in their relationships with white women. For these men, white women's pursuit of them was a driving force in their dating lives.

Another possibility is that these black men were engaged in neutralization techniques to explain and normalize their behavior. Techniques of neutralization refer to how nonconformists explain and normalize their behaviors outside of social norms to maintain their statuses as worthy and moral individuals.[18] In this tactic, people deflect and avoid guilt for behavior with which they are comfortable but that they know others see as out of the ordinary.[19] In the US, black women perceive some black men as relying on stereotypes of white women being more agreeable to justify their avoidance of dating and marrying black women.[20] In order to avoid the stigma of having preferences for white women (especially in light of being interviewed by a black female researcher), black men in Rio de Janeiro may have emphasized being chased by white women, including their whites wives.

Other Carioca black men said that they had hesitated to date white women because they feared opening themselves up to discrimination. Sometimes, this reflected experience. For example, Nicolas was a black man married to Laura, a white woman, and they lived near the city center in a working-class neighborhood. In his interview, he told me how when he had dated Marcela, a white woman, years before, her family did not accept him because he was black (*preto*). He said, "I would sit at the table and some of the people [in her family] would leave the table." Nicolas said that he overheard Marcela's grandmother say that she considered the relationship "unacceptable" because he was a black man. He said he had never said anything to Marcela's family during those incidents. Nicolas said that after dating Marcela, a coworker tried to set him up with another white woman, Carol, and he was initially hesitant: "I was afraid of approaching her because of discrimination. . . . I had already been discriminated against before [with Marcela]. . . . After experiencing certain things, you end up being fearful that it would happen again."

Nicolas dated María Cristina after much prodding from his friend. Her family accepted him, and he learned that some white families would not reject him because of their antiblackness. This fear of discrimination did not emerge as a theme from any of the Angelino respondents, including black husbands and wives. While some black respondents did experience white family hostility, discrimination was not something these partners expressed fearing or preventing them from having relationships with whites.

Romantic careers such as Nicolas's case may explain why black Brazilian men perceived white women as more overt in expressing their romantic interest than nonwhite women. Several men had stories of experiencing racial discrimination in their interactions with white women and their families. White Carioca women who desire a relationship with a black man may have to be more assertive in expressing their desires to assuage the fears that some men have from past bitter experiences.

Matching

Assortative mating is a term used to describe how couples often match on particular social characteristics, such as education. In the United States, interracial couples tend to involve partners who both have college experience, thus they tend to match on education. However, status exchange occurs in Brazilian cross-color unions in which white women tend to have lower levels of education than the darker men with whom they form marital unions.[21] Both dynamics were present among Carioca spouses in which status exchange occurred as well as matching on levels of education (see appendix table 1). However, the majority of Angelino couples indeed involved educational assortative mating (appendix table 2).

While at the population level, these types of couples may or may not "match" in terms of color or education, I found that, indeed, they matched in a way not easily captured by statistics. While white women often described their desires for *negão*, black men described how they had been chased by white women throughout their romantic careers. This matching of desires for color with acquiescence to these desires was a part of the experiences of couples involving black men with white women in Brazil. However, this was true for Carioca couples involving black men and white women with and without status exchange. Among my respondents, I found that educational characteristics of the spouses were not related to matching on desires for *negão*.

For one couple that I interviewed, this matching occurred in a different way. Patrício is a black man in his forties who lives with his white wife, Julia, in a racially mixed neighborhood in Rio de Janeiro. While Julia has a college degree, Patrício only finished elementary school. In his individual interview, Patrício discussed his previous serious relationship with Alessandra, an obese white woman:

"In terms of my financial situation, when I became unemployed, I smoked, and she would buy me cigarettes. She would give me money when I was hard up. She would always help me. Even with food, it was her that would [buy it]; I did not have much to contribute."

Patrício teared up as he revealed how, initially, Alessandra would force him to drink so that he would become aroused enough to have sex with her. With time, he no longer needed to be drunk to have intercourse. Patrício and Alessandra lived together for ten years before she died of cancer. When I interviewed him, Patrício was unemployed and receiving Alessandra's pension.

In her own interview, Júlia, a woman in her fifties, discussed her lifelong desires for *negão*. Like many older white women whom I interviewed, she started dating black men openly once her own parents had passed away. She and Patrício live together in the home that Júlia inherited from her parents. In between interviews, I watched how Julia, also an obese woman, yelled repeatedly for Patrício to come to her aid. He lifted her from her chair and helped her move about the house. Traditional ideas of status exchange would not apply to their situation, since she has a higher level of education and has health issues that challenge her degree of status as a white woman. Rather, they match on several attributes, such as her need for live-in care, his financial need, and her ethnoracial preference. While they may love each other a great deal, their situation complicates using education as the only grounds for assessing assortative mating and status exchange.

Drawn to Stigma: White Husbands in Rio de Janeiro

Similar to white husbands in Los Angeles and white wives in Rio, white husbands in Rio de Janeiro were also drawn to difference. However, their romantic careers were not limited to ethnoracial boundaries. Instead, these were differences based on other stigmatized social categories. For example, Gaspar is a white Carioca man married to Tatiana, a black woman. Both finished college and are in their early forties. They live in a racially mixed, working-class neighborhood not far from the center of Rio with her child from a previous marriage and a child that they had together. In his interview, Gaspar described how he had dated several black and indigenous women before he married and had dated white Europeans when he was living in Europe as a musician. Like several of the Brazilian men whom I interviewed, both black and white, his first serious relationship was with a woman who was older than him. Marina was white (*branca*), and Gaspar liked her intelligence, her almost utopic vision of the world, and her esotericism, which he attributed to her "gypsy" ancestry. They were a couple for five years, but they broke up because she was mentally ill and refused to take medication to cope with the illness. Another girlfriend whom Gaspar dated was blind. Gaspar said he was completely comfortable with her blindness: "She would say, 'Give me your hand, and I will follow,' and for me, that was never an issue. It's interesting; this is something that I ask myself: 'Why don't I see limitations in anyone?' I don't see limitations in people. For me, there is no limitation on humans when one manages to express oneself; if a person can express him or herself, even if he or she has no arm or leg . . . I do not see them with rejection or repugnance or discomfort. It does not bother me."

Gaspar's descriptions of his openness went beyond race, but he was similar to other white men whom I interviewed in Brazil. The white Carioca men I interviewed were often drawn to women who were iconoclasts and social outsiders. In addition to dating nonwhites, several of their narratives of their romantic careers involved girlfriends with health issues, such as drug addiction, obsessive-compulsive disorder, and physical disabilities. Among respondents, these white husbands often had experiences dating members of stigmatized groups whom no one else in my sample mentioned. For instance, white Brazilian wives seemed to have married their husbands because of an overt interest in marriage with *negão* rather than because of a more generalized attraction to members of stigmatized social groups. This pattern of being drawn to members of stigmatized groups did not emerge among Los Angeles respondents.

White Carioca husbands in Brazil did not describe having a penchant for an ethnoracial type, the way that their Angelino counterparts did. The few who had dated black females in the past did not describe them in markedly different ways from the white women they had dated, unlike their female Carioca counterparts. This was also different from Angelino white husbands, who had rarely dated black women before their wives. This pattern is likely due to the greater proportion of Afro-Brazilians in general, including in Rio de Janeiro, where they make up almost half of the population. This provided more opportunities for Carioca white husbands to have had romantic relationships with non-whites than their US counterparts. Although white Carioca husbands were not explicit about their being drawn to difference, it was a pattern that emerged in their narratives of their romantic careers. Social differentiation was a part of the romantic career of white Carioca husbands. However, this differentiation was not based in ethnoracial categories, the way that it was for many white Carioca wives and even for white Angelino husbands.

Discordance in Rio de Janeiro: Black Husbands and Wives in Rio

Some of the black husbands in Brazil that I interviewed referred to their relations with black women as pushing them toward having romantic relationships with white women. For example, Danilo is a college-educated black husband who lives in a racially mixed community (*comunidade* or *favela*) with his white wife, Gabriela, who did not attend college. He said that the first girlfriend he had was black, but it was not a serious relationship, just a "play" girlfriend from his neighborhood: "Even though my first [play] girlfriend was black [*negra*], I always saw black women as if they were my sisters. It's interesting—I always thought, 'Oh, gee, she seems like my sister.' [*laughing*] So I had more of a sisterly relationship than a girlfriend relationship."

Danilo reveals his mainly having romantic relationships with white women as due to only seeing the black women in his racially mixed neighborhood platonically. His prior experiences dating and knowing black women influenced his decisions about entering romantic relationships with them. Very few black men described a lack of romantic desire for black women as a factor in their having relationships with white women. However, among those that did, this narrative of too much familiarity emerged as a theme. This notion of ethnoracial similarity (not differentiation), to the point of seeming "family-like," was mentioned only by black men in Rio de Janeiro and not by any of the black husbands in Los Angeles or any white respondents. I found this ironic, given the tradition of using *sister* or *brother* among African Americans to refer to fellow blacks who are nonrelatives. Terms like *mermão* (short for *meu irmão*) or *broder* (cognate of the English *brother*) are often used in Brazil to mean "my brother," but it is used across colors in Rio de Janeiro.

Another way that black men in Rio de Janeiro framed the influence of their relations with black women was in terms of the rejection that they experienced by black women throughout their romantic careers. Similar to Sérgio's discussion of only having luck with *loiras*, other black men related how black women did not like them. For example, Edvaldo is a black man who lives with Verônica, a white woman, in a distant, mixed, working-class suburb of Rio de Janeiro. Neither had an education beyond high school. He described his experiences dating black women: "I never got along with black women. I don't know, at least the black women that I tried to hook up with, they always looked for white men, you know? They gave preference to men with lighter skin. So I never had a connection with black women, you know?"

Later, he explained an incident at a *pagode* dance party where he asked his friend to introduce him to a black woman. His white male friend explained to him, "This one only likes white men. She doesn't like black men [*negão*] at all." He thought that his friend wanted the woman for himself, so Edvaldo started talking to her anyway.

A little while later, she said, "Oh, my type is really only white men [*branquinho*]. My taste is for white men [*homem branco*]" and such. . . . So I spoke with her, "But why? Why do you not like black men? What did they do to you that was so bad?" So I told her, "Come on, let me fix it" and everything. She was like "No, no. Shoot, it won't work. I am not able to feel any attraction. I cannot see myself with a black man." I said, "Oh, OK, that's fine. You'll be my friend then. No problem. Just introduce me to a friend who likes black men and it's all good."

Experiences of rejection by black women were a part of the romantic career of some black Carioca husbands. This was also a theme in the romantic career of several black wives in Rio de Janeiro. Recall Tatiana and her BMANG friends who collectively started dating white men after maltreatment from prior black boyfriends. Delfina provides another example of rejection shaping the romantic careers of black women in Rio de Janeiro. Delfina is a college-educated black woman who lives with her white, French husband, Auguste, who finished college in France. They live in a predominantly white, wealthy neighborhood of Rio de Janeiro with their daughter and her mother. During her interview, Delfina described her experiences dating Jackson, a good-looking *negão*, when she was a teenager. When he broke up with her, she made a conscious decision about dating black men:

"He was gorgeous, [with] a sculpted body. And he traded me in for a blonde who was ugly as hell. No front teeth. Yes, I suffered . . . but in silence . . . and . . . I got another boyfriend. Gorgeous, a blonde with blue eyes. . . . And I . . . promised that I would never go out with another black man again."

Delfina never did; she dated white men until she married Auguste. One Saturday, Delfina and Auguste kindly invited me to their home for a lavish brunch. Delfina described how when they got married, for bureaucratic reasons, she purposefully dropped one of her last names and added her husband's last name instead. She enjoyed having a French last name in a society where most people, especially Afro-descendants, have Portuguese last names. Fellow Brazilians often inquire, "Oh, are your parents French?" She reenacted her response to them, turning her nose up in the air and saying in a chichi voice, "No, my husband is French." After Delfina explained how people are always impressed, Auguste chimed in, "It's a type of status." Delfina understood Jackson's rejection of her as devaluing her blackness and her overall status. However, similar to the experiences of "elites of color" fifty years ago,[22] her white husband elevated her social status. For Delfina, dating and eventually marrying a white man was a corrective mechanism, a way to save face in her romantic career.

Some black Carioca women were like Delfina and described dating and marrying white men, especially foreigners, as a vengeful response to rejection by black men.[23] Rather than breaking down ethnoracial boundaries, their experiences as jilted lovers led them to draw a social boundary against black men as romantic prospects. Similar to some of the Carioca black men, these women employed ethnoracial differentiation as a strategy throughout their romantic careers. This was different from most black wives in Los Angeles, who did not describe vengeance as a motivation for entering relationships with white men.

The theme of black male rejection of black women occasionally came to the surface in interviews with some of the black husbands in Rio de Janeiro. Some black Carioca husbands described the black women they had dated as "black, but pretty" (*negra, más linda*), a common Brazilian way of describing attractive black women.[24] They would also say that their black girlfriends had been intelligent. When they referred to black women they dated, they would often say that they had "common" features that were "nothing special." However, the tone of their voices would become excited when these black Brazilian men described white women they had dated, including their white wives. Black husbands often discussed at length and extolled the light-colored eyes of these previous partners, a feature mainly dark-eyed Brazilians consider special. They did not mention whether their white partners were intelligent. While European aesthetics and phenotypic characteristics have currency in many places, in my study, black Carioca husbands exhibited this overtly.[25] This pattern reveals the tension between black women being less receptive to black male respondent advances in Rio de Janeiro. It also calls into question the potential differential treatment of black and white women by these black husbands.

This was different from black Carioca wives, who often described the handsomeness of the *negão* and the white men they had previously dated and even married in prior relationships. Black Carioca wives generally described the white men they had dated as good-looking, particularly if they had light-colored eyes, yet they described black men as "gorgeous," often describing them as "tall" and "strong." White husbands in Rio de Janeiro, unlike white wives, often described prior relationships with black women but did not describe them in terms of a color or ethnoracial preference.

Challenging In-Group Preferences

No Ethnoracial Distinctions

Some black respondents, usually black husbands, said that they actually had an in-group preference that they had stayed with until they met their white wives. This was true for black husbands both in Los Angeles and in Rio de Janeiro, including Edward, who opened the last chapter and discussed how "he was too busy looking for the next black woman" until he met Stella. This was also true for Claúdio, a black man who lives in a racially mixed suburb of Rio de Janeiro with his white wife, Fernanda and their daughter Maricela.

> I like dreadlocks; I like cornrows; I like braids. But this openness that I gave to meeting different people allowed me to meet an interesting person who broke some of this. . . . Everyone has a desire in terms of what they want. I have the desire for . . . ten children, but then I meet a woman who says, "No, only two, dude. Are you crazy?" Get it? So having the desire does not mean that it will be realized. [If you say,] "I only want to meet Japanese women," I hope you do. But if you open up one day . . . [and] you're somewhere and you talk with somebody, it may be that all of that changes, because we cannot control our feelings.

Claúdio did not stigmatize individuals who have ethnoracial preferences for romantic relationships. Instead, he describes how being open to the possibilities of life led him to become attached to a person with a different ethnoracial type from the one he had expected. The romantic careers of these men had been ones in which they only had serious relationships with black women until they unexpectedly met the white women who would become their wives.

This understanding of their romantic careers was common among black husbands in both sites, in which chance encounters eradicated their ethnoracial preferences for relationships. Their perspectives demonstrate how scholars who claim that there is no notion of groupness in Brazil[26] have overstated the case; some Afro-Brazilian husbands indeed felt group bounds with black women, even if they were challenged by encounters and eventual marriage to their white wives. This was similar to some black husbands in Los Angeles, such as Edward, who also experienced this. On the other hand, in-group preferences were not mentioned by any of the white husbands or wives whom I interviewed in either site, including those who had dated only whites until they met their black spouses.

Discomfort with Ethnoracial Boundaries

In Rio de Janeiro, I also interviewed a couple of black husbands who had a preference for black women and remained uncomfortable with being married to a white woman. Adão is a college-educated black man who lives with his wife, Marisa, in the condo that she inherited from her parents in a wealthy neighborhood in the South Zone of Rio de Janeiro. They had been friends for many years, had married different people (of their respective colors), and had children with their partners. When Adão separated from his wife, they began to see each other. She separated from her husband, and they soon began dating seriously. When I interviewed him, Adão appeared agitated, frowning throughout the interview, speaking curtly and aggressively. He had been married previously to a black woman, with whom he had two black children.

My relationships always were with black women, and I really support this! I support the idea that blacks have to marry blacks, and this is my position. Politically, that's how I see things, that's what I think . . . so I really had difficulties [in] my understanding that I married a white woman and that I would spend my days with a white woman and not with a black woman with the same origins, the same consciousness, the same possibilities. In reality, [she is] a white woman living in the South Zone with a, a long-standing inheritance from a family that came from an upper-middle-class living in a wealthy neighborhood of the South Zone; it's, it's another reality, you know? So we'll suppose, it's another upbringing, you know? It's another way of seeing the world, and I particularly, I found it difficult to accept, to take her to certain places . . . with me, you know?

Having been active in the black movement since he was a teenager, Adão remained uncomfortable with his falling in love with a white woman, particularly a wealthy one like Marisa. Adão saw her wealth as an additional boundary that created social distance between them. This was very different from the black husbands in Los Angeles; none of them described being uncomfortable with being married to a white woman because of their in-group romantic preferences. Marisa sensed Adão's sentiment. In her interview, she bemoaned his treatment of her:

"He feels strained by being married to a white woman, of being with a white woman with blue eyes and with strong purchasing power—with dough—or living better than [other blacks]. . . . He excludes me, my own husband."

Adão's extreme case shows how not all black partners were comfortable with their spouses' whiteness. Prior experiences in their romantic careers and political convictions left them uncomfortable with the boundaries between them and their white partners. This was rare but occurred among only black husbands, not black wives. Rather than making peace with life turning out differently from what they had expected, like Cláudio, their ethnoracial preferences were a source of tension in their own lives as well as in their relationships. There was no such tension for the black husbands in Los Angeles.

Ethnoracial Differentiation and Preferences in Los Angeles

Unlike their Carioca counterparts, many husbands and wives across colors in Los Angeles were silent about having ethnoracial preferences in their romantic careers. Only a few white Angelino wives described their penchant for the "dark and handsome" types, whom they saw as white ethnics and nonwhites alike. Almost all the white wives in Los Angeles had exclusively dated white men until they met their husbands. While interracial dating is often a precursor to interracial marriage,[27] this was not the case for the majority of the Angelino white wife respondents. If these women had racial preferences, they were not stated overtly during the interview. The racial climate of false "color blindness" in the United States has made it taboo for individuals, including blacks, to discuss racial preferences at all, even though it is clear from other studies that people have them.[28] Brazil, on the other hand, is much less wedded to "political correctness," making racial preferences less taboo to discuss.

Many black husbands in Los Angeles had little or no experience dating black women. The ones who had dated black females in the past did not exhibit distinction in the ways that they described black versus nonblack partners. This was different from almost all the black women who had experience dating black and nonblack men, including whites.

Nevertheless, similar to the white wives in Rio de Janeiro, some of the people in Los Angeles described preferences for ethnoracial others.

Lana, a black woman originally from the Midwest, was the only black person to express a preference for whites. Lana had grown up in a predominantly white suburb and had been living with Larry, a white man. For Lana, her romantic career was colored by being one of the few blacks in her neighborhood and in her high school. When she went to college, she dated Derrick, who was white and the first boyfriend that she ever had, and later dated another white man, named Colin:

"I think a lot of the reasons I am more attracted—I tend to be more attracted—to white men is because that's what I grew up around for the most part and that's just what I found attractive."

Later, Lana said, "It's kind of just generally acknowledged now among my friends that that's just, like, how I am. I like white boys." Similar to the white women in Rio de Janeiro, Lana had a preference for an ethnoracial other, in this case white men. However, unlike the Carioca white women who hailed from neighborhoods with both large and small nonwhite populations, Lana saw her desires as deriving from structural reasons. For Lana, ethnoracial distinction was central to her romantic career but was rooted in externalities of the predominantly white neighborhoods she grew up in and the schools that she attended. However, other black wives in Los Angeles who grew up in similar circumstances did not describe having similar preferences.

While very few Los Angeles respondents voiced ethnoracial preferences in their interviews, the ones who did were most often white men. Most had their first serious relationships with white women who shared their cultural backgrounds. However, several had other romantic relationships with women who were non-Anglo, including Jewish (none of my male respondents were Jewish), Middle Eastern, Latina, or Asian American women (these relationships were common), reflecting the ethnoracial diversity of US society. Unlike so-called rice-chasers,[29] white men who highly desire Asian women, none of the Angelino respondents revealed a fetishization of a particular ethnoracial type. Some white husbands discussed the rejection they had experienced from black women in the past. Despite their flirtation, they expressed how those black women did not take their advances seriously. Nevertheless, several white husbands discussed a preference for non-Anglo women.

William is a white man in his early thirties who lived with his black wife, Betty, and their newborn, Sasha. Like most of the interracial couples whom I interviewed, they lived in a predominantly white, middle-class neighborhood in Los Angeles. I asked him whether he had ever been teased about having a preference for black women: "No. But I mean, I always kind of lean towards darker women as opposed to lighter women, when usually they were white, but they would be brunette or, say, Italian. My very first girlfriend in high school was a Spaniard, and I'm convinced now that she was mixed. . . . She had African features. Definitely. She was very—definitely she was mixed. There's no doubt in my mind."

William saw himself being drawn to women whom he saw as a "darker" type that included people with origins in the Mediterranean. The woman that he describes is someone whom he sees as an ethnoracial other with potential African ancestry. This was similar to other US white husbands who had previous romantic relationships or encounters with women outside of their racial or ethnic groups.

One white husband respondent described a preference for "exotic women," while others described a preference for "strong" women. Although "strong" is a stereotype often associated with black women,[30] the men who mentioned this did not refer exclusively to black women but referred to many women who were often seen as ethnoracial others. Neither blacks in either society nor white Carioca men expressed this tendency. In addition, unlike the Carioca white women who openly adored *negão*, the US white husbands were subtle when discussing their preferences for "ethnic" women. Furthermore, while ethnoracial differentiation was a part of their romantic careers, it did not affect their senses of self as it had for many of the white Brazilian women with a "black soul."

Several black wives whom I interviewed discussed ambiguity in their ethnoracial reflexivity and reflected appraisals.[31] While reflecting on how they thought others saw them, they mentioned that their physical characteristics led outsiders to be unsure of their ethnoracial identities. These women described people not readily identifying them as black because of their lighter skin tone and slender build. They often described themselves as light-skinned and were often mistaken for being "Mexican" or Latina in a city where Latinxs are the largest ethnic group. These findings suggest that although Angelino white husbands were married to black women, they had a preference for those who were physically closer to a European phenotype. This is similar to Powdermaker's study in the 1930s of a Southern black community in which white men preferred black women with lighter complexions.[32,33]

Rather than challenging social norms of whites as ideal, this pattern suggested an antiblack colorism in the romantic careers of these white husbands that reproduced notions of racialized female desirability. Although none of the white Angelino husbands discussed these factors in their romantic careers, it was a pattern that nevertheless emerged. This was not the case among black wives in Rio de Janeiro; some indeed described having ambiguous features, but there were several who did not.

Immigrants and Ethnoracial Preferences

Daniel is a white man in his early thirties who is married to Taiwo, a black woman in her late twenties. Daniel's first serious relationship was in high school with his classmate, Raji, a daughter of immigrants from India. Subsequently, he dated only white women, since, as he said, those were all the women that he had been exposed to. Then he met Taiwo, whose parents are immigrants from Nigeria. According to Daniel, she was one of the few black women who responded positively to his advances. However, he did not describe having ethnoracial preferences nor acting on them in his romantic career.

However, this was not how Taiwo understood Daniel and his white male friends, who shared his middle-class and regional background. In her interview, she discussed their ethnoracial preferences for nonwhite women, especially Asian women, although Daniel is the only one in a relationship with a black woman.

TAIWO: [He said,] "We don't date white women anymore," because they all did before, right?

ME: Why is that?

TAIWO: He says, "White women are spoiled," and I'm like "That is not true. I know so many nonspoiled white women." He's like "Well, the ones I dated were." And then his friends had been telling him that for years. They're like "You need to get an Asian woman." I'm like "That is crazy. That sounds stereotypical, like as if all Asian women will do whatever you say and everything."

Taiwo saw Daniel's friends using the discourse of Asian women as docile, subservient, and hyperfeminine ideal wives. This discourse has its origins in the US military in Asia and US political and economic dominance in the region after World War II.[34] Taiwo's description was similar to that of white male sex tourists who saw the empowerment of white women in their home countries as grounds for enjoying the company of temporary, nonwhite girlfriends abroad.[35] Taiwo's reaction showed resistance to this portrayal of Asian women.

Later in her interview, Taiwo described having Daniel's friend, a white man married to a white woman, visit them in their home. She asked them if they wanted ice cream, and when they said they did, she went to the kitchen to prepare it for them. She described her husband and his friend's reactions when she brought it to them in the living room.

TAIWO: His friend said, "Wow, that's awesome." And Daniel's like "Yeah, you need to get one for yourself."
ME: Because you brought them ice cream?
TAIWO: Yeah, I guess he says, "Man, there are white women that yell, 'Oh, get it yourself.'" I was like "That is so funny to me, because black men who date exclusively white women, I've heard them complain that black women are mean and pushy and always want to be the man of the house, and they dig white women because they're more docile." I'm like "That's real funny." He's like "Well, you're different because you're an immigrant black woman." He's like "You're a child of immigrants. There's a slight difference." And he's like "Asians tend to preserve more of their culture. Even if they're American, they still have their family values from their culture more so, and even if they were born and raised here." I was like "Those are just stereotypes, because I can find you twenty more white women that will get you the bowl of ice cream."

Taiwo's comments show that she saw Daniel and his friend as objectifying her and other nonwhite women as partners to obtain. Taiwo delegitimized these assertions by pointing to their comments as stereo-typical. She also pointed to the ways black men who avoid relation-ships with black women make similar assertions. Several scholars have pointed to men's desires for women on the other side of ethnoracial boundaries for marriage, romantic relationships, and sex tourism.[36] As Taiwo mentioned, this was also true for some black men.[37] Taiwo's inter-view also reveals how immigration was used to bridge over her ethnora-cial differences with Asians, making them all desirable partners. It also shows how even though Daniel did not see himself as having ethnoracial preferences, gendered xenophilia may have still been a part of the mean-ing he gave to his and his friends' romantic prospects.

The majority of Angelino black wives who did not reference eth-noracial ambiguity were second or 1.5 generation immigrants. Similar to prior research on black immigrants,[38] this points to whites' potential preference for immigrant blacks over nonimmigrant blacks. This was different from black women in Rio de Janeiro who described foreign white men as part of their own ethnoracial preferences, not those of their husbands. However, unlike Los Angeles, the ethnoracial preferences of black women in Rio de Janeiro were not related to gender norms.

Body Type and Ethnoracial Boundaries

In comparison to Rio de Janeiro, only a few white wives in Los Angeles expressed ethnoracial preferences throughout their romantic careers. For example, Natalie is a white woman married to Jerry, a black man. They live in a multiracial neighborhood in Los Angeles. In her inter-view, she described how her first serious relationship was with a black man named Sean. In addition, she discussed her experiences dating white men.

> ME: What have been your experiences dating white guys?
> NATALIE: Short. [laughs] I had a couple of brief encounters with white
> guys in college. Unfortunately . . . I found that either my weight
> or my background became some kind of an issue or something
> that they wanted . . . to be different about me. And I was just never
> brought up to believe that you should try to change who you are to
> make someone care about you.

ME: How did they want to change your background?

NATALIE: One specific experience was just—I had a guy that he had a problem with the way I dressed. I was in college. I wore T-shirts and jeans or whatever most of the time, and he wanted me to go out and buy more fancy stuff. Like . . . he wanted me to have cuter party clothes. Stuff like he'd go out to the parties [with] because [Occidental is] kind of—most of the kids who go there are pretty well off. And I would try to explain to him, "I don't have the money to just go out and buy new clothes whenever I want. If my clothes are getting a little ratty, then I have to save up." . . . He didn't object, but I could tell he didn't understand. And he still had an issue with it. I was like "You can't drop it when I tell you there's absolutely nothing I can do about it." [laughs]

ME: What was it like for you as far as people wanting you to change your weight?

NATALIE: I mean, that was most of my early dating experiences. Comments like "Oh, you'd be so much prettier if you'd just lose a little bit of weight" or "Oh, you'd look so cute in these kind of jeans if you were just a little skinnier." And they're like "Oh, your boobs are so nice, but you got such a belly." Stuff like that.

Natalie describes a romantic career of experiencing challenges to dating white men across class boundaries and who tried to change her body type. For Natalie, there were ethnoracial differences in conspicuous consumption related to class difference. This proved to be one of the challenges to her relationships with white men in college. In addition, she implies that there are ethnoracial differences in terms of body type between whites and blacks that made her relationships with white men uncomfortable. The notion that black men prefer fat white women, the ones rejected by white men, for romantic partnership is a popular stereotype.[39] Nevertheless, Natalie's assessment concurs with several studies of body-type preferences between blacks, whites, and Latinxs.[40] One recent study examining a national internet-dating site revealed that white men have an aversion to thick or large bodies, which are preferred by African American and Latino men.[41]

Natalie was not the only white wife that I interviewed who described body type as a factor in her experiences with white men. Ida is a white woman in her fifties who is living with Ollie, a black man, outside of Los Angeles in a neighboring county. Ida also described white male body preferences as part of her romantic career. Her first serious relationship was with a white man, as was her last one, which involved her ex-husband, with whom she had two children. While in the process of the divorce, she described living in a neighborhood that was predominantly black. Unlike the other white wives whom I interviewed in Los Angeles, she described having a past in which she had been immersed in black community life, even learning to do African American hairstyles on children in the neighborhood. She described her experiences meeting and dating men: "I just kind of gravitate to [them], or they see in the eyes, you know? I just start talking to all the black people because I was more comfortable, that's where I came from. [More] than the white. And a lot of the white men, they all wanted that Barbie doll, the blondes and, you know, with big boobs and stuff like that, and I wasn't that."

Ida describes push-and-pull factors in her romantic career that led her to date men of color, predominantly black, after her divorce. In addition, her black social ties and experiences with black cultural life made dating black men more feasible. At the same time, she experienced alienation from white norms of body desirability. Like Natalie and other white wives in Los Angeles, Ida did not describe overt preferences for black men. However, over the course of her dating life, she gained familiarity with black men and saw them as potential romantic partners. Both Natalie and Ida perceived black men as more forgiving in their preferences than white men. While this pattern of body desirability was uncommon among the white wives whom I interviewed, for Natalie and Ida, it was linked to ethnoracial differentiation in navigating their romantic careers.

Most white wives in Los Angeles that I interviewed did not discuss body type as a theme in their relationships with white or black men, including their husbands. In fact, several white wives in Los Angeles expressed annoyance at the stereotype that white women who date and marry black men are always overweight and faced rejection by white men. This was certainly not the case for most of these respondents, who had experienced prior relationships with white men. Their comments suggested that this stereotype was one that white wives in Los Angeles had to navigate and that black wives did not. This may explain why issues of body type emerged among interviews with white wives but not black wives.

Body type also did not emerge as a theme among Brazilian wives of either color. Nevertheless, while I was looking for black-white couples to interview, I encountered a similar stereotype about larger body types while in Brazil. One informant revealed that his father had told him the only white women available to black men were the "fat, ugly ones that white men did not want."[42] However, none of the couples themselves mentioned this in their interview. While Brazilian norms of beauty favor aesthetics understood as European-derived (light-colored hair, thin nose and lips), and its cosmetic surgery industry is one of the largest in the world,[43] lower levels of residential segregation in Brazil may provide less variation between men of different ethnoracial categories. In addition, the historical and contemporary emphasis on race mixture means that the curvy and tanned, but not too dark, *morena* has been traditionally seen as the beauty ideal for all Brazilians. While body types are important in Brazilian society in general, it did not emerge as a theme in the interviews there.

Discordance and Incongruences: Black Husbands and Wives

Black Gendered Rejection

Unlike Rio de Janeiro, none of the Angelino black husbands described experiencing rejection by blacks of the opposite sex. Nevertheless, there were moments when black male respondents would suggest a preference for nonblack women but would quickly retreat from this. For example, Gary is a black man originally from Los Angeles who lives with his white wife, Pavla, an immigrant from Ukraine. They live in a racially diverse neighborhood in the suburbs of Los Angeles. When I talked to Gary about his experiences dating, he described how he did not find black women as attractive as women who were members of other ethnic groups.

> ME: So in terms of dating black girls, how come you haven't had any serious relationships with black girls?
>
> GARY: I don't know. That's a good question. Maybe it could've been just my environment. I wasn't just—growing up in a very multicultural

background, it just, I didn't, I don't think I found them as attractive as other ethnic types, and I didn't—I just didn't go for it. Actually, I take that back. . . . When I was in high school, my prom date, she was black. I really thought she was—I really liked her. She was younger than me, but that turned out—that specific instance turned out to be really bad because she ended up crying in the bathroom the whole night of my prom when I was a senior in high school.

Gary initially offered outside circumstances as the reason he did not date blacks. This was similar to Lana, mentioned earlier, who gave structural explanations for her preference for white men. For Gary, the multiracial environment he was surrounded by was to blame for his lack of attraction to black women, even though they were a part of this environment. Next, Gary described how he did not have any black girls to whom he was attracted or could "relate with." Gary was engaged in neutralization techniques that relieved him of the responsibility for exclusively interracially dating. Unlike the Brazilian white women who blamed their romantic preferences for *negão* on their black spirits or the uncontrollable passions that blackness aroused, for some Angelino black husbands, the environment was a key factor in the role of race in their romantic careers. This was true for some of the black husbands, regardless of growing up in or outside of black communities. Similar to Gary, their attraction to nonblack women was due not to racial preferences in dating and romance but to the environment.

Opportunity structures such as schools and neighborhoods are an important component of cross-ethnic contact and the opportunity for interracial marriage.[44] Being in a multicultural environment likely provided Gary with opportunities to date many nonblack women. At the same time, referencing his black prom date tempers the notion that Gary has a racial preference in romance. This likely reflects the taboo that would attend such feelings in a politically correct US society, where black men were historically lynched for the purported "raping" of white women. This was similar to black Carioca husbands who also attributed the lack of blacks in their romantic careers to outside circumstances. However, given the higher levels of residential segregation in the United States, including Los Angeles, the structural factors likely played a role in the romantic careers of black Angelino husbands. This was different from Lana, mentioned earlier, as well as white respondents across gender and in both sites who shared open preferences based on social or ethnic differentiation. This was also different from many black wives, even those raised in Los Angeles, who rarely mentioned the environment as a force on their romantic careers.

However, this was different from the ways that most black wives in Los Angeles understood black men in their romantic careers. For example, Jennifer is a black woman who lives in an upper-middle class, predominantly white suburban community with her white husband, Mark and their three children. When discussing her prior relationships in general, she said, "African American men or white men—Jewish—I haven't had a problem with any." When I asked her whether she had ever been teased for having a preference for white or nonblack men, she responded that she never had been.

> JENNIFER: I'm trying to think if I have. But I don't—it's nothing that stands out. A couple of people have asked me, and I say, well, if I had been approached by—but I had never been very much approached by very many African American men.
>
> ME: No?
>
> JENNIFER: Nuh-uh. Yeah.
>
> ME: Why do you think that is?
>
> JENNIFER: I don't know why that is. I don't know. . . . There were . . . a couple of times where I was approached, but I was involved in a serious relationship, so I . . . wasn't willing to break off a relationship for somebody else.

While some black women had experience dating black men, others like Jennifer and a few other black women had limited experience dating black men. These were often black women who had not been raised in black communities. Unlike Carioca black women, their limited dating experiences with black men were not linked to avoidance or understandings of rejection. For black female Angelinos, ethnoracial preferences did not emerge as a theme in explaining their lack of experience dating blacks.

One black woman, Helen, described a shift in her romantic career across the life course. Helen is a woman in her fifties and has lived with

Perry for the last several years. Growing up, her mother emphasized that she should marry a white man, but she rebelled, and both her first and second husbands were black. However, her second husband, Jay, abused her both physically and mentally: "My sisters mostly married white guys. I rebelled—'I'm going to marry a black man.' It was a terrible experience. In some way, in my head, I think I go, 'Mom was right because I, literally, have not dated a black man since then, and that was . . . twenty-one years ago.' Literally, [I] have not since then."

Later in the interview, Helen described how, long after the divorce, Jay would harass her:

> Jay used to, like, come over and, like, bang on my door and throw paint on my bedroom window. Then a neighbor of mine said he caught him hiding in the bushes outside my bedroom. Like, just weird stuff. I called the police on him once. I got a restraining order. He couldn't come past the edge of the driveway where I lived to drop off the boys, stuff like that. It was awful, awful. I decided I am never, ever, ever getting married again, ever. That's when I think it was out of fear and just having such the worst experience in my entire life, and I related it to marrying black. I, literally, have not dated one. I tried. I was, like, I would freeze up. My body would go into a craziness, and this was even after, like, four straight years of therapy. That's how much it affected me.

Helen was the only respondent to mention abuse at the hands of a black husband. She uses ethnoracial boundaries to make sense of that abuse, to the point that she experienced a retraumatization when attempting to date other black men. Heeding her mother's directive, Helen's experiences throughout her romantic career have led her to engage in ethnoracial differentiation to exclude black men as potential romantic partners.

No Ethnoracial Distinctions

I expected that the husbands and wives that I interviewed would not make distinctions based on the ethnoracial categorization of their romantic partners throughout their romantic careers. This was true for many respondents; however, a lack of ethnoracial preference was especially common among black respondents in both societies. For example, Ronald is a black man who lives with his white wife, Felicity, in Los Angeles. They met abroad while volunteering for a nonprofit organization. In his interview, Ronald described the serious relationships that he had before he met Felicity. They involved women who had migrated to the United States from Armenia and Taiwan. When I asked him about his experiences dating white women, he made clear ethnoracial distinctions between European white women from France, as well as geographic distinctions within the United States between Texans and Northeasterners. He admitted that, initially, he had not been attracted to Felicity.

> I found her to be stuck up and bitchy, and I immediately assumed that she was a provincial American who, you know, didn't have much world view, and I was greatly wrong. . . . I just like people who are international and, you know, have some world background. I often find—and this is obviously a very snobbish view—but I often find people who just lived in one area to be a bit provincial in their outlook. . . . In a life partner, I probably want somebody who has had some experience overseas at least—if not being from another culture.

For Ronald, ethnoracial distinctions were not an important factor for establishing romantic connections. Instead, international experience was far more important. This was not just something he vocalized but also something that he practiced, according to the women with whom he had previous serious relationships. Ronald was similar to some blacks whom I interviewed who revealed other factors as being more important for establishing romantic relationships, such as having a personality that was "perfect" or being "fun." These were people who had serious relationships with other blacks as well as with nonblacks. These nonethnoracial factors were part of what led them to relationships with their spouses. These responses were rare among the respondents whom I interviewed in both sites.

Black wives in Los Angeles were often overt about not having an ethnoracial preference in their dating lives. This was despite many of them having past serious relationships with white men throughout their romantic careers. For instance, I interviewed Roxanne, a black woman who lives with her white husband, Fred, in a wealthy area of the city. During her interview, Roxanne described her prior relationships with black men, including one who was overt about his preferences for dating white women. (In her interview, Roxanne described her own racially ambiguous appearance as a very light-skinned black woman.) I had met Roxanne through her sister, Kelly who is also married to a white man, Mark. Both sisters had known their husbands since they were children. During her interview, Roxanne discussed how her family reacted to her marrying a white man:

"None of my sisters had problems with it at all. Because we've all dated [white guys]. [My] two sisters that married black guys, they also dated white guys too. They just fell in love and spent the rest of their lives with somebody that was of the same race, and I probably would have, too, if that's who I fell in love with. I wasn't out there looking for a white guy."

Roxanne had dated black men before her marriage, as had most of the black female Angelinos. This contrasted with several black male Angelinos, who, unlike Ronald, often had little experience dating black women. Roxanne's comments reveal a common theme in my interviews with black wives: they did not have ethnoracial preferences in terms of whom they dated and married. This was different from several black Carioca women who had explicit preferences for white men and some whom even saw themselves increasing their statuses through these relationships.[45]

Black wives in Los Angeles discussed their friends seeing them as making the most out of a bad marriage market for black women in Los Angeles, specifically, and the country more broadly.[46] While there has been much mainstream media discussion of black women supposedly being undesirable marriage partners in the US,[47] very few black wives mentioned this. When they did, it was an explanation for how

TABLE 1.1. Romantic Career Based on Ethnoracial Preferences

	Rio de Janeiro	Los Angeles
White wives	+	−
Black husbands	−	−
White husbands	+	+
Black wives	−	−

other people saw her reasons for dating white men, not their own. Similar to black Carioca wives, they also described their friends praising their white husbands as prizes in a tight marriage market.

Conclusion

In this chapter, I examined the role of race and ethnicity in the ways that husbands and wives understood their "romantic careers." I have summarized the findings in table 1.1. I found that while people in both Rio de Janeiro and Los Angeles employed ethnoracial differences to make sense of their romantic preferences, this was especially the case in Rio de Janeiro. Many white wives were overt in their preferences for *negão* throughout their romantic careers. Their black husbands' past experiences of racial discrimination as well as the taboo of preferring white women colored the ways that black husbands framed their romantic careers; they were merely willing recipients of the attentions of white women. As a result, both Carioca white women and black men were engaged in a process of matching, in which the female desire for *negão* corresponded to their partners "giving in" to those desires. Unlike Angelinos, black women in Rio de Janeiro described enacting revenge against black men through their relationships with white men. This was different for their Carioca white husbands, who often had patterns of dating stigmatized women of varying types, including in terms of race and ethnicity. This brings into question whether these white husbands saw their black wives as having equal status.

Spouses in Los Angeles were different from their Carioca counterparts in a variety of ways. Angelinos rarely discussed trial-and-error experiences of learning their own or outsider's ethnoracial preferences the way that their Carioca counterparts did. Instead of a romantic career, they discussed ethnoracial preferences. However, this was taboo, given US society's false attempts at "color blindness." This resulted in less discussion of preferences overall as well as more silence or hedging around the topic. That said, there were a few people who did discuss ethnoracial preferences. A couple of white women described turning toward black men, given perceptions of strict body-type norms of white men. Also, when blacks mentioned ethnoracial preferences, structural conditions were mentioned to deflect the stigma of preferences. In Los Angeles, white men were the most vocal of the Angelinos about their preferences for non-Anglo women across ethnoracial categories—that included black women. However, in Los Angeles overall, there was a greater lack of differentiation, social or otherwise, in romantic partnering.

In both societies, many respondents did not see finding love as an agentic process over which they had control. In Rio de Janeiro, this meant that white women felt a magnetic attraction to *negão*; on the other hand, black husbands saw themselves as willing magnets of white women's desire. Black women often saw the rejection of black men as a force pushing them toward white men. Most respondents who described a proclivity for racial and ethnic others were typically white. This suggests that while the crossing of racial and color "boundaries of love" is happening on both sides, whites are able to do so more openly than their nonwhite partners. Whites are allowed a "privilege of preference" in comparison to their black partners, who rarely voiced such preferences. In Los Angeles, black husbands and wives often pointed to structural conditions such as neighborhood racial composition to explain the "color" of their previous partners.

For the last decade, a number of assumptions surrounding interracial love have emerged. Many scholars have argued that increases in marriage across race and ethnicity are a sign of the blurring of racial boundaries. Another assumption is that interracial love and marriage are a sign that race is decreasing in importance, since racial discrimination purportedly cannot coexist with love across color lines. In intermarriage, romantic partners are supposed to see their partners (and other members of their partner's racial or ethnic group) as equals. The romantic career of these couples shows that the reality is far more complicated.

Many respondents I interviewed entered relationships with people of another color without upsetting the status and privileges associated with whiteness or the stigma associated with blackness. This chapter shows how the search for romantic partners remains one of the few situations in which discrimination or membership in ethnoracial categories is permissible. As a result, many spouses edify ethnoracial boundaries while others, more rarely, subvert them. Finding love is a beautiful thing that should be celebrated. The heart does exist "to love and to be loved," as one black husband, Nicolas, so eloquently said. However, distinction is a factor in love across race and color lines, and as this chapter shows, sometimes it can be front and center.

2

Boundaries of Blackness

Groupness and Linked Fate

Priscila is the daughter of a white mother and a black father who identifies herself as black (*negra*). Both she and her white husband, Jorge,
are college educated and live in a working-class neighborhood in Rio
de Janeiro. Like several black wives whom I interviewed, she and her
husband live with her child from her first marriage to a black man,
her daughter María. In her interview, she explained why she identified
as a black woman: "We self-identify according to what you bring with
you in terms of identity, conviction, desire, understanding of society.
So there are people with the same skin tone as me who would say that
they are *moreninha* [diminutive of *morena*], mulatto [*mulata*]. And I
have a black identity, my father is black, my ancestry is black, and I also
think that all of this is a militant political commitment, of taking on and
bringing about this position, showing how other people hide behind the
miscegenation of Brazil."

When I interviewed Priscila's white husband, Jorge, I asked him if
he would say that Priscila is black. He agreed that he would but did not
discuss these same attributes: "It's because I think that she has the clear-
est ethnic traits: color, nose, mouth, butt. She has various clear traits that
decide it, like her hair. I identify many black things [in her]."

Like several white spouses, Jorge did not mention Priscila's political
commitment to blackness, nor did he discuss her black ancestry as important components of her blackness the way that she does. His description
of her blackness is related to her phenotype or appearance. For him, she is
without a doubt a black person because of these physical characteristics,
even though they are not what she herself mentioned. There is a disso-
nance in terms of how she identifies herself and how he identifies her.

In general, people construct identities based on the repertoires of habits, skills, and styles available within their societies.[1] As Priscila said, this is a process in which people draw on these repertoires to make sense of themselves. The different histories and cultures of Brazil and the United States influence this process for the individuals in the black-white couples. For example, Priscila's description of her blackness references race mixture and intermediate color and ethnoracial categories, which black movement activists have argued are ways to escape identifying as black.[2]

However, it is also more complicated than this. Individual understandings of self are developed through interactions with others and are influenced by reflected appraisals—how one thinks that others see her or him.[3] In other words, human beings use other individuals as mirrors that reflect back to them images of how they are seen. However, living in racially stratified societies can warp the reflections of members of oppressed ethnoracial communities. In *The Souls of Black Folk*, the social scientist and black activist W. E. B. Du Bois discussed the notion of "double-consciousness," in which US blacks navigate a white supremacist society by having to imagine themselves through the eyes of the dominant group.[4] This "second-sight" is a necessary part of living in a racially stratified society. Today, this idea has especially influenced understandings of multiracial identity.[5]

However, in the twenty-first century, double-consciousness may not solely apply to members of disadvantaged ethnoracial categories. With an increase in interracial marriage and multiracial nuclear and extended families, whites may increasingly have this second-sightedness. In addition, in Brazil, race is largely relational, with people often considering their color classification in light of the darkness and lightness of family members, friends, and spouses.[6] Furthermore, Brazilians categorize themselves differently according to the color of the person asking the question.

Interracial couples provide a unique opportunity to unpack this reflexive process of racialization. In the next two chapters, I analyze this "ethnoracial reflexivity," the ways that an ethnoracial looking-glass self emerges for black-white couples in these two societies. Building on Cooley's idea of reflected appraisals and prior studies of interracial couples goes beyond performative components of blackness and whiteness to remove essentialism from the socially constructed nature of "monoracial" categories like "black" and "white" even in the United States. Unlike with reflected appraisals, ethnoracial reflexivity does not presume a congruence between outsider and insider categorization. I also take advantage of having interview data from both husbands and wives to analyze ethnoracial categorization at the couple or "dyadic" level. I develop the notion of "ethnoracial congruence" to assess how a person understands their self-identification, how an outsider (their spouse) views it, and the consistencies and incongruences between the two.[7] These chapters bring to light the perspectives of both men and women on their and their spouses' ethnoracial classifications. This often gets overshadowed in most studies of interracial couples due to their focus on white women. Looking at how both spouses categorize the same partner can uncover similarities and differences in these constructions and can uncover a potential "second-sight."

In this chapter, I examine the "blackness" of the black spouse, and in the following chapter, I will examine the "whiteness" of the other spouse. Throughout both chapters, I describe how spouses understand their ethnoracial self-identification, the way that their partners identify their spouses, the divergences and convergences between the two, and how this compares across these two sites. I also discuss the ethnoracial reflexivity that can emerge for black spouses. I find a greater ethnoracial congruence between partners in Los Angeles in comparison to the partners in Rio de Janeiro. I also find that, surprisingly, class boundaries were more salient for Los Angeles black spouses in their understanding of their blackness than for black spouses in Rio de Janeiro.

Blackness in Rio de Janeiro

Groupness and Politics

Black spouses in Rio de Janeiro drew on a variety of themes in how they gave meaning to their blackness. When I asked black spouses the question "What is your color?" all but one gave the same answer: "black" (*negro*). At the beginning of this chapter, Priscila described her blackness, despite her white ancestry, as a "militant political commitment." This was similar to several black spouses who understood themselves as part of a larger collective of blacks. In fact, the most common way that black spouses described their blackness was in terms of a sense of groupness and political positioning. "Groupness" involves the sentiment that members of a social category "belong together," even if there is little or no interaction.[8] More than just a sense of commonality, groupness involves a level of connection. While some scholars say that racial groups do not exist in Brazil because of racial boundary-blurring as a result of race mixing,[9] other research suggests that groupness is a reality among Brazilian blacks.[10] I found that many black husbands and wives indeed saw themselves as part of a larger "imagined community"[11] of blacks. This groupness was a key component of their ethnoracial reflexivity.

In the idea of linked fate, there is no longer just "groupness," but blacks see their own life chances being tied to blacks as a whole.[12] This idea was created to understand black politics in the United States. Among the black husbands and wives that I interviewed in Rio de Janeiro, the overwhelming majority did not exhibit a sense of linked fate. This was different from many Los Angeles blacks who indeed thought that their chances in life depended on those of other blacks.

Nevertheless, several black spouses described their sense that being black was more than an ethnoracial category but belonging to a type of collective. This was somewhat evident in the last chapter, in which Danilo described black women as seeming like "sisters." Another black husband, Claúdio, described his approach to engaging other blacks. Claúdio lives with his white wife, Fernanda, in the West Zone of Rio de Janeiro, and neither of them attended college. He compared my hairstyle, short dreadlocks, to that of a black man in his neighborhood.

ME: Do you feel connected to other blacks?
CLAÚDIO: I do feel connected. I feel connected because I make myself connect. There is a black man here, for example. He has hair just like yours; it's just with more dreads. . . . His dreads are fuller. They are of the same size. I used to see him . . . back when I had dreads. . . . So he would pass by me even up till today and talk with me. I don't know his name; where he lives, I don't know. I know that he walks around [the neighborhood] and he goes, "Hey, how's it going?" So it's a thing that's a little real "black power." He sees me and speaks. I see him, and I speak. It's an ethnic connection. . . . So at the same time that I connect with him, I feel disconnected, right? I didn't go up to him

and say, "Hey, buddy! Where you live? What's your name again?" I
didn't go there. I feel connected because I make myself connect.
I look at the other guy and say [gives a thumbs-up sign], "Are you
good?" . . . Just like in the Jill Scott music video, when they do their
hand like that [gives a thumbs-up sign again]. It's more or less like
that. . . . There has to be something to identify this connection.

In the United States, African Americans often engage in what is commonly referred to as "the black hello," in which blacks greet one another
when in spaces where they are not in the majority.[13] Claúdio discussed
engaging in a similar action when encountering a black man in his
neighborhood. His comments reveal a pattern among black spouses in
Rio de Janeiro; while they rarely had a sense of linked fate, they still felt
a sense of ethnoracial groupness with other blacks, so much so that he
referenced a salute among US blacks in a music video.

For black spouses in Rio de Janeiro, blackness was not something that
could be taken for granted. Instead, a black identity was a voluntary and
even political act—something to be owned up to or taken on (*assumir*).
For instance, Eloíza has light-brown skin, kinky hair that she chemically
straightens, and self-described indigenous features. She spoke of using
this rhetoric of "assuming" a black identity and how to do otherwise is to
"camouflage" how things really are: "Take it on. Take it on because you
can say that you are white, but the society is going to see you, and it will
see you as black. Because at some point, you will see that the only ones
who get in are what? The white person is there [inside], and you could
not get in because you are black."

For Eloíza and several respondents, experiencing discrimination is a
core part of having a black identity. Eloíza describes racial discrimination as a key component to having a black identity, in which if a person
does not know their "true" racial identity, it will be "revealed" to them
through racist acts. This was similar to one study of black middle-class
professionals in Rio de Janeiro, in which several respondents articulated
black identities in relationship to experiences of discrimination.[14] Eloíza
articulates a notion of ethnoracial reflexivity in which blacks as a group
are the victims of discrimination. However, like blacks in Rio de Janeiro,
they often mentioned discrimination as a dimension to their blackness.

Los Angeles blacks did not describe their blackness as being political or an identity that they had to adopt. White partners in Rio de Janeiro almost never referenced their black spouse's blackness as a group identity, as having a political dimension, nor as a reaction to discrimination. This was despite the general acknowledgment across color that discrimination has a negative impact on black Brazilians.[15] For example, when I asked Vitor, Eloíza's husband, what his wife's color was, he immediately said, "Black" (*negra*). He responded when I asked him why he decided to use the term *black*:

VITOR: Because her race is black. . . . It's not me who decides.
ME: Okay. So who decides [her color]?
VITOR: In Brazil, there are Indians, whites, and blacks [*índios, brancos, e negros*]. . . . And Eloíza is . . . I am *sarará*, in the middle [*meio-termo*].

Vitor evaded answering the complicated question of who decides Eloíza's color by repeating popular understandings of Brazil's three original peoples. I often heard statements similar to this when asking Brazilians for examples of black-white couples to interview. (While they claimed they knew blacks married to whites, these contacts rarely materialized into referrals of actual couples.) Yet Vitor's comments reveal a shallow understanding of blackness despite being married to a self-identified black woman. It was very different from the political assertion of a black identity that Eloíza referenced earlier. Instead, Vitor immediately shifted to his own self-identification, a dynamic that was more common among the husbands that I interviewed. This was largely a pattern that I found among black husbands when describing their white wives, which I discuss further in the next chapter. The only white spouse who referenced their black partner's group-based identity was the one who referenced being negatively impacted by it. It was Marisa, a white woman mentioned in the previous chapter, who discussed her husband's exclusion of her related to his identification with the Brazilian black movement.

The image of blackness that white partners revealed did not neatly align with the ways that black spouses saw themselves as black. On this dimension of black identity, white and black spouses had a low degree of ethnoracial congruence, in which white spouses' understandings of their spouses' blackness did not line up with black spousal self-identification. In other words, the components of the ethnoracial boundaries of blackness were different for black spouses vis-à-vis their white partners.

Phenotype

In Brazil, a person's appearance and not necessarily their ancestry plays a large part of ethnoracial and color classification.[16] This has been historically contrasted with the United States, where ancestry has been more salient in how to classify a person.[17] Several black spouses in Rio de Janeiro discussed their phenotypes, including their skin color, hair texture, and facial features, as explanations for their self-identification as black. It was the second most common way that black spouses explained their blackness. This was different from black spouses in Los Angeles, who did not discuss their blackness in terms of physical appearance during their interviews.

Griselda is a college-educated black woman married to Téofilo, a white man who did not attend college. Alongside education-based status exchange, she inherited a condo in a wealthy neighborhood where they live, and she helped finance her husband's store, which he operates. They live with her two daughters from a previous relationship to a black man. In her interview, she referenced her "potato nose" ("*um nariz batata*") and "thick lips" ("*labios grossos*") as part of her explanation of her blackness. Donato is a black husband who lives with his white wife, Angela, and their daughter in a racially mixed, working-class suburb of Rio de Janeiro. Neither of them has attended college. Some black Carioca spouses, like Donato, referenced both phenotype and biological components in their discussion of their blackness. When I asked him his color, he said black and explained why.

DONATO: Because of my color, because of my blood, I am black. . . .
The blood that runs here [in my veins] is black blood.
ME: But isn't blood red?
DONATO: It is, but it is a blood—how can I say this? The DNA that is here, that runs here, is the DNA of a black man.

In addition to describing his phenotype, Donato references pseudo-scientific claims of racial essentialism. There is no such thing biologically as black blood or black DNA.[18] However, Donato draws on these essentialist notions of race to identify and categorize himself.

Bartolomeu is a black husband who lives with his white wife, Edite, both in their thirties, in a working-class community near the center of Rio de Janeiro. I asked him what his color was, and he immediately said, "Black." When I asked him why, he looked at his outer arms and then quickly turned them over to examine his forearms. By the time of his interview, this was a familiar gesture; when looking for couples to interview, I occasionally asked Cariocas what their own colors were. Many of them would proceed to look at their arms and then turn them over to look at their forearms, insisting that was their true color since it was untouched by the sun. Just like in Bartolomeu's case, this small action showed the importance physical appearance holds to an individual's categorization in Brazil. While a few spouses of either color engaged in this action, none of the Los Angeles respondents did this. This element of phenotype reveals a looking-glass and double-consciousness quality in which Brazilians are cognizant of how they see themselves and how they are perceived as they move in the world. However, they combine this understanding with a "true" color category that is only revealed upon close inspection.

Bartolomeu's wife, Edite, concurred with her husband's assertion that he is black. When I asked her why, she said, "Due to the color of his skin . . . what else?" Several white partners referenced their partners' phenotypes in their identification of their spouses as black. This was also unlike Los Angeles white spouses who did not discuss the physical appearance of their black partners in the meanings that they gave to the partner's blackness. In Rio de Janeiro, the most congruence between black spouses and their white partners was on this theme of phenotype in which four different couples matched. On this dimension, the ways that black partners saw themselves was reflected back in how white partners saw them. The degree of ethnoracial congruence on the dimension of phenotype is likely due to it literally being about physical appearance. Also, since Brazil is less residentially segregated than the United States,[19] blacks and whites in Rio de Janeiro couples likely "see" race similarly within the couples.

Family and Ancestry

Another common way that black spouses described their blackness was in terms of their ancestry and their family. Priscila's comments at the beginning of the chapter show how she draws on her understanding of her ancestry to claim a black identity (despite her white ancestry as well). In part, this is the fruit of the black movement in Brazil, which has made having a black identity a source of pride for many Afro-Brazilians.[20] In addition, having a racially mixed ancestry is an important part of Afro-Brazilians' understandings of their blackness. This is very different from the majority of black Angelino respondents, who did not understand a racially mixed ancestry as central to their blackness.

In another example, Katarina is a black woman who lives a few hours from the center of Rio de Janeiro in a racially mixed working-class suburb. She and her husband, Otávio, did not finish elementary school and live with their two sons. When I asked her what her color was, she said "black" and then explained why: "I think it's because I was born to a family of blacks. My father was black. My mother was black. Both of them [were black], so I am black." Katarina gave a simple explanation of how she understands herself that is rooted in her family genealogy. This was similar to several other Afro-Brazilian husbands and wives who described their blackness in the same way. This is similar to several studies of ethnoracial categorization in which blacks often identified themselves by their ancestry.[21] Ancestry was also a part of how black Angelinos identified themselves. However, it was predominantly black husbands, not black wives, who did so.

White partners in Rio de Janeiro occasionally discussed their spouses' families as a reason for their spouses' blackness. However, black spouses and their white partners hardly ever overlapped in understandings of family in black identities. This was different from white spouses in Los Angeles who rarely discussed their black spouses' families in their identifications. Very few white partners discussed their spouses' families and ancestries in terms of understanding the spouses' blackness. In Rio de Janeiro, ethnoracial congruence was weak on this ancestral dimension of blackness.

Euphemisms for Blackness

In Priscila's interview excerpt at the beginning of the chapter, she describes eschewing terms like *moreninha* and *mulata* to describe herself in favor of a black identity. Priscila was like several black Carioca husbands and wives who expressed distaste for what they saw as euphemisms for blackness. A number of black respondents had similar feelings about terms like *moreno* or *moreninho*. The term *morena* can mean a variety of things, such as "brunette," "brown," "swarthy," or "dark-colored." The term *morena* has a long history of use in popular culture, and many Brazilians identify with the term.[22] However, it is ambiguous, which is one of the reasons that the equivalent of the Brazilian census bureau, the IBGE (Instituto Brasileiro de Geografía e Estadística), does not use it for official counts.[23] (However, the census also doesn't use *negro*, an increasingly popular term for black.) Recent scholarly work shows how Brazilians are increasingly shunning these euphemisms in favor of a *negro* identity.[24] I found this pattern among many black respondents, who often balked at the term *morena*, its diminutives (e.g., *moreninha*), and *escuro* or *escurinho* (dark or darkish), which they understood as euphemisms for blackness. Instead, they favored the term *negro*. Many respondents considered these euphemisms as devaluing blackness. This was different from Los Angeles black spouses, who did not reference avoiding euphemisms or terms apart from *black*.

Some black respondents, all of them black husbands, expressed such antagonism toward these types of euphemisms that they went as far as to say that these terms "do not exist" (*"não existe"*). This was the case for Patrício, a black man married to Juliana, mentioned in the last chapter in the discussion on "matching." When I asked him, "What is your color?" black (*negro*) was his response. I asked him to clarify why he said black and not another color.

PATRÍCIO: I think that my color is black. . . . It's because I understand that it is different. . . . From what I know, I consider myself to be black.

ME: Why? Why black and not another color?

PATRÍCIO: *Moreno*? Dark *moreno* [*moreno escuro*]? I am not a dark *moreno*. I am really black! . . . Because really, on my certificate, it says black. . . . It's from when I applied to enroll in the military. . . . The certificate goes like this—"5'8"; skin color: black [*preta*]; eyes: light brown" or something like that. So then they should have put "color: black [*negra*]." Instead of putting the color *negra*, they put "skin color: *preta*." But a *preta* skin color [*cor de pele*] does not exist. *Negra* the color exists.

ME: What's the difference between the two?

PATRÍCIO: Once . . . I learned this in school, you know? In school is where the teacher said that this color does not exist—the word *preto*. You know? That the word *preto* is tied very much to this thing about color, ink, something with which you paint. It has nothing to do with the name of a race. . . . I consider myself black, you know, because our natural language is black.

In Portuguese, as in other Romance languages, all objects are masculine or feminine and adjectives modify the object they are describing. The word *cor*, or "color," is feminine, so *negra* and *preta* are used for a type of color. Patrício is a man, so *negro* or *preto* would be applied to him. Patrício's interview illuminated many of the patterns of the black spouses, for whom the term *moreno* was not a possibility for describing themselves. In addition, he described how the term *preta* also does not exist for people. He referenced how, in Portuguese, there are two terms for the word *black*: *preta* and *negro*. The term *preta*, as Patrício points out, is often used to refer to the color of things, such as ink, clothing, or other items. The term *negra* refers to the race of an individual (a *preto* book versus a *negro* man). Since people do not come in the actual color black, Patrício rejects *preto* as a term to describe himself. This is particularly striking since the term *negro*, which he prefers, is not an official Brazilian census category, whereas *preto* is one. This may explain his conflict between the military's description and his self-classification.

Patrício was similar to several black wives and husbands because his own white partner did not discuss a concern over euphemisms for blackness the way that they did. Once more, there was discordance within couples, in which white partners largely did not reference the same themes in discussing the black spouses' blackness. This discordance reveals a lack of ethnoracial congruence within couples since the ways that these blacks understood their blackness in terms of these euphemisms was not reflected back in their own white partners' comments.

Several white partners also discussed how euphemisms for blackness "did not exist." They were not, however, the partners of black spouses who had done the same. For example, Carlota is married to Adaír, a black man, and is college educated. They live together in a multiracial, gentrifying neighborhood in Rio de Janeiro. Another Brazilian black-white couple whom I interviewed, Ana María and Cândido, referred me to Carlota and Adair as another black-white couple to interview. However, Carlota was one of the few spouses who did not identify as white, despite her friend's classification. When describing Adair's color and her own, she referenced beer as a metaphor, saying, "There are pale ales, and there are stouts [*chopp claro e chopp escuro*]. So I am a pale ale, and he is a stout." However, she also described him in ways similar to Patrício.

ME: What is your husband's color?

CARLOTA: He is black [*negro*].

ME: Why did you decide on black?

CARLOTA: Why did I decide on it? No, it's like this: we have a habit here in Brazil of saying, "Oh, and your *moreninho* husband?" I said, "My *moreninho* husband?" So there are two possibilities: either he is *negro* or he is *preto*. *Moreninho* he is not. . . . This thing about color is very touchy. There was a survey a while ago in Brazil, a census [that asked], "What is your color?" They identified almost two hundred types: café au lait [*café-com leite*], brownish [*marrozinho*], *moreninho*, mulatto-ish [*mulatinho*], like that. It's just like beer. So you got to the bar and they go, "What kind of draft do you want: light or dark [*claro ou escuro*]?" Right? Because it's like this: the dark is not necessarily the color black [*preto*], but it has a very closed color. But it's a response that I don't know how to give you: "Why did I say he is black [*negro*]"? Because he certainly has a color that is more closed than mine. I am not white, either. Because, it's like this—there are people that have a black [*preto*] . . . that it is almost blue. It's beautiful. Adair does not have that intensity of color. But he is not a color, he is a person. Color is only about pigmentation, about the melanin that you have, right? So that's it.

Carlota was similar to several white spouses who eschewed the term *moreno*, it's diminutives, and the variety of terms that her husband could potentially use. She cites often quoted studies in which Brazilians use hundreds of terms to discuss race and color. For example, in a 1970 study of a small village in Bahia, Marvin Harris found more than 492 terms used to describe thirty-six different people.[25] In a 1976 national survey, over one hundred terms were identified.[26] However, this finding results from placing more weight on the variation in terms than on their frequency or modality. This perspective is problematic in that it often overlooks how the overwhelming majority of people, 98 percent, used the same six terms: white (*branco*), *moreno*, brown (*pardo*), light *moreno*, black (*preto*), *negro*, and light (*claro*). Carlota draws on two of those terms, *preto* and *negro*, to describe her husband, Adair, just as Patrício did. However, Adair, a black husband, did not discuss these euphemisms for his own blackness. Neither did Patrício's wife, Juliana, in discussing her husband's blackness. Even though the same understandings of blackness existed among black and white spouses, there was more variation within couples than across couples along different intersections of race and gender.

This question of euphemisms for blackness "not existing" was found especially among couples involving black men with white women. While several black women also took offense to the use of terms like *moreninha*, they never said that these terms did not exist. This is likely because in Brazil, people often like to "lighten" the color of women but not men. As a consequence, it is likely that Afro-Brazilian men do not get called euphemisms and diminutives like *mulatinho* for blackness as often as Afro-Brazilian women do. In fact, the Brazilian government and the tourism industry have a long history of selling the "licentious" *mulatas* to foreigners as part of experiencing Brazil that continues to the present day.[27] In addition, the term *mulata* is commonplace in popular culture, being the subject of vast amounts of literature and popular songs.[28] This ever-present feminization of the racially mixed Afro-Brazilian means that women may have greater access to terms besides *morena* or *preta* to describe themselves. As Priscila said at the beginning of the chapter, "There are people with the same skin tone as me who would say that they are *moreninha* [a diminutive of *morena*], mulatto [*mulata*]. And I have a *negra* identity." For the black wives whom I interviewed, these euphemisms indeed exist because they supposedly embody them and had even been called by those terms in face-to-face interactions. Nevertheless, they rejected them in favor of calling themselves *negras*. For these women, ethnoracial reflexivity was likely important for how they saw others seeing them, yet they rejected these outsider assessments.

Relational Component

In Brazil, a person's categorization is much more contextual, according to the people surrounding them, than in the United States.[29] People often think about their proximate family members when classifying themselves by color.[30] I found a similar pattern among the black spouses that I interviewed. Many of them described their blackness in reference to another person. For example, Nicolas is a black man married to Laura, a white woman. They live together with her mother and their child near the center of Rio de Janeiro in a mixed-race, working-class neighborhood. In his interview, he identified himself as black. I asked him about the term *moreno*, which I had often heard people use.

> ME: Who is *moreno?*
>
> NICOLAS: Oh, I don't know. . . . My daughter can get a little darker [*ficar mais moreninha*] because Laura is light, you know? But me, *moreno*, for what? Put [your arm] here. [I place my arm next to his.] What is the difference between my color and yours? There isn't any. And I'm even darker, more closed.
>
> ME: Than me? No.
>
> NICOLAS: Look here. I'm more closed. Here, here.
>
> ME: I think that you are lighter than me, a little bit.
>
> NICOLAS: No, that doesn't exist. So those dudes who are pulling that cart, they are black, and I am *moreno?*
>
> ME: Hmm, you do not see a difference?
>
> NICOLAS: The difference does not exist. There isn't one. I do not accept that there is one.

Nicolas' excerpt reveals the relational nature of self-identification that several black husbands and wives described in Rio de Janeiro. He sees his own color in terms of his daughter's color. In addition, he compared his own skin color to my own, coming to the resolution that we are the same color. This was despite my own assessment that we were not the same color. This discrepancy is likely due to the fact that even color is a social construct. For example, research on the blind shows how since race is a social construct, not a biological or physical one, even they are able to "see" race.[31] This may be why Nicolas notices his darker, more "closed" color in comparison to mine, despite my looking at our arms and perceiving that I was darker than him. In addition, as mentioned before, gender biases ethnoracial categorization such that women are often seen as lighter than men.[32] This gender bias may have made it impossible for him to see me as darker than him. Nicolas also compared his skin color to that of men who go about the city collecting junk who are stereotypically black, adamantly espousing a notion of a collective blackness.

Unlike Du Bois' notion of double-consciousness, Nicolas' ethnoracial reflexivity is not limited to being vis-à-vis a distant white gaze but includes a relational comparison to myself, the junk collectors, and even his daughter. This relational element to blackness did not occur among Los Angeles black spouses. In addition, it was rarely a part of how white partners in Rio de Janeiro understood their black spouses' blackness. Consequently, ethnoracial congruence was also low on this dimension, with only one husband and wife matching on understanding the black spouse's color as relational.

Official Documents

In his interview, Patrício recalled the way that he was categorized in official military documents. While he does not agree with the way that they categorized him as *preto* instead of *negro*, this discourse was similar to several black spouses who referenced official documents in their explanations for why they identified as *negro* or *negra*. For example, Edvaldo is a black man who lives in the suburbs of Rio de Janeiro in a racially mixed neighborhood with his white wife, Verônica. Neither of them attended college. When I asked Edvaldo, "What is your color?" he replied that he is black because that was what was written on his birth certificate. I found that referencing official documents was a pattern

mainly among lower-educated black spouses who referred to birth cer-
tificates or military draft documents in their understanding of their
color category. This was different from black spouses in Los Angeles,
who did not mention official documents when they described how and
why they identify as black.

Ethnoracial reflexivity vis-à-vis the state is a concern many have
raised surrounding the use of ethnoracial categories for public policies
addressing racial inequality.[33] Specifically, many have raised the question
of whether using color categories in Brazil would lead to stronger group
identities that could threaten the society's reputation for racial harmony,
having unintended consequences. However, self-classification is already
a part of the lives of the Brazilians whom I interviewed, none of whom
referenced affirmative action programs in assessing their blackness.

A few white partners also discussed official documents in discussing their spouses' blackness. While they were few, they varied across
education levels. For example, Otávio is the white husband of Katarina,
the black woman who referenced being "born to a family of blacks."
Neither he nor his wife finished elementary school. In his interview,
he described how his wife identified herself using terms such as dark
(*escura*) or *negra*. (In her interview, she only used the term *negra*). However, when I asked him what her color was, he said, "She is black [*preta*].
The color black. . . . It already comes on the birth certificate. They put
black as the color." None of the black spouses or their white Angelino
partners referenced official documents in how they understood blacks'
identification.

In Rio de Janeiro, black spouses and their white partners rarely agreed
on the bases for the classification of black spouses. Even when black
spouses drew on similar themes as white partners, they rarely coincided
within the same couple. Table 2.1 provides a summary of the number
of black spouses who used a particular theme to describe how they saw
themselves as black, how their white partners did so, and the extent of
congruence between the two. These findings show a low degree of ethnoracial congruence among black-white couples in Rio de Janeiro, with
at most two but mainly only one couple in which both the partner and
spouse were on the same page of the black partner's self-categorization.
This was different from Los Angeles, as will be shown in the next section.

TABLE 2.1. Rio de Janeiro Couples on Blackness

Theme	Black Spouse	White Partner	Number of Congruent Partners
Family/ancestry	7	3	1
Phenotype	7	5	2
Euphemisms	4	4	1
Groupness/politics	10	1	1
Official documents	5	3	1
Relational component	5	2	1
Total*	22	19	7

* Totals do not add up because many respondents used more than one theme.

Blackness in Los Angeles

History and Resistance to Discrimination

In Los Angeles, I also asked black spouses and their white partners about the categorization of the black spouse. This was extremely awkward. The outsider benefit I enjoyed in Brazil disappeared when I asked Los Angeles couples about their racial identities. Angelinos appeared amused and bemused by the question. For the majority of blacks (and whites) in the United States, how a person self-categorizes their racial identity is often taken for granted. Declaring a black racial identity is not linked to politics or "taken up" the way that it is in Brazil. I had to openly ask respondents, especially black ones, to suspend their disbelief in what surely seemed like a thought experiment.

To explain their blackness, some black spouses discussed how the endurance of and resistance to oppression were central to their identities as black; this included centuries of enslavement, Jim Crow, and the civil rights movement. These black husbands and wives referenced "race pride" and saw heroes like Martin Luther King as important forbearers of their cultural heritage. For example, Quentin is a black man in his late twenties who lives in a racially diverse neighborhood in Los Angeles with his wife, Gloria. He said that being black is about being proud "of who you are and what you are. I mean, be proud of how God made you." While there is some evidence of race pride in large-scale Brazilian surveys, I did not find it among the Carioca black spouses whom I interviewed.

Several black spouses described the experiences of discrimination that they, their family members, and their ancestors had suffered as important elements of how they saw themselves as black people. Black spouses in Los Angeles articulated a narrative of a history of enduring and fighting against racial discrimination. This was different from Carioca black spouses, who rarely mentioned the history of blacks in Brazil, slavery, or the contribution of blacks to Brazilian history as part of their understandings of their blackness.[34] It was also unlike blacks in Peru, for whom slavery and African ancestry were not a part of their black identities.[35] The Cariocas that I interviewed did not deny slavery or slave ancestry. Despite inhabiting the last country to abolish slavery in the Western hemisphere, in 1888, it was just not as central to Cariocas' identities as black as it was to Angelino black spouses.

Why was slavery central to black Angelino spouses' sense of blackness but not for the black Carioca spouses? Although the United States was the first nation in the Western hemisphere to declare independence from a European colonial power, it maintained slavery for almost a century after. This was not the case for most French and Spanish colonies in the Western hemisphere. The heavy participation of Afro-descendants in the wars of independence and the proceeding civil wars meant that freedom was a concession to large numbers of slaves and free Afro-descendants.[36] These terms of abolition allow identities related to slavery to be subsumed under a national identity surrounding independence from European powers.[37] A similar dynamic was not available to most Afro-descendants in the United States; it took a civil war for abolition and the civil rights movement for citizenship to become a reality.

Brazil was different. Instead of a war of independence, it split from the Portuguese empire, declaring itself an independent empire, and became a constitutional monarchy. Although there were millions more slaves brought to Brazil, and slave mortality was higher than in the United States, Brazil also had higher rates of manumission and greater proportions of the African-born.[38] By the mid-nineteenth century, the majority of people of color either were free persons or had been manumitted. Perhaps learning from its northern and surrounding neighbors, Brazilian abolition did not occur through war but occurred over decades through legislation and finally a monarchical edict known as the Golden Law, signed by the Imperial Princess Isabel. When abolition came in

1888, the overwhelming majority of Afro-descendants were already free. For this reason, as in most of Latin America and the Caribbean, Afro-descendant identities after abolition were less tied to slavery in Brazil than in the United States.

On the Margins of Blackness: Class and Ethnicity

Angelino black spouses had a stronger group identity than their counterparts in Rio de Janeiro, with many seeing their lots in life as being tied to those of other blacks. Despite their stronger sense of linked fate and groupness, many of the Los Angeles black respondents described understanding themselves as being on the outskirts of that social group: within it yet at the margins of blackness. Prior research has shown that blacks with higher-status backgrounds have a lower sense of closeness toward other blacks.[39] I found this pattern among the black spouses whom I interviewed in Los Angeles; socioeconomic status was often noted as dividing them from many other blacks.

This influence of class background was likely a product of the types of blacks who intermarry; in the United States, college-educated blacks and whites are more likely to intermarry than those with lower levels of education.[40] This educational difference was reflected in the Los Angeles sample, where the overwhelming majority of black spouses had at least some college experience (appendix table 1). In both sites, highly educated black spouses discussed socioeconomic differences as separating them from less-educated blacks. In Los Angeles, this distinction was the most common theme on blackness that was reported among black respondents. This was different from black spouses in Rio de Janeiro, where even among the most-educated respondents, it only rarely emerged as a theme. This was an unexpected finding, given the influence of class and socioeconomic status on how people are categorized according to color in Brazil.[41]

This class boundary occurred among both black men and women. However, black wives often expressed concerns over appearing haughty in their interviews or as "snobs" to other black people. This was the case for Jennifer, a college-educated black woman who lived with her husband, Neil, and her son from a previous marriage to a black man. They all lived in a predominantly white neighborhood in Los Angeles. When asked about how much she thinks that she has in common with other black people, she said, "Well, it depends." After repeatedly expressing concerns about not wanting to sound "snooty," she explained,

> There's an author that I absolutely love, who is Zora Neale Hurston, and one of her quotes that I love to death—I use it all the time—is that "You may be my people, but you sho' ain't my kind." I think it has less to do with black people in general than those that are probably the same type of background that I have as far as economics are concerned, which probably sounds, like, really snooty and snobby, but it isn't. . . . I went to school at Howard, and typically, the women and men that I hung out with had very similar types of upbringings, as far as they went to private schools or they traveled when they were young. They came from a different socioeconomic class, so in that regard, that saying comes into play: "You may be my people, but you sho' ain't my kind" because I obviously don't identify with every black person, because we have different backgrounds. I mean, if the only thing we have in common is our skin, then that's not much in common at all. I hope that doesn't sound horrible . . . but it's just, like, I'm not going to be hanging out with someone that's got their pants hanging off their ass, that only listens to hip-hop music and nothing else, that has never, you know—not even if they've never traveled, but [they] aren't even up to the idea of traveling or doing something outside of what they normally do. I'm not going to do that, because that's a pigeonhole; that's not who I am, so therefore, I wouldn't have anything to really talk about with someone who sort of lives in this little bubble and never tries to expand or get out of it. I hope that doesn't sound bad . . . because I'm always like "So where do . . . where are the professional black people at in this town" because I don't meet them unless it's work related, and then they're typically producers and actors, but I guess that's it. Whereas, in predominantly black cities like DC, they're everywhere; you just walk down the street, and there they are.

Jennifer draws on cultural understandings of class boundaries among African Americans in which taste, such as a desire to travel or the experience of attending one of the Historically Black Colleges and Universities

(HBCUs), set her apart from other blacks. She also discussed a black middle-class community and environment that she previously had access to while living in Washington, DC, and feels that she no longer has access to in Los Angeles. For this reason, she understands African Americans who are not cultural omnivores (like many middle-class people),[42] only listen to hip-hop, and dress in more of a street style as people on the other side of a class boundary. She sees herself as part of a black elite, referencing an elite black institution and private schools to show how she perceived herself as different from the blacks that she encountered in Los Angeles. While Jennifer uses cultural preferences to draw boundaries against other blacks who are not middle class, she also articulates concerns over appearing conceited. This was similar to several blacks that I interviewed who mentioned class differences, displayed cognizance of those differences, and set themselves apart from other blacks accordingly. For these black spouses, class boundaries complicated their feelings of blackness.

Several white spouses also recognized what they saw as a class boundary between their spouses and many other blacks. Larry is one such white husband. He lives with Lana, a black woman, in a predominantly white neighborhood. Both of them are college educated. Like most Los Angeles couples that I interviewed, both of them moved to Los Angeles from other areas of the country. When I asked him about commonalities that she has with other blacks, Larry described how she had grown up in a town with a large Jewish community: "So I imagine that if you looked at what other black kids growing up in a similar situation [are like]—her parents were doctors, and they're pretty well off—so you look at some well-off black kid in a suburban neighborhood outside any other city, [and] I'd imagine they'd have a lot in common. I think if you looked at Lana and somebody from an inner-city, black neighborhood . . . the things in common wouldn't probably match up as well."

In his interview, similar to spouses both black and white, Larry was uncomfortable with making generalizations and appearing to stereotype blacks. Nevertheless, he described Lana's parents' occupational status as well as the characteristics of the community where she grew up as elements of the distinction that he drew between her and other "inner-city" blacks. In her interview, Lana echoed several of Larry's sentiments.

She acknowledged that racism was what she had in common with other blacks and said that she did not want to "generalize black experiences." Nevertheless, she said, "I felt like my experience has been very different from other black people's, I guess. . . . I think growing up in my income level was unusual from my experience and being a black family." Lana drew on her socioeconomic background to differentiate between herself and other blacks. While the majority of blacks in the United States do not live in poverty, they are overrepresented among the poor in comparison to white Americans or Americans as a whole.[43] Lana makes distinctions between herself and other blacks based on her experiences growing up in a white, ethnic, segregated community and attending segregated, predominantly white schools.

Larry and Lana's similar perspectives were echoed among several other black-white couples in Los Angeles who also experienced convergence on this dimension of blackness. Six black spouses and their own white partners recognized class boundaries as something that complicated the black spouses' blackness. Even though both black men and black wives commented on class distinctions, white husbands were more likely to engage in this class-distinction making.

On the Margins of Blackness: Class and Immigration

For some black spouses, having immigrant origins complicated their understandings of being black in the United States. Five of the nineteen black spouses that I interviewed in Los Angeles—mostly women—had grown up in immigrant families from Africa or the Caribbean, whether they had been born abroad (first generation), came as youths (1.5 generation), or had been born in the United States to immigrant parents (second generation). When discussing their blackness, they described not fitting in with other blacks as children. However, this changed as they became older. The combination of being immigrants and highly educated led to feelings of being within the boundaries yet on the edge of US blackness, problematizing how they articulated a sense of groupness and commonality with other US blacks. Visola was one of these respondents. She was born and raised in the United States to parents born in Kenya and had lived in Kenya for a few years as a child. Visola lives with her white husband, Charles, in a predominantly black neighborhood in Los Angeles. When I asked Visola about what she has in common with other black people, she said,

> I don't know. . . . I think I have a lot in common with a lot of black people, but I think it's just—there's always a twist to it because . . . I think in large part as an adult, I'm more accepted now than when I was growing up, I guess, within the African American community. But there's always that—still that sense of not being completely in. . . . I guess I still go back to that experience when I was in college of some of the African American kids . . . not necessarily seeing me as one of them just because my name was different and I was Nigerian and stuff like that. . . . We could never be full participants . . . in the struggle. And that's kind of what I meant by never really feeling completely accepted by the African American community, because there are people who have said that to me in the past. . . . People feel that I couldn't possibly get it because I was raised in a middle-class household . . . I carry myself in a particular way, [and] I speak in standard English.

Visola describes ethnoracial reflexivity in understanding her blackness in light of interactions with nonimmigrant African Americans. She found that black people do not see her as black in the same way as those who were not raised in middle-class households. Despite the commonalities that she perceives, she has had experiences in which she sees her class background, immigrant ancestry, and mannerisms being read as characteristics of an outsider to the African American community. Her comments were ironic, given she was in one of only two couples who lived in a black community. Still, other respondents from immigrant families made similar remarks, seeing themselves as partial outsiders to US understandings of blackness. A history of overcoming struggle was not salient in these immigrant blacks' understandings of their blackness. In comparison, with a much smaller black immigrant population in Rio de Janeiro (mainly from Angola and Mozambique), immigration was not a part of how black Cariocas understood their blackness.

This immigrant ancestry was a part of how white partners understood their spouses' blackness. This was certainly the case for William, a white man married to Betty, a black woman who emigrated from the

Caribbean when she was young. When I interviewed him, he discussed how despite being a Caribbean immigrant, she has a lot in common with African Americans "because of the way that race works in the US."

> I think that pretty much that anyone with dark skin is kind of lumped into the same group, and therefore they're treated by others in a similar way, as if they are this unified whole—so people talk about the black community. Well, that's ridiculous because there's this much of a rainbow within the black community as there is within the white community. . . . The black community is treated the same as a lump group. She gets treated the same as somebody who grew up in Compton would be treated by a lot of people, so she has that in common. She can talk to somebody who comes from a totally different place. She came from the Caribbean, but she's still going to have a lot in common just in her daily experiences in dealing with people as somebody who grew up in Compton because they're looked at from the outside as the same, so they're going to be treated the same. . . . She's not American, she's not raised here, so she's not an African American by any stretch or any accounting. So I usually just say . . . we invented this term . . . PAD—"person of African descent." It's easier to say than African American, which is super clumsy and nondescriptive. . . . Black has all the negative linguistic connotations that come with it, so the bad guy is always black, and the good guy is always white, so I'm not a big fan. . . . What race is she? She's [of] African descent is far as I'll go.

William was one of the few white spouses who referenced the commonalities that black spouses in general have with other blacks. He described the ethnoracial boundary drawing and discrimination that outsiders engage in by treating people who look like Betty the same, regardless of the neighborhood that they are from or their ethnic background. He also references her ethnoracial groupness, in which she relates to other blacks regardless of their ethnic background. For William, Betty's immigrant origins do not complicate her blackness because of outsiders' potential stigmatization.

There was a great deal of ethnoracial congruence on this dimension of blackness, with three couples discussing the black spouses' blackness in terms of their immigrant heritage. Three out of five black immigrants described their immigrant backgrounds as part of their blackness. However, four out of five white spouses recognized their black spouses' immigrant ancestry as part of their blackness. The two black spouses who did not describe their blackness in terms of their immigrant backgrounds both had mothers who were native to the US. This suggests that the gender of the migrant parent is important for ethnic socialization and understandings of ethnoracial boundaries of blackness.

On the Margins of Blackness: Culture

Black spouses had other ways apart from socioeconomic differences in which they described their statuses as "outsiders" to what they understood as black social norms. Los Angeles black spouses described how they were on the outskirts of black groupness because of their lack of participation in cultural forms associated with African Americans. Some black spouses referenced distaste for the "street culture" and hip-hop that had come to define US blackness in their eyes. This was ironic given the centrality of Los Angeles in understandings and stereotypes of blackness, as seen in gangsta rap and Hollywood films like the classic *Boyz in the Hood* and, more recently, *Straight Outta Compton*, a film depicting the beginnings of Los Angeles' hip-hop scene, involving famous rappers like Dr. Dre and Ice Cube.[44] This was different from Jennifer, mentioned earlier, for whom cultural omnivorism was central to her middle-class blackness. For respondents like her, class was not central to their cultural preferences. Rather than an appreciation for different cultural forms, these black spouses revealed a distaste for these popular or black cultural forms.

For example, Gary is a college-educated black man who was mentioned in the last chapter. He lives with his white wife, Pavla, an Eastern European immigrant.

> I'm not the typical, like, I don't typically relate to the black culture, I guess. A lot of the hip-hop, and that stuff—which is popular, with especially a lot of people in our race—when I was younger, I kind of listened to it, but I never really got it, just because I didn't have a lot of those experiences that rappers have. I don't look at them as role models. I don't look at that lifestyle as something to aspire to, but that's just the popular aspect of it;

but I just . . . I haven't really been . . . immersed in black culture too much like probably my sister has, going to school on the East Coast or you had growing up in Chicago.

Gary spatially locates black culture within the country, describing how blackness is not a strong component of Los Angeles but is something that is found further to the east of the country. Several respondents also regionalized blackness to the South or Northeast of the country, suggesting that despite the large number of blacks living in Los Angeles, black culture is strongest "back East." Like Gary, several respondents described how they did not identify with the cultural elements that are often attributed to US blacks. He described cultural elements such as music and a reverence for rappers that link blacks to one another. However, he places himself outside of this element of groupness. This was a different dynamic from black spouses in Rio de Janeiro, who did not articulate their blackness as outside or inside of cultural dynamics. Black spouses in Rio de Janeiro rarely described a distaste for black cultural elements and did not describe their lack of affinity for Afro-Brazilian culture as putting them on the outskirts of blackness. This is likely due to the nationalization of art forms originally associated with Afro-Brazilians, such as samba, since the mid-twentieth century.[45]

Language also emerged as a cultural element that problematized black spouses' sense of black belonging. Several black wives and husbands described how other blacks interpreted their idiolect as "talking white." Angelino black spouses discussed their speech as a sign of middle-class culture that was a barrier to their relationships with other black people. None of the black spouses in Rio de Janeiro referenced a distinct way of speaking in reference to their blackness. This may be due to the lower levels of residential segregation in Rio de Janeiro and Brazil overall, which prevents the development of separate language communities based on color.

Trevor is a black husband who lives with his wife, Elizabeth, and their two children. Originally from the Midwest, Trevor described how he grew up in a predominantly black neighborhood and that his father owned a business when he was young. Trevor's family would not allow him to answer the phone because customers would immediately think they had reached a white family and had the wrong number. He said that his speech was a cultural marker that served as a barrier to blackness, adding that the way that he speaks is related to his level of education:

"Education really is a barrier in some ways. I do not—I mean, it's not that I'm an education snob; it's just the language issue is just different. I talk differently from a—if I were to go into certain parts of Los Angeles, I don't talk the way they talk, and that's just the way it is, and that's an education thing."

Speech becomes a marker of class that identifies Trevor as different from other blacks who speak using more African American Vernacular English (AAVE). In this respect, class interacts with his sense of groupness with blacks. For Trevor, distinction from other blacks along the lines of language use is a part of how he understands his own blackness.

In Los Angeles, white spouses often referenced their partners' language, emphasizing the performative nature of their spouses' blackness. Unlike black spouses who often saw difference and distinction, white spouses recognized the cultural similarities that their black spouses shared with other blacks. Both white husbands and wives often talked about how their partners would code-switch by speaking differently depending on whether they were talking to fellow blacks or with white people. This was entertaining for one white husband, Vincent, in particular. Vincent is married to Charlotte, and they were one of only two couples whom I interviewed who lived in a black neighborhood in Los Angeles. Both of them had college experience. He referenced her code-switching between Black American Vernacular and a form of Standard American English:

> I notice about Charlotte, when she is talking to me or learned people in her circle . . . she puts on this, like, this white voice. . . . If I was to pigeonhole, I would say she is playing the white role, where she is very nice and very sweet and smooth and articulate, and then she gets on the phone with her sister, and she gets all . . . the Brooklyn accent, like, "No, he didn't!" [comes out]. It's like she slips into it. It is almost like character choices. To see it, it is very funny. I enjoy that.

Vincent referenced language as one element of how he understands his wife's blackness and relationship to other blacks. Vincent's comments suggest that he appreciates this ability of his wife to codeswitch depending on whether she is interacting with blacks or whites. This was very different from Rio de Janeiro, where only one of the white spouses discussed the black spouse's language (or culture more broadly) as part of the calculus of their being black.

Not speaking varieties of black vernacular or listening to hip-hop left these respondents feeling on the fringes of black social life. This was likely exacerbated by the majority of them living in predominantly white neighborhoods. However, several of these same respondents, mostly black husbands, had a cultural outlet that enabled them to continue to feel connected to blacks: playing basketball. Several black respondents, mostly black husbands, described the importance of basketball to their sense of black groupness. For example, Edward is a black man who is married to Stella, a white woman, both of whom are college educated: "I mean pretty much from the time I left New York . . . if it wasn't for my personal life and my personal interests that maybe are shared by predominately black people . . . if I didn't like playing basketball so much . . . I wouldn't even meet black people."

For Edward and other black husbands, basketball was a way to feel connected to other blacks. Several black men described how through playing basketball, they encountered other black men. This desire to be in black spaces with cultural activities that they understood as black was present among black spouses in Los Angeles far more often than in Rio de Janeiro, indicating the stronger sense of groupness that Angelino black spouses experienced. In Rio de Janeiro, black spouses, usually husbands, referenced *baile charmes*, soul dance parties, as sites where predominantly people of color, especially blacks, would spend time. However, they did not describe them as places in which they felt connected to other black people, and neither did their white spouses. They also did not mention soccer as an important sport for experiencing black solidarity. This is likely because soccer in Brazil is a national sport. While mainly blacks are represented on national teams, it is not associated specifically with Brazilian blacks the way that basketball is among US blacks. White Angelino partners rarely mentioned basketball as a cultural form related to their spouses' blackness. However, many of them referenced class and other distinctions between their black spouses and other blacks. Similar to Rio de Janeiro, white partners often did not recognize the elements of groupness, cultural or otherwise, that their black spouses did.

White Spouses: The "African American" Label and Multiraciality

Several white partners in Los Angeles referenced their spouses' blackness in ways that were discussed rarely, if not at all, by the black spouses themselves. A common response to their understanding of their spouses' identities was one that Irene gave after saying that her husband, Orion, is "African American": "That's what he calls himself." Not only did white spouses defer to the racial categorization that they understood their black spouses had and used, but they weighted the label *African American* very heavily in their discussions of how they understood their spouses' blackness. This was in comparison to their black spouses who rarely, if ever, used the term *African American* to describe themselves. One recent study found that whites react more positively to the label *African American* than to the label *black*, which signals to them a lower social class and lower status, and whites related it more to negative emotional tones.[46] This positive association for whites to the term *African American* may explain why white spouses were more likely to use it and identify it with their spouse.

White spouses, particularly white husbands, were more likely to reference race mixture in their black wives' ancestries. For example, Perry is a white man who is college educated, like Helen, who is black. They were one of the few couples who were interfaith as well as interracial, with Perry being Muslim and Helen being Catholic. They lived in a predominantly white, wealthy neighborhood in Los Angeles. I asked Perry about Helen's race: "I guess she's black. I know she's a little bit mixed race. Her dad came from the Caribbean. I think one of her grandmothers married a Jewish guy, and she's Catholic."

Although white husbands often discussed how their black wives had racially mixed origins, their black wives did not reference nonblack ancestors in their understandings of their own blackness. Since most of the black husbands had two black parents and few had nonblack ancestry (in comparison to the black wives), white wives were less likely than white husbands to reference their black husbands' racially mixed ancestries. Some black wives acknowledged in their interviews that they realized that they appeared ethnoracially ambiguous to nonblacks and were often confused for being Latinas. This was similar to one study in which the black wives and white husbands both appeared to be white.[47] Nevertheless, none of the black women referenced their ambiguous phenotypes in terms of how they understood their own blackness, even though their white husbands did. This was similar to some black women in Rio de Janeiro who also experienced some outsiders, including their husbands' white family members, not categorizing them as black. Nevertheless, similar to these Los Angeles black wives, that ambiguity was not a part of how they identified themselves. In respect to being "African American" and multiraciality, the image that white spouses in Los Angeles reflected did not perfectly align with how black spouses saw themselves.

As seen in table 2.2, Los Angeles black spouses articulated their blackness in terms that were very different from their Carioca counterparts. Despite the history that they share with other blacks, they also described how they were distinct from them. These black spouses referenced factors such as education and language as barriers to feeling like true group members. White partners often saw similar themes composing their spouses' blackness, including within the same couples. As a result, ethnoracial congruence within couples was higher among Los Angeles couples in comparison to the Rio de Janeiro couples overall. The factors

TABLE 2.2. Los Angeles Couples on Blackness

Theme	Black Spouse	White Partner	Number of Congruent Partners
Different from other blacks	9	5	2
Class boundary	13	8	6
Language/culture	6	5	3
Groupness	8	2	2
Oppression	8	2	0
Multiraciality	3	5	2
African American	0	7	0
Total*	20	15	13

* Totals do not add up because many respondents used more than one theme.

that constituted the boundaries of blackness were more similar for black and white couples in Los Angeles than in Rio de Janeiro.

Conclusion

In the United States, blacks who interracially marry have been seen as "sellouts" for centuries. When Frederick Douglass, the famous abolitionist, married a white feminist, many blacks called his second marriage a sign of his derogation of black beauty and black women everywhere. (Of mixed ancestry himself, Douglass jokingly replied to the accusations, "My first wife, you see, was the color of my mother, and my second wife the color of my father. . . . I wanted to be perfectly fair to both races.")[48] The Black Power movements of the 1960s and '70s in the United States also highly stigmatized interracial marriage.[49] Black women in particular were likely to criticize men in the movement for "talking black but sleeping white." Even today, the interracial marriages of famous black men have fueled accusations of their being sellouts,[50] discrediting their blackness and commitment to black causes. As mentioned before, in Brazil, these sentiments have been largely limited to black movement circles, despite the interracial marriages of movement leaders, such as Abdias do Nascimento. However, in a variety of nonactivist social settings, I occasionally heard Brazilians across color disparage nonwhite soccer players and their preference for blonde girlfriends and wives.[51]

As seen in this chapter, black spouses in Rio de Janeiro often articulated their blackness in ways that their white spouses did not see. Groupness, family ancestry, phenotype, official documents, relationships, and euphemisms for blackness were the dominant ways that black Carioca spouses understood their own blackness. This was in contrast to Los Angeles blacks, who had a stronger sense of "belonging together" yet

TABLE 2.3. Boundaries of Blackness in Rio de Janeiro and Los Angeles

Boundary Characteristics	Rio de Janeiro	Los Angeles
Groupness	+	+
Linked fate	−	+
Congruence	−	+

saw themselves as on the margins of black groupness. Boundary construction against other blacks, especially through the use of class boundary making, problematized their feelings of black cohesion. More than for black Cariocas, culture was a salient theme in how Angelinos understood their blackness.

Table 2.3 provides a summary of the social construction of blackness within these couples in these two sites. Carioca spouses had a lower degree of ethnoracial congruence in comparison to their Angelino counterparts. White partners in Rio de Janeiro rarely overlapped with black spouses in terms of how they saw their spouses' blackness. The most salient theme of blackness for black spouses in Rio de Janeiro, a sense of groupness, was invisible to their white partners. In comparison, couples in Los Angeles had a higher degree of ethnoracial congruence, with husbands and wives drawing on the same cultural repertoires for understanding the spouses' blackness. However, themes such as the African American label and emphasizing the nonblack ancestry of the black spouse were more important for how white partners understood their spouses' blackness than for how black husbands and wives understood themselves.

This chapter illuminates how couples understood the composition of ethnoracial boundaries of blackness in very different ways. There was more agreement or ethnoracial congruence among Los Angeles couples than among those in Rio de Janeiro. However, in both sites, the elements that were the most salient for black husbands and wives were not the ones that were salient for their white partners. This reveals not just that racial boundaries in Brazil are less stable than in the United States but how they are unstable in the very constitution of what makes a person, the black spouse in this case, black.

Strikingly, despite seeing their spouses on the boundaries of blackness, neither white partners in Rio de Janeiro nor Los Angeles engaged in tactics demonstrating a breach of the boundaries of blackness. Rarely did white partners talk about themselves in relationship to their spouses' blackness. This was different from the tactics of both black and white spouses when it came to whiteness, as will be seen in the next chapter. Similarly, white partners rarely referred to their similarities to their spouses in terms of socioeconomic status, culture, or themselves being the descendants, however distant, of immigrants in understandings of their black spouses. For this reason, both partners were involved in the reproduction of the boundaries of blackness. There was no bridging, blurring, or shift in the articulation of blackness. Rather, they were involved in its reproduction. Boundaries may be more flexible in the Brazilian context, but when it came to blackness, both partners reproduced them in both sites.

This chapter shows how black identities in interracial couples are far more complicated than a simple "sellout" label. Too often, ethnoracial categories are taken for granted as already existing in the world, leading us to ignore their socially constructed nature, even for "monoracial" categories like being black. As a political scientist, Cathy Cohen pointed out in her analysis of US black mobilization around the AIDS crisis: black solidarity is not something that can be taken for granted.[52] She demonstrated how socioeconomic status, sexuality, and other social categories increased fractures in "black community" politics. As more blacks intermarry and, as shown in this chapter, immigration problematizes what it means to be black in society, new ways of understanding race are necessary for a grasp of black social worlds.

Ethnoracial reflexivity builds on prior discussions of the looking-glass self, double-consciousness, and reflected appraisals without taking for granted that how outsiders see a person is incorporated into their sense of self. More than just looking at how being in an interracial relationship shapes an individual's racial identity, the concept of ethnoracial reflexivity reveals interactions and intersections between how a person is identified and how they identify themselves. It builds on ideas of the self as being reflected through a "looking glass" and "double-consciousness" by breaking a racial self into the components of how a person sees themselves and how they are seen by another person. The social construction of race did not cease to exist for blacks or whites in these couples despite being married to a person of a different color. Instead, black and white spouses were both engaged in the construction of ethnoracial boundaries of blackness as it pertained to their respective societies and made sense of where the black spouse fit within those confines.

3

Boundaries of Whiteness

Flexibility and Shifting Meanings

In the summer of 2015, Rachel Dolezal made headline news when the media revealed that she had claimed to be black and was head of the Spokane, Washington, chapter of the National Association for the Advancement of Colored People (NAACP). However, she was white.[1] Dolezal was a part-time professor of Africana studies, a discipline created through black mobilization when blacks were rarely hired at universities. Dolezal was a graduate of the historically black Howard University, where she had sued the university for antiwhite discrimination only to adopt a black identity for several years. During an on-camera interview, she implied that an older black man was her biological father. Dolezal had married and then later divorced an African American man and was a mother to two black "sons" who had once been her adopted brothers. She wore her hair in popular hairstyles typical of black women, including hair weaves and braids. She did not completely trust her parents' word of their white ancestry.

What prompted the media blitz was the fact that Dolezal had reported several antiblack hate crimes to the authorities, including death threats and lynching imagery. In a televised interview, a reporter insinuated that Dolezal had fabricated the crimes, which she denied. Reporters from the media found Dolezal's white parents, from whom she had been estranged, in Montana. They showed proof of Dolezal's life before her assimilation into blackness, including showing photos of a teenage, blonde Dolezal. Dolezal continued to state that she was black because she is the mother of two black boys, has had a "visceral" connection to celebrating blackness since she was a child, and has subsequently owned "what it means to experience and live blackness."[2] However, there was an ethnoracial incongruence between how Dolezal saw herself and the way that most of the United States saw her.

When making sense of race and color, scholars have often focused on the lives of nonwhites. This is particularly the case when it comes to understanding racial identity and racial group formation. However, in the last two decades, there has been a burgeoning interest in whiteness in the United States,[3] including studies of how whites understand their own racial identity.[4] Whiteness studies are far more nascent in Brazil.[5]

In this chapter, I use the concept of ethnoracial congruence introduced in the last chapter to understand the social construction of whiteness for these black-white spouses. I examine how white spouses understand themselves as white, how their black partners do so, and the extent to which those perspectives are congruent. In addition, I discuss ethnoracial reflexivity in terms of how whites understand how outsiders categorize them and incorporate it into how they see themselves in ethnoracial terms. I find that whites in both sites experience greater flexibility with ethnoracial boundaries than their black spouses. This was especially the case in Rio de Janeiro, where white spouses drew on the cultural repertoire of race mixture to push against and pull ethnoracial boundaries. In Los Angeles, white spouses often shifted the discussion about whiteness to one about ethnicity. In both sites, patriarchy enabled husbands to bridge over ethnoracial differences with their wives.

Brazilian Whiteness in Rio de Janeiro Spouses

Brazil and the United States have had different approaches to understanding racial categories. Many factors influence an individual's racial categorization in a place like Brazil, where racial boundaries are more porous and flexible. Age, region, education, and even the race of the person asking the question can all affect the type of response an individual gives when asked, "What is your color?" In Brazil, as in much of Latin America, a person with known black or indigenous ancestors can consider herself and be considered "white" by others. Most of the spouses categorized as white by fellow Brazilians (twenty-five out of twenty-seven) did just that, identifying themselves as white.

The idea of "bleaching out" descendants of slaves and indigenous peoples through emigration from Europe was promoted by the Brazilian state at the beginning of the twentieth century.[6] At the same time, blacks were prohibited from immigrating to Brazil. The government provided free transport to Brazil as well as parcels of land once they arrived as an explicitly prowhite public policy, one of the first examples of race-based affirmative action in the society. The recipients of these benefits largely went to the southern and southeastern regions of the country, including Rio de Janeiro. The state of Rio Grande do Sul was a major recipient of European immigrants, especially from Germany and Italy. Several white spouses that I interviewed were the children and grandchildren of people who were a part of this whitening process. These white spouses identified themselves and were identified by others, including their black partners, as white despite many also having African and indigenous ancestors.[7]

Phenotype

Some of the white Cariocas that I interviewed did not find their whiteness problematic at all. They pointed to their physical appearance as evidence that they belonged firmly in the bounds of whiteness. For example, Deisy is a college-educated woman with light hair, skin, and eyes who lives in a middle-class, racially mixed suburb of Rio de Janeiro with her black husband, Wanderley. When I asked her what her color is, like several respondents, she mentioned her Iberian origin in which her ancestors are from Spain or Portugal. She also engaged in a discourse of relativity,[8] situating herself among white family members to make sense of her own color. Although Los Angeles white spouses referenced their ancestry as well, they did not discuss their appearances or their family members to give credence to their self-identification as white.

Later in her interview, Deisy clarified her identification as white: "I am white. I usually say that I am a 'sour white' [branca azeda], Caucasian. Here, we call it, over on Orkut [a formerly popular Google-based social networking site], I write Caucasian because I am a sour white. . . . When a person is very white, we say they are sour white. . . . Because of the color of my skin, I have to say [I am white]. When I have to write this, when it is necessary to identify myself, I am white. My ethnicity is Caucasian."

Being a sour white is a reference to an individual being as white as milk. It is sometimes used as an epithet[9] because of the negative qualities of being very white in a tropical environment, where it is better to be able to tan, not burn, in the sun. Very few of the white spouses referred to themselves as "sour whites," yet it was common for white spouses to reference paler skin, light-colored eyes, and straight, thin hair in calculations of their whiteness. This was true even for the white spouses who had indigenous or Afro-Brazilian ancestry along with their (mostly) European ancestry. Like Deisy, several white spouses saw their whiteness as unequivocal and normal. This was a gendered practice, with largely white wives, not white husbands, drawing on phenotype to explain their whiteness. This is likely due to Brazilians tending to see women as being lighter in comparison to men.[10] This was also different from Los Angeles white spouses, where none of them referenced their phenotype when discussing their whiteness. Only a few of their black partners linked their white spouses' race to their physical appearances.

One of the ways that white spouses in Rio de Janeiro discussed phenotype in understanding their whiteness was by drawing on how outsiders saw them. I asked Marisa, a college-educated white woman from the wealthy South Zone of Rio de Janeiro, what her color was. Married to Adão, a black man, Marisa replied that she was white and said, "Because it is what they say. I am white with blue eyes. . . . Everyone has said that since I was born." Marisa recognized how outsiders saw her and referenced it in her understanding of her self-categorization.

In another case, Ulises was a white man who did not attend college and who lived in a racially mixed, distant suburb of Rio de Janeiro. Married to his black wife, Flávia, who was college educated, their relationship involved status exchange. Ulises was similar to other lower-educated white spouses who referenced the effect of the sun on their skin: "I am white, but you see that my skin is not white. Due to the sun, I get tanned [moreno]. But now, the color of my real skin is white, as I was born."

For both Marisa and Ulises, physical appearance to outsiders factors into their calculus of their whiteness. They espouse ethnoracial reflexivity in understanding their whiteness, taking into account their interactions with others and how others see them. For Ulises, that even included perceiving how he thought that I saw him and explaining away discrepancies between his physical appearance and his understanding of himself.

Black partners also frequently discussed their white spouses' phenotypes to make sense of how they saw them as white. For example, Caetano is a black man in his sixties who migrated from the Northeast of Brazil with his white wife, Brígida, decades ago. When Caetano described his wife in passing in the interview, he often referred to her by saying, "She is white and has green eyes," her eye color accentuating, even enhancing, her whiteness. Brígida made passing references to "my color, the color white" during her interview. This ethnoracial congruence was similar to only a few other couples in which both white spouses and their black partners referred to phenotype in understanding the white spouse's whiteness. However, it was only on occasion that black partners described how people outside of the relationship saw their white spouses; ethnoracial reflexivity was rarely a part of how blacks saw their white spouses.

Redrawing Boundaries and Race Mixture

As mentioned in the introduction, ethnoracial boundaries—just like other forms of social boundaries, such as gender—involve a dividing of "us" versus "them." One strategy for engaging ethnoracial boundaries is to redraw them by expanding or limiting the range of people that are included within a category.[11] This was the most common way that white spouses described their whiteness. If whiteness were a box in which to place people, white husbands and wives in Rio de Janeiro would frequently jump in and out of it. When describing their color and racial identity, white spouses would often pull and release ethnoracial boundaries to include and then exclude themselves. This was especially, though not solely, the case for lower-educated whites with no college experience. The well-known fuzziness of Brazilian ethnoracial boundaries became evident when examining how white spouses understood their whiteness. This was different from black spouses (and their white partners), who understood blackness as being more stable. It was also different from both white and black spouses in Los Angeles, who had very rigid ethnoracial boundaries to negotiate.

In Rio de Janeiro, white husbands and wives engaged in this boundary redrawing in several ways. The way that they excluded themselves from whiteness was to reference race mixture in their ancestry. Similar to research on white identification in Brazil,[12] the overwhelming majority of the white spouses that I interviewed described race mixture in their ancestries, citing black and indigenous ancestors. For example, Laura is a white woman who lives with her husband, Nícolas, in a working-class neighborhood in the North Zone of Rio de Janeiro. When I asked Laura what her color is, she said she was white, noting that her birth certificate erroneously classified her as brown (*parda*). However, over the course of the interview, she clarified what being white meant for her:

"We are in a country that has a lot of mixture, and I only have white skin, but I am not totally white, right? I am white, and he is black, but our daughter, my daughter, is white . . . [but] not pure white, the white race [*raça branca*], you know? For me, white like that is somebody who is really white, [the color of] milk, green eyes. I don't think that I am totally white. Because I come from a lot of mixture, many years [of it]."

As in much of Latin America, Brazilians largely determine whiteness by skin tone.[13] Laura draws on this physical characteristic in determining her own racial identification. Like several respondents that I interviewed, she referred to different types of whiteness that exist in the Brazilian mindscape. She termed the whitest *really white* (*branco branco*), but many respondents used the term *the Aryan* (*o ariano*) and *Viking* as the epitome of whiteness. The majority of respondents, like Laura, have nonwhite ancestry and therefore consider themselves less white. Unlike whites in North America or Europe who are understood to have no racially mixed ancestry (despite reality often to the contrary), for many respondents, Brazilian whites are not "really white." Los Angeles spouses made no such references to "real whites."

Whites in Brazil, especially middle-class ones, often have an understanding of a global whiteness based in Europe and North America.[14] In their eyes, these are the whites who do not have any nonwhites in their family trees, are very pale, have straight hair, and have light-colored eyes. Several respondents made references to these really white Aryans, to which they often compared their own whiteness. One white husband, Harry, is a college-educated American who lives in Rio de Janeiro with his Afro-Brazilian wife, Silvia. A pale man with freckles and light-colored hair and eyes, he described himself as the standard of whiteness that Brazilians often reference. This Northern European variety of whiteness, which is rare in Brazil, is highly prized.

Brazilian icons like the television actress and singer Xuxa[15] and the supermodel Gisele Bundchen, both *gaúchas* (people from Rio Grande do Sul) from the whiter, southern areas of Brazil, fall into this category. In a few rare cases, race mixture was how white spouses explained that they were not white at all. The two spouses who were labeled as white by Brazilian informants (as well as their black spouses) and did not see themselves as white drew on similar arguments of a racially mixed ancestry to exclude themselves from whiteness. Unlike Afro-Brazilians who often use understandings of racially mixed ancestry to affirm their blackness,[16] the white spouses that I interviewed used race mixture to explain why they were white but not *that* white. Nevertheless, for most white spouses, this was how they simultaneously included themselves, yet excluded themselves, from the white category, redrawing ethnoracial boundaries. Los Angeles white spouses did not interact with ethnoracial boundaries in the same ways.

Isidoro is a pale, white man with a college degree who lives in a distant suburb of Rio de Janeiro with his black wife, Raquel. When I asked Isidoro what his color is, he said,

> ISIDORO: Oh, I am considered, for statistical purposes, as white, you
> know? But it's funny; I'm not able to see myself like that. . . . I
> am white; I am black; I am Japanese; I am Spanish; I am Jewish; I am
> everything. If I had to spin it to say what is my color, technically I
> am white, but that is not how I feel. . . . I am white, the grandson of a
> Jew and an African, of a Spaniard with an Indian.
> ME: And you are white?
> ISIDORO: I am white. I have curly hair. If I let my hair grow out, it
> would curl. I don't have straight hair, you know? . . . I am not able
> to understand this posturing. I think this posturing is the fruit of
> ignorance, you know?

Isidoro's comments reflect a theme common to whiteness studies, in which whites do not see themselves through a racial lens.[17] By seeing himself as "beyond" race, Isidoro enacts one of the privileges of whiteness: the ability to deny or be unconscious of one's own race despite reaping the advantages of whiteness. He uses his race mixture to problematize being labeled as white according to his appearance. This was very different from black partners in Rio de Janeiro, as seen in the previous chapter, who often took on a black identity rather than having it assigned or pushed on them, as white spouses like Isidoro experienced.

Nevertheless, unlike white or black spouses in Los Angeles or even black spouses in Rio de Janeiro, Isidoro was like several white spouses in Rio de Janeiro who understood whiteness as something being imposed on them from the outside that they refused to internalize. In Isidoro's case, statistical purposes forced him into a white category. However, his comments reveal his ethnoracial reflexivity, in which he sees how others see him and uses his racially mixed ancestry to reject it. This was different from white spouses like Marisa who incorporated how outsiders saw her into her understanding of herself as white. This was also very different from white spouses in the Los Angeles sample who never discussed a difference between how outsiders, including statisticians or the state, saw them and how they saw themselves in terms of race.

Isidoro also pointed out how his hair curls, implying by this that he has African ancestry. This is because couples (as well as informants) in Rio de Janeiro often believed that no person of solely European descent has curly hair. Isidoro's comments were typical of many college-educated white spouses, especially white husbands. Similar to Laura, he drew on understandings of race mixture to challenge his whiteness and even delegitimize the whole idea of racial categorization. This was different from black spouses in Rio de Janeiro who did not see a conflict between their racially mixed ancestry and their racial identification as black. This was also different from Los Angeles white spouses who did not problematize identifying themselves nor being identified as white.

One reason this was a phenomenon among white husbands may be related to the role of gender in race and color categorization in Brazil. As mentioned before, Brazilians prefer to lighten women and darken men when categorizing others. As it was largely men who darkened themselves, gender was likely a factor in why they were more likely to hedge or invalidate claims to whiteness. Since skin color is not as salient for white or black "monoracial" identities in the United States, this was not a dynamic that I encountered in Los Angeles.

As a college-educated man, Isidoro was similar to other college-educated white husbands who found being categorized as white problematic, even when they adhered to a white identity. This was similar to Mexico, where those with higher socioeconomic status, such as college-educated individuals, were less likely to identify as white.[18] These findings are likely because colleges and universities in Brazil are overwhelmingly white. As a result, these respondents may be the least white of the whites in colleges and universities.

In addition, college-educated white husbands, similar to Isidoro, were the most likely to have had personal contact with European notions of whiteness. For example, Gaspar lives in a racially mixed neighborhood in the North Zone of Rio de Janeiro with his black wife, Tatiana. As an artist, Gaspar had lived in Europe for a few years. He distinguished himself from "whites" in Europe, saying that he experienced racial discrimination when he lived there. Gaspar was one of two white spouses who refused a white categorization for themselves, preferring the term *mixed* (*mestiço*) to describe himself. College-educated white spouses are more likely to have spent time abroad. They are also more likely to live in or near tourist areas of Rio de Janeiro (the wealthiest, whitest areas of the city), which provides them with more contact with foreign whites. Lower-educated white spouses rarely discussed their whiteness vis-à-vis an international audience. Highly educated men either rejected the term altogether or used other terms like *mestiço*, whether by itself or alongside self-categorizing as white, to identify themselves. This was different from Los Angeles, where none of the spouses who were identified as white by outsiders and black partners had a different self-categorization.

Although white spouses referenced their racially mixed ancestry, it was rare for their black partners to do so. Isidoro's black wife, Raquel, had a different perspective on her husband's whiteness. Like several black wives, Raquel discussed her husband's tendency to get burned by the sun when they go to the beach and his need for sunscreen. She also explained his being white due to his being the "descendant of Spaniards," drawing on his Iberian ancestry. Raquel revealed that one of her friends even jokes about Isidoro's whiteness, saying, "He is very white. He doesn't even look like he is from here, from Brazil. He looks like he is from another country." This same friend referenced his long moustache, which makes him look like a foreigner. Furthermore, Raquel discussed Isidoro's love of literature, which makes him speak a very refined

Portuguese and compels him to correct other people's Portuguese, including Raquel's friends. These factors together make Isidoro seem more like he is from Portugal than Brazil.

For Raquel, like many black wives, her white spouse is unambiguously white. Despite white spouses problematizing their whiteness because of factors such as racially mixed ancestry, their black partners drew clear boundaries against them. This was particularly the case for couples involving white husbands and black wives. A number of the black wives I interviewed compared their white Brazilian husbands to *gringos*, a general term in Brazilian Portuguese (with origins in Mexican Spanish) for foreigners. For those that were married to actual *gringos*, black wives drew on a presumed lack of race mixture to draw sharp racial boundaries against their white husbands. These black partners used these factors, together with references to foreignness, as a way to reproduce sharp boundaries against their white spouses, often against white spouses' wishes, which placed white spouses squarely in the category of whiteness.

Race mixture was not a common theme that black Carioca partners used to refer to their spouses' whiteness. As a result, there was little ethnoracial congruence between black-white couples on the dimensions of race mixture. One reason for this may be that black partners are not as aware of the intricacies of their spouses' ancestries. Another reason may be that black partners often saw their white spouses as distinctly on the other side of a color-race boundary. This was very different from how those same white spouses saw themselves, moving the boundary of whiteness to include and exclude themselves. Black partners, on the other hand, redrew the boundary of whiteness to include their white spouses. This discrepancy in categorization did not exist among Angelino black-white couples.

Strikingly, whites in Brazil experience the most consistency in racial categorization of all color categories. In an analysis of national survey data, 75 percent of whites in Brazil identified themselves and were identified by others as white.[19] The white spouses who challenged their categorization by others as white were few, with only three out of twenty-seven white spouses completely rejecting a white identity. Given the centrality of race mixture to the Brazilian national identity, it is likely that for these spouses, claiming a white self-categorization would compromise their national identities as Brazilian.[20] Given Raquel and her friends' comments, this is a reasonable assessment.

Boundary Pushing

Another way that white spouses negotiated ethnoracial boundaries was to push against them. White spouses were not able to cross ethnoracial boundaries because the overwhelming majority of respondents did not change their own memberships to a different category. Instead, white spouses, usually white wives, engaged in affiliative ethnicity in which they were drawn to an ethnoracial identity that was not their own.[21] As the first chapter described, an attraction to difference can lead individuals to engage in romantic relationships across racial and ethnic boundaries. Several white Carioca wives described attempts to darken themselves through their relationships with black men. This did not cause them to change racial categories in terms of how they identified themselves; they still saw themselves as white. Yet they approximated blackness, pushing against boundaries of whiteness yet not puncturing through.

Idália is a woman with a light tan, blue eyes, and long blonde dreadlocks. I met her through our mutual "loctician," a hair stylist specializing in dreadlocks. When we met at the hair salon, she found out about my study of black-white couples in Rio de Janeiro and volunteered herself and her husband to be part of the sample, identifying herself as white and her husband, Róbinson, as black. A high-school graduate, Idália lives with Róbinson, who attended college, and their black, adopted son in a racially mixed suburb of Rio de Janeiro. Status exchange may characterize their relationship from the outside, but they see each other as social equals.

In her interview, Idália alternated between identifying herself as brown (*parda*) and white. She said that she was darker than her white cousin who is so white that her blue veins show through her skin yet lighter than this white cousin's sister, a *morena* with what Idália saw as more indigenous features. Idália said that she felt like a "sour white" when she takes off her clothes and notes her white skin, yet her official documents, such as her birth certificate, identify her as brown. Noting her own dreadlocks, Idália said, "People don't understand how it is that

I have such smooth hair, and I make my hair kinky like a black person. Everyone straightens their hair, and I make my hair kinky." She explained, "[It's] because I am a white black woman (*branca negra*), you know? I think blacks are beautiful! I think the hair is beautiful; I think the way you guys do your hair is beautiful, and I think your bodies, your skin, [are beautiful]. I do. It's not that I'm dissatisfied with the way that I am. But I would like to be a black woman. I think that I am a black woman internally, you know? And that's how I like it! I think it's beautiful; I like it."

Later in her interview, Idália gave an example of how she performs blackness.

> Just yesterday, I was in the street with my son; my son also has dreads. So we passed two women, and they said, "Her head's probably full of lice!" So I responded, "You're the one who has lice! And you've got it there." [She points in between my legs.] I gave her a response right away, you know . . . an aggressive one; I was aggressive. Because if she comes to me and even a peep comes out of her, I lose it right then and there, you know? I don't want to hit anyone, I don't like hurting anybody, but I don't let anyone do this to me or to my family—or any person I see that's weaker—so I will interfere, you know? That's why my husband calls me "Ghetto Blonde [*Loira do Morro*]." Because generally, it's the black girls that live in the favelas that are more aggressive. They're bolder . . . and they get into fights more, you know? They're not afraid of anything. So he calls me "Ghetto Blonde." "Here comes the 'Ghetto Blonde'!" So much so that he stays quiet—the one who argues is me.

Morro is a reference to the *favela* or shantytowns where many working-class and poor people, mostly of color, live in Rio de Janeiro. The closest English equivalent would be the ghetto, although it is not a perfect translation. Both Idália and her husband identify aggressiveness and poverty with black women. By performing aggression, Idália pushes against the ethnoracial boundaries. In Brazil, *loira*, which translates directly as "blonde," is often a euphemism or substitution for "white." The "Ghetto Blonde" label shows how Idália pushes against the boundaries of whiteness through her performance of aggression against people in public who offend her, which she attributes to lower-class black women; she sees herself as pushing against the boundaries of whiteness and aligning with black women. Through her presentation of self, Idália pushed against racial boundaries, approximating what she saw as "black womanness" in her hairstyle and her mannerisms. However, the "Blonde" reference suggests that she never fully escapes her whiteness.

Idália's understanding of herself as a white black woman was similar to something that I heard from other Brazilian white women respondents. Another college-educated white woman, Nádia, described herself as a "frustrated black woman" (*negra frustrada*)—frustrated because she is not black. Yet another white woman, Verónica, who finished high school said, "I love blacks so much that I had the desire to be a black woman." These white wives in Rio de Janeiro described an admiration for black cultural traits that white spouses of either gender described less often in Los Angeles. Many of the Carioca white wives that I interviewed saw themselves as pushing against racial boundaries in terms of their presentations of self, hobbies, religious practices, sexuality, and, of course, family formation. Their desires for being black also often included desiring blackness as a sexual object, as seen in their espoused preferences for *negão*. However, several white wives also described frequently attending racially mixed or predominantly black events playing *samba* or *pagode*. Others engaged in Afro-Brazilian religions like Candomblé and Umbanda. There were several white spouses in Los Angeles who had a similar appreciation for black culture and spending time in black social settings. However, none of the whites in the sample pushed against the boundaries of ethnoracial self-categorization the way that white Carioca spouses did. Their taste for blackness did not shape their senses of themselves as white the way that it did for white spouses in Rio de Janeiro.

It is common for individuals to privilege their in-group when they experience hostility and discrimination from outsiders.[22] However, these white wives disidentified with fellow whites in favor of the outgroup through an affiliative ethnic identity. Most of these white wives had experienced stigma because of their "taste" for blackness. Through going beyond a fetishization of blackness and *negão*, these women flipped notions of white supremacy and black inferiority on their head.

By challenging the hierarchical order of ethnoracial categories, these women were engaging in a boundary-making strategy. This was not a strategy that I found along other race and gender intersections.

This attitude toward their whiteness revealed a gendered type of flexibility in racial boundaries that blacks did not have. None of the black Carioca respondents, including wives, whom I interviewed described a desire to be white or described frustrated struggles for whiteness. In a context of black consciousness and mobilization, such sentiments would likely be stigmatized. None of the black Angelino respondents did so either, for the same reasons along with the more fixed ethnoracial boundaries.

This sentiment of affiliative ethnicity was rare among white husbands in Rio de Janeiro. This is likely because, as several Carioca informants told me, being a black man was very much in style, not being a black woman. These white women may have been riding the wave of "coolness" that the black movement ushered in as an unforeseen consequence of black consciousness raising. (Ironically, as will be discussed in chapter 6, the black movement was one social setting that was off-limits to these white women). This gave them increased access to black men. While this dynamic was present among white spouses in Los Angeles as well, especially white wives, it was more common among Carioca whites. This difference may be due to the higher levels of segregation in Los Angeles,[23] which prevent whites' access to black communities.

Black partners in Rio de Janeiro often recognized the boundary pushing of their white spouses. For example, Tatiana is a black woman who lives with her white husband, Gaspar, and their two children in a racially mixed neighborhood in the North Zone. As mentioned earlier, Gaspar was one of two white spouses who refused a white categorization for himself, preferring the term *mixed* (*mestiço*). He did not know the tribe of his grandfather yet still felt a link to indigenous people that compelled him in the past to do volunteer work on a reservation.

In her interview, Tatiana said that she and her family frequently attend predominantly black events in which Gaspar and their son are the only whites there. Tatiana referred to him as a "frustrated black man" (*negro frustrado*). She claimed that he is in denial about his whiteness. She said that one of her nicknames and terms of endearment for him is "white boy" (*branquinho*)[24] to tease him about this. Like many black partners,

Tatiana saw her husband pushing against racial boundaries while not crossing them. Several black wives placed their husbands squarely in the white category, reconstructing racial boundaries in their classification, despite white husbands showing the most resistance to this label. Black husbands, on the other hand, generally recognized their wives' color difference but were less likely to resist the idea that their wives approximated blackness.

Race, Color, and Bridging Boundaries

Skin color largely drives ethnoracial categorization in Brazil.[25] However, they see race and color as analytically distinct concepts.[26] While some research has found that for Brazilians, the term *raça* translates as "force," for the Cariocas that I interviewed, the translation was closer to the English word *breed*. For this reason, both black and white spouses expressed confusion over the term. In addition, since the Brazilian national identity is so tied to having a racially mixed ancestry, the very notion of the couples that I interviewed being "interracial couples" was highly problematic, since presumably every individual is "interracial." Nevertheless, because different mixtures of races can lead to differences in skin tones, even among siblings with the same ancestry, Brazilians recognize color distinctions among them.

Unlike Los Angeles couples, Brazilian couples often distinguished between race and skin color in their understandings of blackness and whiteness. White spouses, especially white wives, often drew a distinction between themselves and their black partners. However, these were largely distinctions of color, not race. They did not understand themselves as racially distinct from their black spouses. For instance, I had interviewed Brício, a black man, and his wife, Bárbara, a white woman. Brício recommended Nádia, mentioned at the beginning of the chapter, and her husband, Leandro, as a black-white couple for me to interview. Nádia described an interaction with Leandro about allowing me to interview them.

> Brício came over, you know, and talked about your research and everything. . . . I said, "Of course, we accept; we want to participate, right?" So then, I spoke with Leandro, so he said, "But hey, why participate in

this research? We are not different racially. . . ." What I think is that we have arrived at a level of miscegenation that it is difficult for you to find a race, an ethnic group, that is in fact pure. So then, I think that we end up confusing everything—race, ethnicity—with skin color. Because I think that skin color is one thing, and race, ethnicity, is another. So like, I am different from him, I think, in skin tone, and so we confuse this with being white and being black. You looking at him, you see that Leandro is a strong mixture of blacks and Indian, and I know that he also has French in his family . . . and I know that I have black in my family, that I have Indian, that I have German.

Nádia's comments show how she sees Leandro consistently challenging the color distinctions that she attempts to draw, thus shifting her perspective on difference. Here, Nádia understands Leandro as using the discourse of race mixture to bridge over potential differences. Rather than emphasizing their different colors, she is able to place emphasis on how they are both the progeny of race mixture and thus of the same race. Although many African Americans and white Americans often have nonblack and nonwhite ancestors, respectively, among the Los Angeles respondents, they did not detangle a racial self-categorization from a skin color categorization the way Carioca spouses often did. When Los Angeles spouses did reference race mixture, it was often white husbands discussing their white wives' blackness, not the reverse.

For black Carioca husbands, the depth or thickness of the ethnoracial boundary between themselves and their wives was thin or easily crossable through the discourse of race mixture. For example, Sérgio is a black man who lives with his white wife, Hilda, in a racially mixed suburb of Rio de Janeiro. Both are in their late twenties, and he is currently in college. In her interview, Hilda revealed that she identifies herself as white because she felt that other color categories such as black, Asian, or indigenous (*negra, amarelo, ou indigena*) did not apply to her and that others would laugh at her if she identified in any other way. Looking at their wedding photos and coming to their house when both were present, I perceived Sérgio as darker than Hilda, but Sérgio said, "She is the same color as I am." Nonetheless, he agreed that Hilda was white, while he considered himself black.

A few black spouses were similar to Sérgio, invalidating the notion that a color distinction existed between them and their wives. This strategy was employed mostly, though not exclusively, by husbands, especially black husbands. They did this through a number of ways. One of these was to reference their own color, especially mentioning how they were not different in terms of color. Neither white nor black husbands saw themselves as very different from their wives, unlike black and white wives. The construction of masculinity in marriage, in which wives become part of their husbands and their families, may explain why husbands did not sense the color differences that their wives did. In other words, having social status on one dimension (gender) allowed them to bridge over boundaries on a different dimension: race and ethnicity.

As a self- and outsider-identified *negro*, how can Sérgio think of himself and his wife as the same color despite their different racial categorizations? In part, this is because he does not see the difference in skin color that exists between himself and his wife (that I and others saw). But it is also because he draws on his wife's other physical characteristics to demarcate her as white, such as her hair texture, which she told me that she straightens with heat. These other physical characteristics, such as not being very tall and her large nose and not just skin color, were a part of his calculus for understanding his categorization of her as white. However, her other characteristics mean that for Sérgio, in a racial and color hierarchy, Hilda is low on the totem pole of whiteness and, thus, not very "distant" from him. This was similar to other black husbands who emphasized how their spouses were not "really white" and thus closer to them in a gradated system of both race and color.

This perspective contrasted with the thick boundaries that black wives in Rio de Janeiro perceived between themselves and their white husbands. It also contrasted with the black husbands in Los Angeles who saw their wives as more distinct than black husbands in Rio de Janeiro considered their own wives. Furthermore, this was not a perspective that emerged when discussing blackness for these couples. This boundary-bridging was a dimension of whiteness but not blackness, likely because of the lack of political mobilization around a white identity in the same way that there is for a black identity.

Table 3.1 summarizes the ways that black and white spouses in Rio de Janeiro understood whiteness. Redrawing boundaries was the most frequent way that white spouses understood their whiteness. This was different for their black partners who more often concentrated on the strategy of bridging boundaries. This was also the category of the most congruence.

There was a great deal of ethnoracial congruence in boundary-bridging among black-white couples in Rio de Janeiro. In fact, as seen in table 3.1, this was the dimension of whiteness that had the most congruency between couples. This is likely because of the strong role of race mixture in national identity in Brazil. It is also likely due to the weaker group identity that exists among members of the same ethnoracial category in comparison to the United States.[27]

Whiteness in Los Angeles

Unlike Carioca respondents, white Los Angeles spouses could articulate what they had in common with other whites and discuss distinctions between themselves and whites with different educational backgrounds. This is because the level of ethnoracial "groupness" in the United States is much higher than in Brazil.[28] While questions surrounding a white group identity were often dead ends in Rio de Janeiro, they led to lively discussions with white spouses in Los Angeles. White Los Angeles respondents could articulate what they had in common with other whites and discuss distinctions between themselves and whites with different educational backgrounds. For example, Madison

TABLE 3.1. Brazilian Couples on Whiteness

Theme	White Spouse	Black Partner	Number of Congruent Partners
Phenotype	10	7	3
Boundary-work			
Redrawing	11	5	2
Boundary-pushing	16	12	6
Boundary-bridging	10	9	4
Total*	21	22	13

* Totals do not add up because many respondents used more than one theme.

is a white woman who lives in a middle-class suburb of Los Angeles with her husband, Kevin. Both of them went to college, and they just had their first daughter, a newborn named Alexa. I asked Madison how much she thought that she had in common with white people. She said,

> I guess a lot. I feel like I have a lot in common with all kinds of people, but I guess if I were to try to—if I had to remove myself and kind of look at it like the perspective of other people, I guess I would have more in common with white people, but that's because maybe my appearance, maybe the way that I dress. . . . I guess maybe mannerisms and my—just the way that I speak might be considered whiter, but as far as the way I feel, my feelings, my religious beliefs, and my values, everything more that I identify with, I feel like is kind of more of a universal thing.

Madison's comments reveal a number of themes that I found among Los Angeles respondents. Several white spouses discussed how their appearance, the way that they dress, the way that they speak, and the way that they dance were emblematic of their whiteness. Many whites in my sample mentioned aspects of cultural consumption that either made them similar to or different from other whites of different socioeconomic status. They mentioned factors like reading books over watching television, traveling, and even identifying with stuffwhitepeoplelike.com, a satirical blog enumerating things appealing to white, middle-class, young urban professionals, including microbreweries, Asian women, independent music, and religions their parents do not belong to. They often saw factors such as these uniting them with individuals with higher levels of education across race. This was different from Brazilian whites, whose understandings of whiteness did not intersect with the meanings they gave to class. While educational attainment led whites in Rio de Janeiro to describe their whiteness in different ways, they did not describe education as a factor in their white identification. None of the Brazilian white spouses discussed cultural attributes that distinguished whites from blacks. Even though Madison mentioned that her other characteristics are more universal, she was able to articulate some things as white attributes. This was also not a pattern among black spouses, who did not discuss their spouses' whiteness in those terms.

Bridging Boundaries of Class

When discussing their whiteness, white spouses in Los Angeles were more likely to bridge boundaries of class. In Rio de Janeiro, questions about similarities with whites of the same and different educational status were often met with responses about similarities with specific individuals. In Los Angeles, where most white spouses had at least a college degree, many were articulate about differences and similarities across class. However, several discussed bridging across class boundaries. This was more the case with white wives than with white husbands in Los Angeles. For example, in her interview, Madison also discussed the things that she had in common with whites with lower levels of education.

> MADISON: Not very much, probably not, but I have all kinds of friends too. I mean, I have friends that never went to college. I probably don't have as much in common with people who—I know it sounds really sad, but I guess I just don't have as much in common. I don't know, just not very—not as much. . . . There probably isn't as much that I have in common with those people than with people who are educated. I know—I feel guilty saying it, but it's, I just, I don't seem to have some of the same interests.
>
> ME: Like what? What do you mean?
>
> MADISON: Like I'm not that materialistic. I feel like of the people that I know that are white, that are not as educated, they tend to dwell a lot, or they talk a lot about "He said this; she said that" and materialistic things. I'm just not into that. I'm more into talking to people about politics or . . . just the conversation, the kind of conversation is different . . . but it's not always true, because you know what? I have friends that are definitely—they're not as educated, and we have a lot in common as far as, like, just having fun and hanging out. . . . I have a lot of different kinds of friends. So I shouldn't really say that, but it's—I think if I had to, I would say I wouldn't have as much in common with them. . . . But the truth is that it just, I'm very, like—you can have a lot in common with someone that isn't as educated, you know? I mean, there's my mom, for example, like, she never went to college; I mean, she just recently took some online courses, if that

even counts. She's more self-educated; she reads the paper every day, and I consider her, like, one of the, you know, wise and, and intelligent people that I know. So it's like, you know, and she has [a] very humble, very humble background, you know, so. You just don't know people until you just sit down and talk to them and really get to know them.

Madison's interview revealed how she recognized distinctions between how whites with and without higher education act. She initially does not see herself as having very much in common with those with lower levels of education. She describes what she sees as their materialism and their gossipy tendencies. Perhaps in an attempt not to appear class conscious or "snooty," like the black women in the previous chapter, Madison hedges her comments on these distinctions. She does this by emphasizing her relationships with friends who do not have college degrees as well as her mother, who has a lower level of education than she does. Bridging class differences to maintain racial solidarity has a long history in the United States.[29] While Madison does not refer to racial solidarity in her response, she does demonstrate a drawing and subsequent erasure of class boundaries among whites. This suggests a higher level of groupness among Angelino whites in comparison to Carioca whites.

Sometimes white spouses, particularly white husbands, used class and upbringing to bridge over racial distinctions. This was the case with Daniel, a white husband who lives with his wife, Taiwo, in a suburb of Los Angeles. When I asked about his commonalities with other white people, he said, "I think I have a lot in common," yet he immediately transitioned to a more universalist discourse, saying,

I think I have a lot in common. What's interesting is that over my life, I've realized that for me, it's a much more cultural issue than a race issue. I have a lot in common with [Taiwo] because of the way they grew up. They were never rich growing up. Even though her dad was a professor, he's a literature professor, so he never got paid that much. Both parents always worked, they never had a lot growing up, and what they did have they sent home, so it's not like they lived on it or splurged or anything like that. I grew up largely the same way. We had five kids. My dad's always been a saver, so we lived on less than what we had, so even if we had it, we didn't know we had it as kids. I tend to think that it's much more of a cultural thing. I can tell you that there are white people that grew up very differently than I did. I have nothing in common with them. I have very little in common with them; but her—I think we have an amazing amount in common because of the way we grew up. We both grew up in the Midwest.

Although he attributes their similarities to "culture," Daniel emphasizes socioeconomic similarities between himself and Taiwo to bridge across their ethnoracial distinction. Angelino whites often claimed class and "culture" or upbringing were more important than race for identifying with other people. This was not a pattern that emerged among Carioca whites. Unlike black husbands and wives who saw themselves on the margins of blackness (and unlike their white counterparts in Rio who did not always recognize themselves as white), white husbands and wives in Los Angeles recognized their whiteness but immediately referenced other aspects of their lives as being more salient as references for social boundaries. This functioned to shift away from talk of ethnoracial difference to social distinction of other types.

Black partners also engaged in bridging across other social boundaries when discussing their spouses' whiteness. Similar to Rio de Janeiro, it was largely black husbands who engaged in this bridging. However, unlike bridging over class boundaries, they largely built discursive bridges over an implied ethnoracial boundary. For example, in his previous statement, Edward also built a discursive bridge over categorizing his wife as white by linking to a discussion of his own blackness, emphasizing their shared Americanness. Similar to black husbands in Rio de Janeiro, black Angelino husbands also used discursive bridges to discussing their spouses' whiteness. However, unlike Carioca black husbands, who emphasized race mixture, Angelino black husbands often linked their identification of their wives' race to their categorization of themselves as black.

Ronald is one of a few people who have parents of different races yet identifies himself as a black man. He is married to Felicity, a Jewish white woman. The son of a multinational corporate worker, Ronald grew up living in many different societies. Ronald drew on his wife's Jewish ancestry in his articulation of her whiteness as well as his experiences growing up in Ireland.

Being Jewish sets her off [of other whites]. . . . And by whites, I don't mean Europeans or Australians or Canadians; I mean white Americans. . . . Her being Jewish is still—makes her different. For example, I'll give you two examples. We've both faced discrimination, I guess you could say, in our lives. Um, me and my Scottish school people would call me Paki or chocolate bar or whatever else. . . . Paki is astounding because I'm not even Pakistani. Get the race right. Felicity, on the other hand, she lived in an affluent, or she still, her family still does live in an affluent part of Albuquerque, and a lot of her friends were white. Uh, when she was a girl, and then they all got into country clubs, and she never got an invitation because she was Jewish . . . so she's been actually discriminated against. . . . So they all, most of her friends became all sorts of Mexican friends. Her closest friend is Hmong. She's got friends from all over the world. You know, Dutch, people from all over the place. . . . I guess she identifies a lot more with white culture than with the American white culture than I do and lower-class African American culture [too]. I don't. Middle-class African American culture, I think for the most part, is very, just American culture.

Ronald's description of his wife shows that he draws similarities between her experiences being discriminated against as a Jewish woman and his own facing racial slurs as a child. He also discusses how growing up abroad means that Felicity has more in common with African American culture, including lower-class African Americans, than he does. Other black husbands, the rest of who were not married to Jewish women, engaged in similar practices describing how they and their wives were not very different despite their different racial categorizations. They often bridged over their wives' whiteness, which they converted into ethnic meanings, as mentioned in the previous section, such that their white spouses did not seem very different from them. White women in relationships with men who are not white often have their whiteness challenged.[30] However, in this scenario, it was the husbands themselves who were challenging their whiteness. This was not a dynamic that occurred among white husbands discussing their wives' blackness in either site.

Black wives in Los Angeles, on the other hand, rarely bridged racial identity in discussing their white husbands. A few Los Angeles black women described their white husbands' staunch belief in the American Dream ideology and its promise of equal citizenship for everyone. Several black wives said that their husbands did not understand race relations and its falsification of that ideology. Like black women in Rio de Janeiro who also drew boundaries against their husbands, black women in Los Angeles were less likely to discuss their white spouses as similar to them. This was likely a result of their differing views on the role of racism in preventing equal opportunities for all.

Changing the Boundary Meaning

Rather than reproducing, pushing against, or blurring ethnoracial boundaries, some social actors completely change the meaning of those boundaries.[31] This was a boundary strategy in which several spouses engaged when discussing the whiteness of the white spouse. For example, Perry is a white man originally from Colorado who lives with Helen, a black woman, near the beach in Los Angeles. They are both college educated and in their fifties. I asked Perry what it meant for him to be white, as he had identified himself: "I don't really think about it, to be honest with you. . . . We're supposed to have Scottish blood and some British and some German, and at one time, when I was younger, I knew one of my great-grandfathers was German, so I was kind of like, 'Well, maybe I'll take German in school. . . .' What it means to me to be white? I don't know. I guess it just means that most of my ancestors were white. I kind of think of myself as sort of a Heinz 57."

In the United States, white is the default, mainstream category, such that whites rarely have to think about their whiteness.[32] Thus it is typical that Perry says he does not think about his whiteness very much. Many other white male Angelinos did not consider their whiteness salient, even though they are in interracial marriages. However, this was also true for white spouses in Rio de Janeiro, who also did not think about their whiteness despite not being the mainstream, default category of the society.

Similar to other respondents in both societies and across colors, Perry used a biological notion of his ancestry, couching it in terms of "blood" and genetics. However, unlike white spouses in Rio de Janeiro who problematized a white label by distancing themselves from whiteness through race mixture, several white spouses in Los Angeles did so by shifting from a language of race and being white to US notions of ethnicity based in distinct European nation-states. It was common for white husbands in Los Angeles to consider identities such as Scottish, British, and German as separate, discrete identities within themselves. White spouses turned away from US racial categories to a focus on a multinational European ancestry. By doing so, they complicated notions of their categorization as white. This was very different from white spouses in Rio de Janeiro, who discussed European (Portuguese, German, or Italian) ancestry as an *explanation* for their whiteness. In Los Angeles, white husbands and wives referenced discrete nation-based understandings as a *complement to* a white identity that provided nuance to their whiteness. While white Carioca husbands and wives described their non-European ancestries (even specific ancestors) in piecemeal ways, they did not discuss their European ancestries in this way. None of the Rio white spouses understood their whiteness as a collection of different and distinct European ethnicities (even when this was their actual ancestry), like the famous ketchup brand.

Perry's understanding of his ancestry is a form of symbolic ethnicity,[33] in that it is not a salient part of his everyday life and is not affiliated with any type of discrimination or negative outcomes, yet it compelled him to learn about European history and the German language. Like Perry, several white spouses completely changed the meaning of whiteness from a discussion of race to one of ethnic options from which they selected.[34] This was true for white spouses, including those with Jewish identities.

As seen in table 3.2, black partners changed the meaning of whiteness from one of race to one of ethnic options more often than their white spouses. This was especially common among black husbands, including Trevor, who did just that. He and his wife, Elizabeth, who is white, both have postbaccalaureate degrees and live in a predominantly white neighborhood. I asked Trevor about Elizabeth's race.

TABLE 3.2. US Couples on Whiteness

Theme	White Spouse	Black Partner	Number of Congruent Partners
Boundary-work	8	8	3
Ethnic options	6	10	2
Color-blind universalism	9	5	1
Affiliative ethnicity	4	5	1
Total*	12	16	6

* Totals do not add up because many respondents used more than one theme.

TREVOR: [She's] Caucasian, and she comes from a mixture of Germanic and Celtic background.

ME: Okay. And why do you say she's Caucasian?

TREVOR: Actually, she has also Germanic and Celtic on the European side, and she also has some, it's very low level at this point, but there is some Native American Indian background there too.

Similar to Nádia's comments about confusing race, ethnicity, and skin color in Brazil, people in the United States often use the words *race* and *ethnicity* interchangeably.[35] Nevertheless, there was a clear pattern of several black partners answering a question about their spouses' race by discussing their ethnicity. As seen in his interview, Trevor uses the early twentieth-century pseudoscientific taxonomic category Caucasian to categorize his wife.[36] He describes his understanding of the ethnicity of her immigrant ancestors who migrated to the United States. In addition, similar to black husbands in Rio de Janeiro, and a few husbands in Los Angeles, he described her Amerindian ancestry, emphasizing race mixture in her background.

Trevor's wife, Elizabeth, did not mention her nonwhite ancestry in her interview. Unlike white spouses in Rio de Janeiro, whites in Los Angeles rarely mentioned nonwhite ancestry in articulating their whiteness. In my sample, only one Los Angeles white spouse referenced his Mexican and indigenous ancestry. This may not necessarily be due to a lack of race mixture in the ancestry of US whites; it is a common practice for whites to have indigenous ancestry yet still consider themselves and be considered by others as white.[37] In addition, the United States has a centuries-long history of "passing," in which African Americans with more European features would leave their communities of origin to marry and disappear into white populations.[38] As a result, unlike in Brazil, many whites with black ancestry may not know about it.

Edward was another black husband who engaged in bridging discourse. Edward is a black man who is married to Stella, a white woman. They live together in a racially mixed neighborhood in Los Angeles. When I asked Edward what his wife's race is, he initially said Stella was German but then corrected himself and said that was her ethnicity. Then he said that she is "Caucasian American." He elaborated on how he understood her:

> Well . . . she's an American, so she is versed in American culture and American way of life, and it probably wouldn't be . . . an accurate description to say that, I couldn't say that she is—although her ethnicity is German, she's not; she's American. She's versed in American culture. It's kind of like I'm versed in American culture although my roots may be African. So I might describe myself as, so I would describe myself as African American. Sibling on sibling, Stella's family may be from Germany. My roots may be from Africa.

Edward referenced Stella's ethnic option as German, emphasizing his understanding of her ancestral roots in Germany. He expands this discussion to be about not only her individual categorization but also her natal family. He then draws on his own blackness to understand her whiteness, emphasizing their shared American nationality. Similar to black husbands in Rio de Janeiro, black Angelino husbands bridged over their spouses' whiteness by linking their identification of their wives' race or color to how they categorized themselves. He then switches to an understanding of her based in a shared Americanness, one of the few instances of boundary-blurring that occurred among the couples that I interviewed. Strikingly, he was one of the few respondents who did not use the term *white* to describe his white spouse. This may have facilitated the boundary-blurring that he engaged in.

Table 3.2 shows low ethnoracial congruence on this dimension of whiteness. There were only two couples in which both spouses discussed the ethnic ancestry of the white spouse. This is likely because these ethnic options were not as salient for white spouses as they were for their black partners. This is in contrast to white spouses in Brazil, who often discussed their European heritages to provide reasons for their white identities, which their black partners rarely did.

Color-Blind Universalism

Fred is a white husband who lives with his black wife, Regan, in a predominantly white suburb of Los Angeles. When I asked him about what he has in common with other white people, he said, "Some, I don't know. I mean, it depends." When I asked what he meant, he said, "Well, because there's some dumb people out there, everywhere," suggesting he was not like stupid white people any more than he was like dumb people of any color. Similar to many of the white spouses, he used color-blind universalist discourse to understand his whiteness and to erase ethnoracial boundaries. Similar to Rio de Janeiro, white spouses in Los Angeles often referenced general, universal characteristics that cut across race, more so than their black partners, when discussing their whiteness. While some white women emphasized their distinction from people with negative attributes in the way that Fred did, it was more common for white men to do so. As seen in the previous chapter, color-blind universalism was not a theme that emerged when discussing blackness.

It was less common for black partners to understand their spouses' whiteness in terms of color-blind universalism. In fact, only one couple experienced congruence along this dimension of whiteness. This occurred with Kelly, a black woman, and her husband, Mark, a white man. A wealthy and highly educated couple, they live in a predominantly white neighborhood of Los Angeles with their three children. When I asked her about Mark's race, she said that he is white because she knows his background and because of his physical appearance. Moving to a discussion of ethnic options, she said that rather than the Italian and Mexican heritage of his mother, he looks more like his father's Irish and German side. When I asked her about the qualities that he has in common with other white people, her discourse shifted to one of color-blind universalism.

KELLY: Mark has only things in common with people that he likes. It doesn't matter what color you are because there are people that he just will not get along with, and it does not matter what color you are.

ME: What kinds of people are those?

KELLY: People that are rude, people that he might think are narrow-minded. He just doesn't have patience for them. When we went to [a friend's] birthday celebration, Mark had the opportunity to meet a bunch of people that he had not met before because they were all people that I had worked with . . . on the Obama campaign, so he got to meet the people I was spending every weekend with . . . and he really, really enjoyed them, and there were all kinds of different people. . . . Nobody he didn't like, but then, those people he would have something in common with, you know? He's really open to a lot of different people, but if you make a comment or something, then it's very hard for him. . . . He won't make any efforts to extend his friendship with you.

Kelly was one of the few black spouses who saw her white spouse as practicing color-blind universalism in terms of his social relationships. Rather than race being a factor in the types of people that he has things in common with, Kelly understood him as using personality characteristics to do so. Blurring ethnoracial boundaries occurs when social actors emphasize other distinctions that cut across categories.[39] Kelly blurs ethnoracial boundaries by emphasizing other characteristics, such as being rude and narrow-minded. However, she was the only black partner who understood color-blind universalism as part of the spouse's white identity.

Affiliative Ethnicity and Its Limits

Although a sense of affiliative ethnicity with blacks was pronounced among Rio de Janeiro spouses, it was still present to a limited degree among Angelino white spouses. These white spouses discussed a preference for African American culture, often surrounded themselves with African Americans (often men) in their social lives, and described a high degree of comfort when they are among African Americans. However, rather than pushing against racial boundaries by challenging or problematizing their whiteness, white spouses in Los Angeles did not claim to take on some aspect of a black identity and still categorized themselves racially as white.

Gender was a factor in this process. While fewer whites in Los Angeles than Rio de Janeiro experienced affiliative ethnicity, in both places it was more common for white females than white males. This was similar to "Puerto Rican wannabes": white teenage females who took on black and Puerto Rican affiliative ethnicities through their dress, mannerisms, and relationships with black and Puerto Rican men.[40] Twine had similar findings among white women in Britain who engaged in black hairstyling of their biracial children, West Indian cooking, and displaying a great deal of respect for elders.[41] Engaging in these practices allowed them to achieve the status of "honorary blacks" among the black women whom they were close to.

Isabelle is one such white spouse. She lives with Oscar, a black man, in a distant suburb of Los Angeles. Unlike most interviews that I conducted, she was in the vicinity as I was interviewing Oscar. Oscar became drunk over the course of his interview, repeating himself and becoming confused by my questions. As I was interviewing Oscar, out of the corner of my eye behind him, I could see Isabelle silently shake her head as Oscar spoke. Before ending the interview early, to come again when Oscar was more sober, he discussed how he understood Isabelle's race. Her face turned bright red as he spoke, "I can't tell from your skin if you're black or white because they call Isabelle the 'White Nigger.' . . . She's the blackest white girl you will ever know. I swear [to] God. She's got soul, and she can handle her own, you know what I'm saying?"

Oscar's comments suggest that he sees Isabelle as an "honorary black," despite her skin color. In his interview, he said that "everybody" saw her this way, implying that it was not just him but also others who recognize Isabelle's affiliation with blackness. His interview suggests that he sees Isabelle successfully crossing ethnoracial boundaries.

Although Oscar's statement evidently embarrassed her, Isabelle verified in her own separate interview that she spends time with Oscar and his black, male friends and that she ends up as "one of the guys." They were the only couple to experience ethnoracial congruence around a black affiliative ethnicity for white spouses. Isabelle admitted that their nickname for her was indeed "White Nigger." In one example, Isabelle gave a portrayal of Oscar's friends taking her side when Oscar teases her:

ISABELLE: You know, they don't really tease me in a bad way. It's all in terms of endearment. You know, either they just laugh about "Oh you can't cook this" and [I say], "Watch me cook it." . . . They'll say, "Oh, you can't cook greens" or "You can't cook this." But if you ask . . . his friends, all the black people that come here, it's like "Isabelle cooks better than you now," you know? And then they have a nickname for me, you know—that—it stays within the group. But it's not really teasing, but it's just . . . a term of endearment, and you just don't say it, you know, outside and everything else.

ME: What's your nickname?

ISABELLE: White Nigger. [*laughs*] . . . Isn't that what he said?

ME: Well, in the last interview that's what he said, and you were like "Oh, my God!"

ISABELLE: Well, yeah, because I don't, you know, it's a term of, it's just—it's a term of endearment, you know, because they always tease me like, you know, I don't know if it's *tease* [her emphasis]. [I]t's a term of endearment, but it's only within our thing, you know? When they get out in their "Yo Mama" jokes and everything . . . because we have the domino parties—we play dominoes and barbecue, grill out and all that stuff they call it—but, but they always go "Hey, White Nigger." Like "Yes, Big Dick?" I call him. We just have that. . . . I'm usually one of the guys; I'm really just one of the guys. It's always me and *guys* (her emphasis).

Isabelle's interview suggests that cultural markers matter for successfully navigating black social life. Based on these comments, Oscar and his friends see Isabelle as crossing racial boundaries through her participation in black cultural life, including knowing how to cook "soul food" like collard greens. In addition, Isabelle's comments demonstrate how, through her husband's friends, she is able to participate in a male-dominant African American sociocultural life, from "Yo Mama jokes" to playing dominos. Similar to Idália's "Ghetto Blonde," "White Nigger" suggests Isabelle has successfully taken on mannerisms traditionally associated with blacks. It is striking that Isabelle is usually the only female at these events. This is likely due to the perception that black women are often hostile to couples involving white women with black men.[42]

White women are often "unwhitened" through relationships with men of color and can be victims of "racial abuse" at the hands of white family and community members.[43] However, they can simultaneously inhabit privileged spaces in communities of color, especially in spaces dominated by men of color. This privilege allows them greater maneuverability when negotiating ethnoracial boundaries. Brazil's more flexible ethnoracial boundaries meant that white wives' attempts at affiliative ethnicity with blacks allowed them to problematize their whiteness. Unlike Cariocas, white spouses in Los Angeles with this affiliative ethnicity could not deny or complicate their own understandings of their whiteness, even those with a racially mixed ancestry. There was no Los Angeles counterpart to the *negras frustradas*. For example, throughout her interview, Isabelle referred to herself as a white woman. Also, "White Nigger" was an accepted label placed by others but not a term that Isabelle used for herself.

Later in her interview, Isabelle continued to discuss the interactions that she has when in all black male spaces with Oscar. Her speech was full of hedging and discomfort.

> ISABELLE: You know, but um, I mean, they like, you know, they like, they tolerate me, you know? They like me, but you know, they're the ones that when they start drinking, they'll do the white jokes, [the] not nice white jokes.
>
> ME: Oh yeah?
>
> ISABELLE: Yeah.
>
> ME: Like what?
>
> ISABELLE: I can't remember, because I just put them out [of my head].
>
> ME: Okay.
>
> ISABELLE: But like, you know, kind of derogatory, trying to be derogatory, but I'm twenty years older than them. And I don't let it bother me. And it's when they're drinking all their rum and everything and, they always [say], like . . . "Oh that's right, you're white," you know, or something like that.

Isabelle's comments show that despite her successfully performing blackness and having others recognize her affiliative ethnicity, she remains firmly embedded in the white racial category. Derogatory, possibly even racist, jokes are a way of reminding her of the ethnora-cial boundary that exists despite her affiliative ethnicity. Similar to other white Angelino spouses with affiliative ethnicity, Isabelle's whiteness was never fully erased or challenged. None of the Carioca white spouses described experiencing such derogatory jokes that reminded them of their whiteness (even though black partners sometimes referred to them). The rigidity of racial boundaries in the US context, along with its gendered component, meant that the little flexibility of crossing racial boundaries that some white spouses encountered was very temporary and did not affect their ethnoracial selves.

Conclusion

In Rio de Janeiro, Dolezal—like many white wives whom I interviewed—would have likely been seen as a *negra frustrada*, a frustrated black woman. Her blackness would have been less problematic since, as seen in the last chapter, for Cariocas, being black is an identity that one assumes. The more flexible boundaries of Brazil would have allowed her to face less stigma for assuming a black identity. Also, with the reputed race mixture that even whites celebrate in Brazil, she likely would have been able to claim a black identity. Similar to other white women in Rio de Janeiro, she took on an affiliative blackness.

However, as seen among white wives of those affiliated with the black movement, even in a place where racial categories are fluid, being involved in Afro-Brazilian social justice would have called Dolezal's racial categorization into question. In any case, a woman like Dolezal would likely not have made headlines. Given Brazil's fluid racial cate-gories, she would have likely been more successful at circumventing racial and color boundaries in her life.

Dolezal's situation, similar to the white women in Los Angeles, showed the rigidity of racial boundaries in the United States. How-ever, the white wives in Los Angeles' self-categorization did not change despite their affiliative ethnicity. Dolezal suffered by trying to assert an individual construction of race rather than recognizing its socially constructed qualities, losing her teaching job and her position at the NAACP because of her violation of the US racial system of categori-zation. The social construction of race does not mean solely that it is invented but that it is an invention that people work together to create and recreate every day. Like using a branch to hit a tree, Dolezal experienced the widespread backlash to breaking US social norms of white and black categorization.

In this chapter, I show how the porosity of racial boundaries in Brazil gives Carioca white spouses more flexibility when identifying themselves, in comparison to their black spouses as well as white spouses in Los Angeles. This allows Carioca white spouses to be simultaneously included and excluded from whiteness. Whiteness for white spouses in Los Angeles is far more fixed, with white spouses often completely changing the meaning of race to one of ethnic options. This chapter goes beyond previous work illustrating the variety of ways that interracial relationships affect white identities[44] to show the reflexive nature and social construction of race by both people in the relationship.

Ethnoracial categories are both internally and externally determined, with actors signaling their identification to members and nonmembers of their categories.[45] In this chapter, I found that whiteness in Brazil was often articulated through ethnoracial reflexivity in which white spouses described how others saw them as they made sense of their self-identification. While physical appearance was important, having black or indigenous ancestors was part of the way that whites made sense of whether they were white or "Aryan." Other whites, usually college-educated white men, denied being white altogether, in spite of the opinions of their spouses and others. Carioca black husbands and wives typically validated their spouses' whiteness, although the boundary-work of these black partners differed according to gender.

Examining white identities revealed the much-lauded flexibility of ethnoracial boundaries in the Brazilian context. White spouses and their black partners redrew, pushed against, and bridged them in articulating whiteness in the relationships. For Los Angeles whites, groupness was stronger and was linked to white spouses bridging across class differences to reveal commonalities with less-educated whites.

However, rather than engaging ethnoracial boundaries, white spouses changed the meaning of them, emphasizing ethnic identities based in an ancestral nation-state in a sleight of hand. They also communicated a color-blind universalism in their understandings of their whiteness.

It was their black spouses, usually black husbands, who used discursive strategies to bridge over ethnoracial difference.

In both sites, denials of racial boundaries as well as pushes against them reveal the greater flexibility whites have in Rio than their black spouses, as seen in the previous chapter. White spouses were able to include themselves in a white category in one moment yet were able to push, pull, and reconfigure racial boundaries to problematize their whiteness. This chapter shows how the cultural repertoires surrounding whiteness that are available in both Rio de Janeiro and Los Angeles allowed whites to maneuver racial boundaries. However, these maneuverings largely left out issues of racial inequality and hierarchy hidden in the two sites. Neither husbands nor wives of either color in either site discussed the advantages of whiteness and even avoided such discussions when I raised them. This was very different from the black respondents, as in the previous chapter, who experienced far less flexibility in their racial senses of self and for whom discrimination and disadvantage were often front and center. In comparison to black spouses, as seen in the last chapter, white husbands and wives had more flexibility with racial boundaries than their black partners, although the gender difference was wider in Rio de Janeiro. This chapter adds to this new tradition by revealing how nonelites construct the boundaries of whiteness for themselves and those they love based on the repertoires—whether a racially mixed ancestry or references to nation-states—available in their societies.

Table 3.3 shows how boundaries of whiteness compare in the two sites. Groupness was a stronger characteristic of how couples

TABLE 3.3. Boundaries of Whiteness in Rio de Janeiro and Los Angeles

	Rio de Janeiro	Los Angeles
Theme		
Groupness	–	+
Congruence	–	–
Strategy		
Bridging	+	+
Pushing	+	–
Changing meaning	+	+
Redrawing	+	–

understood whiteness in Los Angeles in comparison to Rio de Janeiro. However, in both sites, there was little congruence between couples on the ways that spouses discussed the whiteness of the white partner. At the same time, including bridging, changing the meaning, pushing against, and redrawing boundaries of whiteness, Carioca's boundary strategies were more varied than the Angelinos. This finding adds greater nuance to the long-held understanding that ethnoracial boundaries in Latin America are weaker; we can now see that the wider range of strategies available to Brazilians is likely an important part of this flexibility.

4

Black, White, Mixed or Biracial

Identifying the Children

Yvonne is a white woman who lives with her self-identified black husband, Aaron, and their two children, a boy and a girl, in a predominantly white neighborhood right outside of Los Angeles. When I interviewed her, she was pregnant with a third child, a daughter. I asked Yvonne about the expectations that she had about her children before they were born as well as her child who was on the way. She discussed Aaron's parentage involving his black father and white mother as well as her own ancestry.

> We had no idea what our kids would look like just because my dad is a natural blonde. Aaron's mom is a natural blonde. He's got an African American father on his side. We have such a mix of DNA that is coming into each of them that we just had no idea how it's going to play out. Truthfully, the browner they are. . . . I'm hoping he gets a little darker. . . . Aaron obviously has the more dominant genes, and I'm pretty fair and recessive as they come. So I knew I was up against some pretty dominant genes. Our daughter has the curly hair and the darker color. I mean, I tease that I married [Aaron] for his DNA because I'm so fair and [have very] straight hair. I'm like, the curlier and browner they come out, the happier I am. I just love that. . . . I want them to identify with being African American and having the physical traits. I just love Aaron and who he is. I love seeing little mini Aarons running around.

Parents have many hopes and expectations for their children before they are born, including the children's health, gender, and physical features. In racialized societies like Brazil and the US, these expectations can reveal a logic, a hierarchy of desirability, and processes of racial socialization. Through "racial schemas," people understand and racially categorize individuals, reflecting the societies in which they live.[1] This concept of racial schemas is useful for comparing the logic of race mixture in the United States and Brazil, as manifested in the children, the products of race mixture. Looking at understandings of the children of black-white couples reveals the extent to which they blur or break down ethnoracial boundaries. While this does not negate the love parents have for their children, it can have implications for their children's well-being and even their socioeconomic status.

In this chapter, I examine a subset of fourteen black-white couples with children from their relationships (see table 4.1 and appendix table 3). Most of these couples were composed of white wives with black husbands. I discuss parents' racial schemas in terms of their expectations surrounding the phenotype and racial categorization of their children, how they and others react to the child's actual appearance, and the ways parents racially socialize their children in these two sites. Overall, I found that parents in both places did not expect their children to be white. Brazilian parents expected their children to be black like their black parents; US parents understood their children to be in a different category, both white and black.

Should the children of interracial couples qualify for positions set aside for African Americans? Brazil is already debating this very issue.[2] There has been much controversy surrounding Brazilians of racially mixed ancestry who apply for university slots and government positions as Afro-Brazilians when their blackness or brownness is questionable.[3] One student was even expelled from the State University of Rio de Janeiro despite claims of a black grandmother.[4] In 2016, Brazil created state tribunals to classify job applicants and assess the validity of their claims of self-categorization to eliminate fraud.[5] Such measures

TABLE 4.1. Interracial Couples with Children from the Relationship

	Rio de Janeiro	Los Angeles	Total
Black husbands with white wives	4	6	10
Black wives with white husbands	7	4	11
Total	11	10	21

raise the question of their relation to early twentieth-century pseudoscientific claims of the ability to measure race. In the United States, there is growing concern over the origins of blacks at elite colleges and universities.[6] With higher numbers of interracial marriages and biracial children, there are strong policy implications for how parents categorize their children.

I examine the implications of these factors for parental understanding of their child's eligibility for university policies targeting underrepresented minorities. These include quotas for Afro-descendants in Brazil and US affirmative action diversity initiatives. In Rio de Janeiro, parents had expectations for black children before they were born; this shifted depending on the child's actual appearance. These categorizations did not shift upon discussion of qualification for affirmative action in university admittance. In Los Angeles, parents saw their children with both feet firmly planted on either side of a black-white color line. However, questions surrounding eligibility for affirmative action led them to place less weight on the children's white ancestry and more on their black origins. Parents did not display an emphasis on other crosscutting social cleavages (i.e., "My child is American / Brazilian / Christian / a human being") that would suggest a blurring of ethnoracial boundaries. Rather, understandings of an ethnoracial "us" or "them" remained intact no matter how parents categorized their children; parents did not blur ethnoracial boundaries in their understandings of their children's classifications. I end this chapter with a discussion of children's role in understanding race mixture and racial boundaries generally in these two societies. This chapter reveals the flexibility of ethnoracial boundaries in the case of Rio de Janeiro spouses and how Los Angeles parents can be involved in the everyday construction of new ones in the form of "the biracial."

Parental Schemas in Rio de Janeiro

Like Los Angeles, black-white couples in Rio de Janeiro more often included black men with white women than the reverse. This was reflected in the couples whom I interviewed, with more couples involving black husbands and white wives. However, the sample of couples who had children from their relationships was different. As seen in table 4.1, most parents that I interviewed in Rio de Janeiro were couples involving black wives and white husbands. Several white wives and black husbands revealed that they had been in prior relationships with same-color partners and had children from those marital unions. This pattern was the likely result of greater opposition to black men and having children with them. I also suspect that the influence of colonialism on Brazilian understandings of race mixture makes family formation between white men and women of color more palatable. I did not find a similar pattern among the Los Angeles couples.

Racialized Expectations

When I asked respondents in Rio de Janeiro about expectations of their children's appearance before their birth, parents in both sites generally mentioned the health and well-being of their children, including an absence of deformities. However, upon further probing, it became clear that almost all study participants had expectations and preferences regarding how their children would look before they were born. According to the racial schemas of parents in Rio de Janeiro, the children of their black-white relationships ought to yield black children. In slavery-era Brazil, as in the United States, the children of black female slaves inherited their mother's slave status regardless of their paternity; this was during a time when being black (*negro*) was synonymous with being a slave.[7] In fact, children of white masters and black slaves had higher rates of manumission than the children of black men in both societies. However, the fact that they were born into slavery may have influenced the assumption that black parentage outweighs white parentage. Judging by the expectations of parents of both colors in Brazil, while Brazil does not have the one-drop rule and phenotype largely determines categorization, the expectation of black offspring nevertheless remained.

Conforming to this expectation, Vitor expected his daughter to be black. He is a white, college-educated man who lives with his wife, Eloíza, and their newborn, Karina, in the racially mixed city center. I asked him whether he had any expectations concerning his daughter's appearance, and he said, "No. I knew that she was not going to come out white; she was going to be black. Especially because it is the gene that dominates; the black gene is dominant."

Vitor drew on a pseudoscientific understanding of the expectations surrounding his daughter that involves genes, although race is not a biological construct but a social one. In the whitening norm prevalent in Brazil in the first half of the twentieth century, race mixing supposedly led to lighter offspring due to the supposedly stronger genes of whites.[8] His understanding of the intersection between race and genes is a reversal of that norm. Instead, he articulates a darkening hypothesis and ideology in which race mixing with a black person should lead to darkening over generations because it leads to children that are black. This may be influenced by his perspective as a white person, since in every black-white couple, one person could be darkening while the other is lightening over generations.[9] However, this perspective was common across the color of the spouse.

Some of my participants produced children who were not black, despite their mixed heritage. The Brazilian racial schema clearly makes this possible, since phenotype rather than ancestry largely determines the racial or color categorization of an individual. For this reason, unlike in the United States, a child with a black father and a white mother could be classified as white. However, parents admitted that they had been surprised when their children were white. Tatiana, who is a college-educated black woman, was shocked by the pale skin of her son Zeus by her white husband, Gaspar. She felt her son didn't look like her. She laughed as she said, "It was one of those things when you look and you find it so weird, like 'Is he really mine? Was he switched for another?'" She and a number of Brazilian wives described inspecting the color of their newborns' testicles because they believed a white-looking baby would darken over time if his testicles were dark. She was shocked to find that, like the rest of Zeus's body, they were white.

Unlike Los Angeles couples, some Carioca white spouses admitted they were disappointed that their children were white. While Gaspar did not mention this to me in his interview, Tatiana confessed that Gaspar wants their son, who is now six, to be darker. Gaspar often tries to expose him to the sun to tan, despite Zeus's sensitive skin. The *negras frustradas* I described in the last chapter, who desired to darken themselves, were pleased if their children were dark. However, those like Angela, whose children were lighter, were disappointed. Angela is a white woman with a high-school education who is married to Donato, a black man of the same education level. They live with their daughter in a racially mixed distant suburb of Rio de Janeiro: "When my daughter was born, she came out white. . . . I said, 'Geez, God punished me. He didn't give me a black child. . . .' When I held her in my arms, I said, 'You couldn't have been black [*preta*]? Why did you come out white? God doesn't listen to me, does He?'"

Angela's comments reflect the disappointment that she experienced in having a daughter who was white despite being white herself. This was unlike parents whom I interviewed in Los Angeles who never thought of their children as white and certainly did not refer to desires of darkening themselves through their offspring. For Angela, race mixture was a way to help her achieve the black family she had always desired. Her child's whiteness was proof that she had failed in her attempt.

Other mothers in Rio de Janeiro, both black and white, were happy when their children did not have the kinky hair associated with blacks. Many used the term *bad hair* (*cabelo ruim*) to refer to kinky hair. Otávio is a white husband who did not complete elementary school, like his black wife Katarina. In his interview, he revealed that Katarina claimed that she had chosen him in part to avoid having a child with kinky hair. Delfina, a black college graduate, had similar desires and tied her preference for straight hair to her child's gender:

> I was worried about the hair; I didn't want hard hair at all because it is very difficult to manage [a] girl's hair. When we knew it was a girl, [I said], "My God in heaven, if she comes out with bad hair, I'm screwed [*estou frita*]!" . . . My only concern was that she would be a girl with bad hair. Like, if it's a boy, he can have bad hair because with a boy, it's short hair, little curls, but with a girl [it's more difficult].

Several people echoed Delfina's sentiments about the difficulty of styling kinky hair. They referenced the idea that black hair requires special products. None of the parents were upset when their children had straight or wavy hair, but most women who expressed a strong preference for it tied that to gender. In the Russian roulette of hair textures, several Carioca mothers were happy that they had won. This was different from Los Angeles couples who did not specifically describe desires for children with nonkinky hair or an aversion to styling black hair.

Family Reactions

Carioca couples had far more contact with their extended families than Angelino couples did. Within this context, the mothers of the couples, particularly white mothers, were particularly likely to express an opinion about their children's physical characteristics. For example, while Angela wanted her daughter to be black because she desired darkening herself, she said that her mother was elated. According to Angela, she had said, "Oh, I prayed so much for her to come out white [*branquinha*] without bad hair." For his part, Angela's husband, Donato, said he did not expect their daughter to be born really white and that he hoped that she would be healthy. However, his mother would ask him over and over again, "How will she come out? Do you think she'll come out dark [*escurinha*]? Do you think she will come out white? How will she come out?" He said that his response was always "I don't know, Mom. There is no way to know. God is the one who determines it, right?" Fathers of the black-white couples were never mentioned as having preoccupations surrounding the appearance of children, only mothers and other female relatives. This is likely because women are the ones tasked with child-rearing and would more likely engage in styling hair or putting sunblock on the children.

Gaspar described how the white appearance of his son Zeus led to difficulties with Tatiana's extended black family. As Gaspar said, they had expected Zeus to "turn out blacker than he is, that he have kinkier hair [and] thicker lips," all traits associated with blacks. While Tatiana had said Zeus didn't resemble her, Gaspar said that Zeus had inherited Tatiana's fine facial features, but nonetheless, Zeus's light skin and light-brown, wavy hair set him apart from Tatiana's black family. According to Gaspar, Tatiana's relatives called him "Whitey" (*Branquelo*) on occasion, purposely excluded him from the other children in the family, and bullied him verbally and physically. They also engaged in aggressions masked with humor such as not giving him a chair to sit on with the other children in the family, pushing him, and yanking his ear. One of the most recent incidents was during Christmas when Tatiana's family members called him "Japanese boy" and "Portuguese boy" while shoving him. Gaspar understands these aggressions as stemming from the child not meeting his black in-laws' physical expectations.

Categorization

Interviews with parents in Rio de Janeiro revealed great variance in their categorizations of their children (see table 4.2). During their interviews, they occasionally categorized their children in passing or described their children's colors. If they did not over the course of the interview, the majority were asked directly about how they categorize their children. While all the mothers revealed clear ways that they understood their children, some of the fathers' responses could not be placed into any particular category. This was due to their own musings and inquietudes about how to categorize their children without coming to a decision. Still, as seen in the table, the majority of the fourteen parents were able to do so. Although parents often used multiple terms to describe their children, there were no cases in which one spouse thought their child white and the other thought him or her black; the other parents used a mixture of race and color terms, often terms that were euphemisms for black.

As seen in table 4.2, while all Carioca parents acknowledged the race mixture of their children, the majority of parents classified their children as black (*negra, preta*) and, to a lesser extent, dark (*escura*). This categorization had the most congruence; there were five couples in which both parents identified their children as black. This agreement occurred across education levels of the spouses.

TABLE 4.2. Parents' Categorization of Children in Rio de Janeiro

	Mother	Father	Congruent Parents
Black (*negra, preta, escura*)	6	6	5
White	4	3	2
Middle term (*meio termo, mestiço, meia e meia*)	4	0	0
*Moreno/a***	3	4	1
Not white	2	2	0
Total	14	11	5

* Totals do not add up because many respondents used more than one term.
** As mentioned earlier in the book, *moreno/a* is an ambiguous term with many different meanings. Several parents used the term to describe their children's color and appearance but not to classify them into a particular category. Fewer still were those who simply remarked that their children were "not white."

Nevertheless, Cariocas' understandings of their children's racial categories reflected Brazil's flexibility in racial schema and ethnoracial boundaries. While most parents expected their children to be black, if their phenotype required it, they understood their children as white. As seen in table 4.2, the white category was the second most chosen category for their children. It was widely adopted by couples involving black husbands and white wives.

The fact that none of the respondents described expecting that their children would be white, even couples including the lightest of black partners (by my own estimation), suggests the influence of blackness as tainting whiteness—a notion that produced the one-drop rule in the United States. While several parents adopted this explanation for why their children could not be classified as white, others still understood their children as white. Adopting a white classification occurred across parents' education levels but was particularly common for couples involving black husbands and white mothers. This was at odds with the white wives' discussion of the potency of the *negão* in chapter 1. Nevertheless, this finding was consistent with the findings from a national study in which children were more likely to be classified as white if the father was black or brown.[10]

Parents also used middle categories to categorize their children, using terms like *middle-of-the-road* (*meio termo*), *mixed* (*mestiço*), and *half and half* (*meio a meio*). Mothers, especially—though not exclusively—white mothers, were more likely to identify their children using these terms. No one used the term *mulato* spontaneously to identify their child. One black mother, Priscila, mentioned that this was due to the term *mulato* having the connotation of Brazilians seeking to escape being labeled as black. It is also likely due to its associations with hypersexuality[11] that are inappropriate for children.[12] As seen in table 4.2, none of the fathers used such terminology, even white fathers. This is likely due to these white mothers, much like with the US "mark one or more" (MOOM) option on the 2000 census,[13] seeking recognition of their maternity in their children's categorization. As a result, there was no congruency in using these middle terms among parents.

Carioca parents without ethnoracial congruence usually had less than a college degree. However, no Carioca parents used complete opposite black and white categories to categorize (or even describe) their children. For example, both Edite, a white woman, and Bartolomeu, her black husband, have low levels of schooling. Bartolomeu described their children as brown (*morenos*), and Edite described them as blacks. In the other two couples who identified their children in different ways, white mothers used terms such as *half and half* (*meio a meio*) or *in the middle* (*no meio*). The fact that no Carioca parents used complete opposite black and white categories suggests that common understandings of Brazilian flexibility in racial schemas are slightly overstated; incongruences between parents were differences of degree, not contention surrounding opposite ends of the spectrum.

Parenthood Questioned

In the United States, on May 21, 2013, a white father took his two daughters to a Walmart in the Washington, DC, area.[14] After he picked up his black wife and they drove home with their children, a police officer came to their house to make sure the girls had not been kidnapped. He explained that a Walmart security guard had asked the officer to check out the situation. It was later revealed that a fellow customer had told the security guard that the children "did not fit" or "match up" with the father because they were of different colors.

This was an extreme case of situations that multiracial families can encounter when parents' paternity or maternity is questioned. While it is easy to dismiss these incidents as US phenomena, several respondents in Rio de Janeiro experienced similar situations. For instance, Nicolas is a black man and is married to Laura, a white woman. Neither Nicolas nor Laura had attended college. They live in a racially mixed neighborhood near the center of Rio de Janeiro. During his interview, he made references to our shared dark skin tone. One day, he was walking in the neighborhood with his daughter when she was a baby and she started to cry. He described the scene:

A white woman stopped [and] called the police over, because I was carrying a white child in my arms and she was crying a lot. So he came and spoke to me, and I said, "Try and take her from my arms." So he tried, and the little girl cried. So then she hugged me and said, "Daddy." If I had not shown that she was my daughter, I would have gone to the police station. . . . [The white woman just] saw my color. She said, "That young, dark [*escuro*] man, that black man, is with that white child, and she is crying a lot." That's what she said. If she had said, "Gee, I don't know why that kid is crying, maybe it's not the father," so then, it's OK. . . . Now the way that it was done to me, it was very bad, very suffocating.

In this situation, Nicolas makes an attempt at a form of race work that Steinbugler calls *visibility management*: attempts by interracial couples to deal with discrimination in public.[15] By having his daughter name him as her father, he tried to be seen by the officer and other outsiders as the legitimate caretaker of the child instead of as a kidnapper. If he had not done so, he might have been accused of committing a crime.

Situations as alarming as Nicolas's were rare in Carioca couples' experience, but Wanderley and Deisy, who are both highly educated, seemed used to having their parenthood questioned. In his individual interview, Wanderley told me that after they agreed to my interview, Deisy asked him about his greatest frustration being in a black-white couple. He responded, "Not being recognized as the father of my children." She told him, "Oh, I have to prove to everyone that they are my sons!" In their case, even though they both agreed that their sons are black, both partners experienced not being seen as the parents of their children. Other parents described similar frustrations. Five wives and four husbands decried this treatment by outsiders, although only one couple experienced congruence on this dimension.

Given the potent narrative of racial harmony and race mixture that is so prevalent in Brazil because of racial democracy ideology, this was an unexpected finding. The experiences of these couples show that families that exist at the nexus of current categories and racial boundaries are problematic, even in a society as racially mixed as Brazil. While black fathers experienced this issue in Rio de Janeiro, it did not emerge as a theme among black fathers in Los Angeles. The one-drop rule was likely more relevant for black fathers than other parents.

Racial Socialization Practices

One study of white women who had children with black men in Britain found that some mothers developed a "racial literacy" that included: recognizing racial discrimination as a contemporary social problem, understanding how other social locations like class and gender mediate experiences of racism, recognizing the cultural and symbolic value of whiteness, understanding that racial identities are an outcome of social practices, knowing how to discuss race and racism, and the ability to interpret racial codes and practices.[16] As I spoke to Carioca parents about how they racially identified their children and how others reacted to their children's appearances, particular themes spontaneously emerged in terms of how they build racial literacy among their children. In Rio de Janeiro, many spouses spontaneously described the ways that they tried to build racial literacy in their children. However, this was something that mainly black spouses, both husbands and wives, brought up over the course of their interviews. White Carioca parents rarely described teaching their children anything about how race operates in Brazil; if they were concerned about it, they did not spontaneously mention it. In fact, a couple of white women explicitly said that they did not teach their children anything about race. These women said they found it important to share the idea that race does not matter and that their color is not a determinant of their life chances. This was different from Los Angeles, where both black and white spouses understood and conveyed racial literacy to their children.

In both sites, parents described the importance of finding black figures with whom their children could identify. Tatiana's son Zeus, who is considered white, nonetheless has a strong black identity at the age of six. Tatiana admitted that she and her black natal family find the paradoxical juxtaposition of his black identity with his white phenotype absolutely hilarious. Once, when she and Zeus were watching a film that showed children in Africa, she said to him, "Look, our cousins, our brothers, our uncles, our aunts." However, he misinterpreted her comments, as she explained:

"So he tells his friends in the square, 'Oh, I'm going to Africa. I have some cousins there [*laughs*]. . . . My cousins live over there in Africa. I come from there too.' [laughs] It's hilarious! I think that I am filling his head too much. I don't know. Poor thing. He thinks he came from there on a plane. I've already told him that it's not the case, it's a question of origin, but he is too little to understand."

Rather than recognizing whiteness, Tatiana was passing on a more Afrocentric racial literacy to Zeus that was about the cultural and symbolic value of blackness. Notably, Tatiana referenced African origins but not slave ancestry; Cariocas of both races rarely described slave ancestry as something to pass on to their children. Instead, they provided a sense of an imagined community with black people living in Africa today, which nonimmigrant Los Angeles respondents did not.

Bureaucratic Institutions and Affirmative Action in Rio de Janeiro

One of the reasons bureaucracies collect data on race is to implement policies promoting the inclusion of people of color into institutions, such as schools and universities. A site of discomfort for the parents whom I interviewed was dealing with bureaucratic settings in which they had to classify their children. This anxiety was gendered, with mothers usually referencing it as an issue spontaneously without being asked about it specifically. This was due to their being the ones confronting bureaucracy in registering their children for administrative purposes, such as the first day of school. Similar to US mothers of such children who were uncomfortable with the one-race option on the US census,[17] Brazilian mothers found this requirement confusing. They were often unsure about which box to choose and often sought further instruction to make such decisions. They described administrators who said they should identify their children as black because of the benefits that can accrue to being an Afro-descendant. This was similar to Los Angeles mothers who also expressed this process as a concern.

In Brazil, the use of quotas to include Afro-Brazilians in public colleges and universities has been highly controversial. Almost half of the country is composed of brown or black individuals, but whites are the overwhelming majority of college students in the public universities, which are more prestigious, and the most desirable public-sector positions. The Brazilian Supreme Court upheld the use of quotas to address these imbalances in 2014.[18] In practice, quotas reserve some university slots for poor students of any race and others for indigenous peoples and Afro-Brazilians.

I asked parents in both sites about the relevance of affirmative action policies for their children; it did not emerge spontaneously in the interviews. When I asked Deisy about her experience with the Brazilian quota system, Deisy admitted that her son had gained admission to the State University of Rio de Janeiro through the system but that his offer was rescinded once the administration learned of his high family income. Being black was not enough to gain him admittance as a quota student. Deisy said, "You had to be really, really poor" to gain university entrance through quotas for that university. As the case of Deisy and Wanderley's son suggests, some institutions will not give these slots to Afro-Brazilians unless their family income falls below a certain threshold. However, in popular parlance, quotas are often understood as an issue affecting blacks and not about income.

Nationally representative studies show that the majority of Brazilians are in favor of quotas for higher education.[19] However, the majority of parents that I interviewed were against the use of quotas. Ironically, among Rio de Janeiro respondents, those with the lowest level of education—who would gain the most upward mobility from quotas—were the ones who were the most against them. Respondents with the lowest levels of education were the ones who were the most against the quota system in general, despite quotas also being available for the poor. This may be due to a lack of familiarity with university systems in general or the influence of overwhelming antiquota discourse frequently in the media.[20]

Parents who identified their children using middle categories thought that their children would qualify for quotas for Afro-descendants (afrodescendentes). However, I found that even the possibility of benefits did not make Carioca respondents who identified their children as white comfortable changing their children's classification. In this respect, Brazilians were not flexible in racial classification during their interviews. Although all of these children had one black and one white parent, if they considered their children mixed (mestiço) or black, they thought that they qualified for the use of racial quotas. If they were white, they did not.

Parental Schemas in Los Angeles

Extended Families

The family structure in the two research sites resulted in couples in Rio de Janeiro having far more contact with their extended families than they did in Los Angeles. Los Angeles parents, and couples in general, were frequently migrants from other areas of the country. As a result, their extended families often lived far from Los Angeles. This may be one reason couples in Los Angeles did not describe the appearance of offspring as problematic for extended families. Another possibility is that couples did not relate those experiences or issues in order to appear to be politically correct.

Racialized Expectations

In Los Angeles, husbands across colors referenced desiring an inheritance of their wives' good looks. Several parents, especially white husbands, hoped that the child would inherit the light-colored eyes of the white parent. Following a new racial logic, Los Angeles parents often expected their children to encompass a "biracial type" and named specific physical characteristics associated with this type. Specifically, parents expected their children to have "curly hair" and "caramel-colored" skin, which, as one black husband put it, was "a mixture of the two colors." Thus they had an idea of what "typical" "mixed" children look like and expected their children to conform to it.

For example, Pavla is a white woman married to Gary, a black man. Both have college degrees. Originally from Eastern Europe, when I met Pavla, she had straight, reddish-brown hair. When I asked her about the expectations of what her child would look like before he was born, she said:

PAVLA: Yes. I always wanted my baby to have curly hair.
ME: Is it because you have straight hair?
PAVLA: Yeah. I like curly hair. I don't know why. I love it, so when I was pregnant, I would tell Gary, "Oh, my God, he's going to have curly hair; he's going to be so cute." And then, I always imagined—you see all these mixed babies. I always thought they were the cutest babies

ever, mixed babies . . . because they have the perfect skin. Like, my skin is like—I burn myself if I lay down in the sun, and you know, stuff like that, so I think my baby has the perfect skin. I like their type of hair. It's so beautiful. It's like soft but curly—I don't know. I just think they're so cute.

For Pavla, her expectations and desires for her child's appearance came together in a biracial type with particular skin and hair characteristics that she understood as different from her own. Racial mixture in the family-formation process helped her realize her appreciation for the biracial type. In addition, Pavla's comments show a negotiation with racial hierarchies in which she replaces whiteness as a beauty ideal with biracialism.[21] She uses the ideology of "hybrid vigor" to give meaning to her child's looks, in which race mixture produces "super babies" with perfect physical features. Like many parents whom I interviewed in Los Angeles, Pavla subscribed to the positive stereotype that all children of interracial couples are attractive. Her child's race is a central part of how she understands his attractiveness and looks in general. Although black and white parents in both sites generally saw their children as attractive, as most parents do, in Los Angeles, they were more likely to attribute this beauty to the children's racially mixed ancestries. Their attractiveness was a racial attribute, not just an individual one. Parents in Rio de Janeiro discussed assumptions about their child's categorization but did not tie how they categorized the child or their race mixture to their child's attractiveness.

Similar to Rio de Janeiro, parents in Los Angeles, usually mothers, expressed shock that their child had a lighter skin color than they had anticipated. However, in Los Angeles, they compared their expectations not to a black type but to a biracial type. For example, Betty is a college-educated black woman who lives in a predominantly white neighborhood with her husband, William, who is also college educated. Similar to other Angelinos, she had expected a "caramel-colored" child and was surprised that her child was much lighter than expected. When I asked her if she had expectations surrounding her child's appearance, she laughed and said, "Yes! I hoped he was gonna be dark. . . . I just wanted him to look black. Very obviously black. [Because I thought it would be] way easier for him—to fit in. [*long pause*] But now it looks like he's going to be . . . Mexican or . . . anything *but black* [her emphasis]. . . . I was so freaked out when he was born because he was a little white baby [*laughs*]."

Betty's remarks reveal that she was hoping that her son would have a darker skin tone that would make his black ancestry more obvious. Her comments also reflect the multicultural nature of Los Angeles, very different from Rio de Janeiro, and expressed concern about her son being mistaken for a member of another ethnic group. Similar to a few of the black parents that I interviewed, this was based in desiring accurate understandings of his racial heritage. Another possible, but less likely, interpretation (given her other antiracist comments in her interview) is that her desire for her son not to be seen as Latinx was based in anti-Latinx sentiment. Her last comments revealed her sentiments about having a child that is perceived as white to outsiders.

Parenthood Questioned

Betty's discomfort also likely stemmed from not wanting to be confused for a paid caretaker instead of being his actual mother. This is an issue common among mothers of racially mixed children, especially black mothers.[22] Similar to parents in Rio de Janeiro, Los Angeles parents, especially white mothers, described having their parenthood questioned by outsiders. For instance, Alison, a white woman, described how she was burping her son on the bus in Los Angeles and an older lady got on the bus, sat next to her, and said, "Oh it is such a shame that parents don't stay at home with their children anymore. They get nannies to take care of them." Being mistaken for the paid caretaker rather than the biological mother was painful to Allison as well as other respondents.

This questioning of parenthood by outsiders sometimes took on a more sinister tone for black parents. For example, Visola is a black woman married to Charles, who is white. Together, they have a son, River, and live in a predominantly black neighborhood in Los Angeles. Several years ago, when he was four months old, she took him to her neighborhood post office. At the time, she said that he had very light skin and straight hair. She narrates,

So I was standing in line behind this older African American gentleman, and he kept staring at me and [River]. I had [River] in my arms. . . . Then finally, he turned around, and he was like "That can't possibly be your child. . . ." I said, "Excuse me, sir?" He was like "That baby in your arms looks nothing like you. That can't possibly be your child. Are you the nanny?" I looked at this man, and I was dumbfounded. I looked at him, and I'm like "Excuse me? This is my child. This is my son." . . . [H]e goes, "I guarantee I'm going to see this child on the news tonight, and when I do, I will call the police and tell them where I last saw him." That's what he said to me, and he walked out of the post office.

Alison and Visola's experiences were similar to those of couples that I interviewed in Rio de Janeiro, in which parenthood was questioned for individuals in these black-white couples. However, in Los Angeles, it was largely women who experienced this hostility. In Rio de Janeiro, it was less of a gendered phenomenon, with men also having their paternity questioned. This pattern shows that policing racial boundaries in the family was a phenomenon in both societies, but in the United States, it is likely more tied to issues of maternity than paternity. This was a striking finding, given that historically in both societies, slave status was determined by the mother's status. Also, since both black and white mothers were questioned—although white mothers were rarely accused of kidnapping—US notions of maternity, not the one-drop rule, are a likely culprit for these societal differences.

While having their parenthood questioned was a downside of being an interracial couple, my Los Angeles interviews revealed that biracial children were a source of praise and validation from outsiders as well. Several parents experienced strangers frequently giving them compliments on their children's physical appearance. For example, Kevin is a black man who lives with his white wife, Madison, in a predominantly white suburb of Los Angeles. He explained the last time that someone gave validation and support to his being in an interracial relationship:

"Daily. Well, lately with the baby . . . when people ask, they see pictures on my phone, [and] they go, 'So what's your wife look like?' And I'll scroll through, and I go, 'Here's me and my wife' or 'Here's the family.' And they're like 'Oh, that's why your baby's so cute.' Like 'Mixed races always have the most beautiful kids,' and they'll go on and on. . . . For me, I mean, whenever somebody's going to say that, that's validating a positive aspect of the relationship that I'm in."

For Kevin as for many other couples in Los Angeles, such reactions were a source of pride. One white father, Mark, is married to a black wife, Kelly, and lives in a predominantly white suburb of Los Angeles. He said that his children were "gorgeous" and that he "struts" when he goes out with them, in part because they are so good-looking. This was not a theme among the parents in Rio de Janeiro, an unexpected finding, given the idealization of racial mixing in Brazilian culture. However, "biracial" children are more common in Brazil than in the United States, and the concept of the *mulata* is highly sexualized but racially equivalent to such terms as *mestiço*. Carioca parents did not express the same degree of valorization of their children because of their racial ancestry the way that Angelino spouses did.

Racial Identification

While the one-drop rule has been prominent in understandings of race mixture in the United States, there have been other ways of talking about the offspring of black-white relationships. Black communities have used the term *mixed* for decades to refer to these children. However, changes in the census have been linked to an increasing recognition of nonblack, especially white, parentage for those who were once deemed only black outside of black communities.[23] The option to "mark one or more" on the US census, which emerged through the mobilization of white mothers of interracial unions, recognizes nonblack ancestry in mixed children.

Reflecting changing attitudes toward racial mixture in the United States, the Los Angeles parents that I interviewed, unlike Carioca parents, did not expect to have black or white children. Rather, they understood their children as biracial and were engaged in the everyday construction of this intermediate racial category. They articulated a very specific form of biracial categorization of their children, a "border" one, in which children do not have to choose between racial identities because they are *both* black and white.[24] The majority of Angelino couples claimed this additive identity for their children, articulating the race of each parent as encompassing different "sides" of their children.

Many said their children could take advantage of "the best of both worlds" by drawing on both black and white cultural and social network resources embedded in both sides of the extended family. This was very different from parents in Rio de Janeiro who generally expected their children to be black before they were born.

Ironically, the only US couple in my study who racially identified their children as black was the one with children who are arguably more white than black. A college-educated couple involving a black male and a white female, Yvonne and Aaron live in a predominantly white neighborhood near the beach in Los Angeles. In their separate interviews, they both described their children as black. Aaron was raised by his black father and identifies as black despite having a white mother himself. When Aaron discussed how he classified his children, he said that however they identify is "not a big deal" for him. Nevertheless, he said,

> I think of them as black, and I will tell them that they're black when they ask, so that's why I think I'm black. I come from the black—not just a black parent but the black condition too. . . . My relatives were slaves in this country. It's an experience that is unlike any other experiences in this country. I'm summarizing a couple hundred years of history, but that history defines the black race, and that's what I am. . . . I'm slightly uncomfortable with it because I don't really know what that's going to mean for people, if it's going to have meaning for them or people. [I'm] only uncomfortable relative to the easy definition of being black; I'm not uncomfortable with the notion that they have a multiracial background. . . . Are they multiracial, or are they black, and what does that mean? I think of them as black. I will tell them they're black. If they push back and say that they're multiracial, it's not going to cause a fight, OK?

Aaron's wife, Yvonne, agreed:

> Yeah, they've got a mix of different races and backgrounds in them, but it's—you know, you want to embrace the African American piece of you. Even though—whatever percentage it breaks out to, but there's just such a history and just such an identity of being African American that we want to make sure they embrace. They're going to know their history

too. They have a grandmother that emigrated from Scotland. They're not going to lose the other part of themselves, but there's just—you don't embrace being white. Being white doesn't—it's such a broad term. I think within being white, there's just so many other cultures and identities and pieces of that, that being African American—there's a whole history and culture that you really—I don't want to lose that, and it's something that's really important. So it's something that having that as a stronger piece of their identity—they'll have to work to keep that a little bit.

Both Aaron and Yvonne draw on the particular history of African Americans in the United States to make sense of how they racially identify their children. They draw on a shared understanding of slavery, saying that this history has implications for the way that their children today are racially classified. This couple was more specific than most in referencing elements particular to African Americans in the United States. The other couples, despite often having a black parent who was the descendant of slaves, did not frame their children's racial identification in terms of that history or the social condition of African Americans. Instead, they discussed representing the different parents as pieces of their children's race. This appeared to be Yvonne's concern, given her discussion of her children's "percentage" black. It was important for these parents to maintain blackness as an identity. Yvonne compares this with understandings of a white identity that she does not see as rooted in an ethnic cultural heritage. She references a Scottish ethnic heritage but does not use it in the same way she does an African American racial identity. For Yvonne, "African American" is both a racial and an ethnic identity.

At first glance, Yvonne and Aaron's racial identification of their children seems to follow traditional definitions of blackness according to hypodescent. However, they use understandings of black history, not biological ancestry, to identify their children as black. By valorizing black ethnic identity, not adjudicating pseudobiological fractions of blackness, they deviate from traditional notions of hypodescent.

Racial Socialization

Among the Los Angeles respondents, the majority of parents did not spontaneously describe building racial literacy or engaging in racial socialization of their children. Race was not an issue that emerged over the course of parents talking about their children. In the Los Angeles interviews, although racial literacy rarely emerged in the interviews, when it did, both black and white spouses discussed it. White husbands were the least likely to mention it.

One theme that emerged among both the Los Angeles and Rio de Janeiro couples was parents emphasizing a knowledge of the children's history. For example, several Los Angeles respondents said they were planning to teach their children about their black ancestry. When I talked to Aaron about how he identified his children racially, he said,

> Our great ancestor Gabrielle, who Gabby was named after, was a slave. We named her [their daughter] . . . Gabrielle Ann. Gabrielle after this woman who was a slave, the first person in my dad's family that was in this country, and after Yvonne's grandmother Ann, who was the first woman in her family who was in this country; and we wanted to give Gabby a new history, a new name, a new meaning. We wanted to kind of think about the way those histories merged. It's a really difficult thing to cross that ocean—and I mean that, I think, literally and metaphorically—to come here. It was hard for Yvonne's grandmother to do it with a dead husband and a baby to raise, and it was difficult for my ancestor to do that strapped to the hull of a ship. We wanted that to be reflected in [our daughters].

For Aaron, teaching his daughters their family history, especially their slave history, was an important component to teaching them racial literacy. For Aaron, naming his daughter after her slave ancestor was part of building his daughter's racial literacy. Through this choice he ties blackness to a history of slavery.

Parents in both sites were interested in toys for their children that reflected a nonwhite racial identity. In Rio de Janeiro, parents, typically mothers, expressed a need to find black dolls as a means to emphasize that black beauty exists. In Los Angeles, only two respondents referenced this, both of them white men. In one instance, the father described the hardship he experienced trying to find birthday party items with images of the Green Lantern, a superhero who has had both white and black incarnations. He wanted the black version for his son. This racial sociali-zation, however, was a bigger issue for parents in Los Angeles than those in Rio de Janeiro.

Bureaucracy and Affirmative Action

Like their Carioca counterparts, Angelino mothers described their difficulty in filling out forms that asked for their children's racial classifi-cation. However, in Los Angeles, mothers wanted to be able to reflect all of their children's ancestry on such forms. They often said they wished checking multiple boxes in the sections asking the child's race was an option. While the US census has had a MOOM option since 2000, many other official documents do not. Like their Carioca counterparts, moth-ers often sought the guidance of administrative officials, who vacillated between ascribing white or black identifications, depending on insti-tutional interests—typically of the school their child attended. Namely, officials advocated that mothers identify their children as black when it was advantageous to show diversity and white when it was advantageous for a school to seem to have more white students.

Since the issue of affirmative action was not in the public sphere as much as in Rio de Janeiro, several Angelino parents had not given the issue much thought. Still, when I asked them whether their children qualified for affirmative action programs, the majority of parents said that their children would qualify for programs designed to increase racial diversity. When asked why, they gave a variety of reasons. For example, Angelino parents emphasized that their children's eligibility depended on the purpose of the policies, such as whether their goals were to increase black numbers specifically or minorities in general. Kevin, the black husband mentioned earlier, reflected on this in his interview:

"I think in today's mixed-race era, being a child of a mixed race could be a benefit. . . . I think people are looking for diversity, and I think they're looking for—they'll continue to look to add different kinds of people to business situations, you know, different organizations. I think it's a plus."

Several parents thought that their biracial children could benefit from programs that aim to encourage diversity, in keeping with the idea that affirmative action programs improve diversity more than redressing past wrongs suffered by minorities. Thus Angelino parents who understood their children as being both black and white saw them as not white when it came to eligibility for affirmative action programs.

Other parents thought that their child being both black and white meant that they qualified for programs and university slots designated for African Americans. Madison, for example, categorized her child with Kevin as biracial—both black and white. However, she admitted that it would probably be to her daughter's advantage to identify as African American to benefit from affirmative action programs and policies. Kevin did not refer to advantage, but he agreed that their daughter should be able to benefit. When I asked him about his newborn daughter's future eligibility for affirmative action programs and policies, he said, "As long as one of your parents is, she could still say she's not white. So yeah, she would benefit." Parents like Kevin and Madison felt their children's whiteness would be erased or ignored in relation to affirmative action policy. They hardened the boundary between biracialism and whiteness while erasing the boundary between blackness and biraciality. This contrasted with Carioca parents, who felt their children's eligibility for quotas depended on the children's physical appearance. This strategy implied that white as a racial category continued to be more exclusive to Angelino parents.

Conclusion

With same-race parents in the US, the assumption is that their children will inherit their parents' race. However, with interracial couples, there may be different assumptions and expectations about the race of the children. These understandings of race mixture can reveal the racial logic of the society in which they live. In this chapter, I discuss parents' racial schemas in terms of their expectations surrounding phenotype and racial categorization, how parents and others react to the child's actual appearance, and the ways parents racially categorize their children in the two sites. Finally, I examine the implications of these factors for parental understanding of their child's eligibility for university policies targeting underrepresented minorities, specifically quotas for blacks in Brazil and US diversity initiatives that include blacks.

This variation in the two sites in expectations and categorization of the same child of a black-white union demonstrates the greater fluidity between ethnoracial boundaries that exists in Brazil in comparison to the United States. In Rio de Janeiro, parents often expect to have black children due to mixture with a black parent. However, there is a greater flexibility in identification in that a child's phenotype determines the category they fit into, such that a child could be white, black, or mixed (*mestiço*). Affirmative action eligibility did not cause parents to waver in their assessments of their children's race, particularly for white children, whose whiteness made them ineligible despite having a black parent.

When Los Angeles parents described their child's race, they often described it as additive: both black and white. They maintained the same biracial categorization of their child before and after their child's birth. Since phenotype is not a component of racial identification in Los Angeles, this identification persists, regardless of the way the child looks. Nevertheless, when the child's eligibility for affirmative action is in question, even Angelino parents become more flexible in their assessment of their child's race, with parents emphasizing blackness if they consider it advantageous. Sometimes they understood the biracial categorization as a type of minority status that is unique and adds to attempts at increasing diversity. Other parents conflated a biracial categorization with blackness, hardening the boundary against whiteness. While parents acknowledged that their children were white as well as black, they did not see that as removing a minority status.

This chapter shows how parents in black-white marriages engage in the social construction of ethnoracial boundaries for their children. Parents are involved in the assortment of their children into ethnoracial categories that vary according to the racial schemas of their societies. This assortment process has implications for how they steer their children toward or away from the use of race-based programs in their societies.

In the next two chapters, I examine how people in black-white couples negotiate ethnoracial boundaries as they engage in social life as a couple. I show how they understand white extended family members drawing boundaries against black partners and how it differs in the two societies. I also analyze how they make sense of interactions with strangers in public as a couple. These chapters reveal more of the social element in the construction of ethnoracial boundaries.

5

"A Fly in the Buttermilk"

Black Spouses in White Families

Neil is a white man married to Jennifer, a black woman. Both of them went to college and met and fell in love while living in Oklahoma. Together, they moved to Los Angeles, where they live in a wealthy area. Like several white husbands married to black women in both sites, Neil is helping Jennifer raise her child from a prior relationship with a black man. When I asked him about his family's response to their relationship, Neil mentioned that his parents still live where he grew up, in the Midwest: "I think that they didn't have strong opinions in the beginning because they just weren't there, and people weren't really aware. . . . They just knew her name kept coming up. Other than that, they just knew that I was kind of forming a greater friendship and a greater kind of relationship with this woman, but since they weren't there, they didn't really have an opinion, other than the fact that it was making me happy, so I think they were happy with it." Neil's story of his family's reaction to his relationship with a black woman is not the common US narrative of black-white couples experiencing hostility from white family members. Too often, scholars focus on the rejection and hostility that occur when people of color enter white families, often ignoring the extent of social cohesion that can occur in these families.[1] However, social cohesion is not an apt description of extended family life, since Neil's parents have participated very little in his family life, which was also the case for several white men whom I interviewed in both sites. While Jennifer was marrying into the family, the distance that this couple experienced—like many other Los Angeles couples that I interviewed—meant that her integration into the extended family was very limited. In addition, white masculinity provided a shield for couples like Neil and Jennifer such that they experienced little opposition from white family members.

Families are an important institution in which care, financial resources, and affection are distributed. Like schools and neighborhoods, families in post-slave societies are often segregated by race and ethnicity. While this is more the case for the United States, it is also true to some extent in Brazil.

Although there have been increases in interracial marriage in both the United States and Brazil in recent decades, they occur simultaneously with continued white advantages across a variety of socioeconomic outcomes. In racially unequal societies where whites are dominant, how white families integrate black spouses into themselves can have repercussions for the life chances of both partners in a couple as well as their children. Black-white intermarriage has the potential to provide black spouses with access to resources embedded in white social networks. On the other hand, intermarriage can also open up black partners to acts of discrimination from white extended family members that they might not have experienced otherwise.

Previous chapters in this book have mainly described the ethnoracial boundaries of categorization. In this chapter, I discuss how black-white couples negotiate the ethnoracial boundaries of white families. I discuss the different tactics of action, discursive strategies, and cultural repertoires that black-white couples and their families draw on to understand the integration of black partners into white kin networks. I unpack how race and gender combinations, along with educational status, affect this integration and how different notions of masculinity and race intersect to produce differences in white family reactions to contemporary race mixing. I find that Carioca white extended families were overt about their discomfort with intermarriage with blacks, despite their own black ancestry, in what I call the *irony of opposition*. On the other hand, Angelino white families were careful to practice a color-blind mode of opposition initially. This often transformed into a more overt form of opposition. In both sites, marriages involving black men were more stigmatized; by contrast, white men enjoyed autonomy from their white families in their romantic and family formation decisions. I show how entering white families can be an uncomfortable process for black spouses in both sites.[2]

Family Structure and White Family Reactions

Similar to other studies of race mixing in both sites,[3] none of the couples in either of the sites spontaneously expressed extended white family members as a cause of worry or concern in their relationships. It was only upon asking specifically about the reactions of the white partner's family to the relationship that black-white couples in both sites revealed the opposition that they faced. Overall, opposition was more common if the man was black and the woman was white, and hostility was more common in Angelino's families, though it was by no means absent among Carioca respondents.

Rio de Janeiro has lower levels of residential segregation than Los Angeles, which allows for greater contact between people of different colors, which may promote acceptance of intermarriage.[4] Also, within the Brazilian racial logic, the same family can have children of different colors. In addition, family life in Rio de Janeiro was very different from the family life of Angelino respondents. In Rio de Janeiro, like in most of Latin America, extended families play an important role in the social lives of couples. Visits with the natal family, especially the wife's family of origin, were frequent among respondents, with couples often seeing them every week. Several couples that I interviewed in Rio de Janeiro even lived with the wife's parents. This often meant that Carioca white family members who were initially opposed to a black husband became acclimated to him. In Rio de Janeiro, several of the black men who had been accepted by their wives' families related stories of family opposition in their previous relationships with white women. For this reason, many were grateful not to face that situation with their current partners' families.

This was unlike Angelinos, whose natal families often lived in distant cities or states. This was because several couples, like interracial couples in general,[5] had migrated to the city from other areas of the country. This meant that the integration of black spouses into white families was a much longer process for Los Angeles couples than for couples in Rio de Janeiro. Couples in Los Angeles saw their natal families with less frequency than Rio de Janeiro couples, in what I call an *exclusionary integration*—black spouses were often integrated into the white families but at a distance because of geography. The only exception was Visola and Charles, a couple involving a black woman and a white man, who had one of Charles's family members living with them. Nevertheless, even US whites' extended families that were initially against these relationships came to accept their black in-laws into their families.

Nevertheless, the death of older white family members was a strategy that I sometimes found among couples involving college-educated white wives with black husbands in Rio de Janeiro. A few white women in their forties and fifties revealed that while alive, older white family members had been against their previous romantic relationships with black men. These white wives often had previously married white men and had white children with them. They took advantage of the death and absence of these natal family members to have relationships with black men. For example, Juliana is a college-educated white woman and is in her fifties. She lives with Patrício, a black man, in the home that she inherited from her parents. Juliana recalled that her parents welcomed blacks in her home as guests and friends, but when Juliana developed a romantic interest in black men, her mother began to hassle her, using the epithet *crioulo*, a derogatory term for blacks. There is no direct translation, but the term is similar to *nigger* in the United States.

> She had jokes that would annoy me a lot. Like "Princess Isabel." Do you know who Princess Isabel was in Brazil? She created the Golden Law liberating the slaves. She would call me "Princess Isabel" because I "would go crazy for niggers [*crioulo*], you know?" She would say, "Gosh, you go crazy for niggers." She would say this in that exact way. She would call me "Slave Ship" [*navio negreiro*]; slave ships brought blacks to Brazil in the era of slavery, right? She would talk like this: "Don't you look in the mirror?" So that I would look in the mirror and see that there was a color difference.

Juliana understood that her mother had a firm color line when it came to considering blacks for romance. In a pattern that I found among several white Carioca women, Juliana had casually dated black men but never entered a long-term relationship with a black man until after her parents had died. Without older family members to police ethnoracial boundaries, older Carioca women seemed to enjoy the autonomy that their white male counterparts experienced, since the opposition had passed away. This dynamic occurred only once among the Los Angeles couples and was not a theme that emerged among them.

Rio de Janeiro: Black Integration into White Families

Gender, Color, and Intersections of Hostility

In both Rio de Janeiro and Los Angeles, couples involving black men married to white women described hostility from white families. The construction of black men in both societies is likely a factor explaining this. In the United States, black men have historically been seen as one of the greatest threats to white womanhood, justifying segregation and acts of violence, including lynchings. Today, black men continue to be seen as "criminally inclined, promiscuous, and dangerous."[6] While Brazil lacks the US history of lynching blacks, the media often portrays black men in the media as diabolical and criminally dangerous.[7] At the same time, white women are idealized as symbols of female beauty and femininity in both countries.[8] In addition, US white women are represented as naturally belonging to white men.[9] Interracial marriages with black men are more common today in both societies,[10] but this history makes white women's marriages to black men more threatening to social norms than white men's marriages with black women.

In addition, white men being romantically or sexually with women of color is reminiscent of colonial and postcolonial periods of both societies. Both societies have long histories of white men having unfettered access to black women's bodies, whether slaves or free, as well as to the bodies of indigenous women.[11] This pairing is far more resonant to both nation's histories and notions of white male agency and superiority. This likely partially explains why couples involving white husbands did not experience as much hostility as those involving black men with white women.

White Male Autonomy

In both research sites, couples involving black women with white men referenced a lack of opposition to their relationships from white families. Similar to Neil's story at the beginning of the chapter, white men were privileged in these relationships by virtue of their race and gender.

Just like with the experiences of interracial couples in Colombia,[12] white men were able to enact hegemonic forms of masculinity by acting autonomously in their romantic relationships. In Rio de Janeiro, several white men commented that no one really knew about their previous relationships, including interracial ones, so their parents had no opportunity to take issue with them. For example, when I asked Teófilo, Griselda's husband, about his family and friends' reaction to his relationship, he said, "No one said anything to me. When they found out, I was already with Griselda. No one said anything. They accepted Griselda. Now, if they are against it or not, I don't know. . . . There were a lot of people who did not know. Many people did not know that I had separated [from my previous wife]. . . . So when they discovered that I was no longer married and that I was with Griselda, people were shocked."

In their relationships, the white men in my study acted very independently of concern for their families' approval, to the extent that people were not always aware of their interracial relationships. Circumstances do not even allow Teófilo to distinguish shock over his divorce from shock due to his involvement with a black woman. His comments suggest an indifference that he had to outsiders' reactions to his relationship.

Similarly, Otávio is a white man who did not finish the second grade. When I asked him about his family's reaction to his relationship with his wife, Katarina, a black woman with a fourth-grade education, he said this was irrelevant: "No, my family does not get involved at all. . . . See, if I am of age, no one has to involve themselves with what I do or what I don't, you know?"

Women did not reference their age in their discussions of how their families treated them. Both Teófilo's and Otávio's comments were typical: white men operated much more autonomously in their relationships than their white female counterparts.

Black males in both sites also experienced some degree of autonomy in their relationships vis-à-vis their families. In Los Angeles, however, black husbands expressed greater interest than white husbands did in whether their families of origin accepted their spouses. In addition, their wives' white extended families often challenged their autonomy in their romantic relationships. Unlike their black male counterparts, in both sites, autonomy was part of the meaning that white men gave to their relationships and was a cultural repertoire that they drew on to give meaning to their interracial marriages.

Racial Ambiguity

Interviews with respondents in both sites revealed another factor that may explain gender differences in white family acceptance. Many of the black women in the sample had been told they were not really black. For example, Eloíza is a Brazilian with facial features that she says are indigenous, despite identifying herself as a black woman. In her interview, Eloíza said, "His family thinks that . . . I am not a black woman. His sister, who went to college, I spoke to her, 'My goodness, Suelaine . . . your mother, I can understand, since she has little education, but you?' 'But you are not a black woman,' [Suelaine replied]. I said, 'No, Suelaine, I am not a black woman, so what am I? A Viking? . . .' She subscribes to the idea [because] . . . they don't want to see me as a black woman, because they think that black people are ugly."

Eloíza's in-laws refuse to acknowledge her as a black woman, even though that is how she self-identifies and how her husband and other Brazilians identify her. This discursive strategy of white family members was to contract ethnoracial boundaries of blackness to exclude black wives from that category. This was not a pattern among the black men whom I interviewed in Rio de Janeiro, who across skin colors did not experience ambiguity surrounding their blackness.

Overt Opposition

One discursive strategy that Carioca white families employed when black spouses started dating and even married white partners was to express overt hostility. The Carioca couples that I interviewed described white family members as using overt racial language to express their displeasure at the introduction of black partners. This was similar to a study of interracial couples in Cuba, where having black romantic and marital partners was also frowned upon.[13] For example, Konrad, a college-educated black man in his forties, is married to Ofélia. A white woman, Ofélia did not attend college, characterizing their relationship as involving status exchange. Despite Ofélia "marrying up" in terms of socioeconomic status, in separate interviews, both spouses said that her mother initially did not approve of their relationship.

> So, one time [Ofélia] told me that her mother said . . . "If you are thinking that you are going to marry a black man, that you're going to have a child and I am going to be there doing cornrows on the head of a black [child] . . . it's not going to happen. . . ." So then, I would go to her and her mother's house. At the beginning, her mother didn't want me to go there, right? She would not let me in, so I would stay downstairs, and [Ofélia] would come down, and we would go out.

According to Konrad, it was only after Ofélia got sick and could not leave the house that her mother allowed him to enter it. His interview excerpt reveals that Ofélia's mother initially reconstituted an ethnoracial boundary that placed him on the side of the "other." Over time, however, Ofélia's mother came to accept the relationship and now even lives with them. White parents in Brazil used explicitly racial terms in a way that never occurred among US respondents. This may be related to the lower education of whites who intermarry in Brazil. In Brazil, less-educated whites are more likely to intermarry than highly educated whites. One study of US whites showed a correlation between expressions of overt forms of interpersonal racism with lower socioeconomic class.[14] While it is unclear whether the same pattern exists in Brazil, this may explain the overt opposition that black spouses experienced who entered the social space of the white family. This may also explain why similar experiences of overt opposition were rare among Los Angeles spouses, since they were of higher socioeconomic status than the Rio de Janeiro couples were.

Insults through Humor

An absence of vehement opposition is not the same as complete acceptance or indifference. Even when black partners are integrated into. white extended families, on occasion, they can experience inclusionary discrimination in which they become integrated into these families yet are not on an equal level with whites.[15] Another discursive strategy that white Carioca families employed when black spouses married into their white families was the use of humor. Carioca couples, but not Angelino ones, described their white extended families as using light-hearted yet openly racist humor to refer affectionately to black spouses. Jokes can be a "combination of friendliness with antagonism" and are part of an overall structure of relations.[16] Studies of race in Peru, Mexico, and Brazil have shown how humor is a form of hegemonic discourse reminding blacks of their lower status position.[17]

For example, Angela and Donato are a black-white couple living in a racially mixed suburb of Rio de Janeiro. Both finished high school. In their individual interviews, they both said that Angela's parents love and accept Donato, but Angela notes that her mother makes uncomfortable jokes. She calls Donato *Foguinho*, after a silly black character on television. She also calls him *neguinho*, which is a diminutive of *negro* and is often used as a term of endearment, including within families. However, depending on the way it is used, *neguinho* can also be a racial epithet. Angela's mother has teased her about Donato being ugly. This is similar to many studies in Latin America showing how blacks are often understood as having "ugly" features.[18] These are all ways of highlighting an ethnoracial boundary between Donato and the white family and making it clear that he is not on the "us" side.

In her interview, Angela described her brother's behavior toward Donato:

My brother likes him a lot. He doesn't have anything [mean] to say about him. He'll screw with him, [saying,] "Ah, you monkey. . . ." Before [our daughter] was born, he said that the decoration of her room was going to be a bunch of vines. . . . I was going to put in a bunch of bananas because she going to come out a little monkey, he would joke. . . . He would joke, but it always was that type of joke, in relation to blacks, but you would see that it was with respect; it was not to offend. Because sometimes you can joke with a person but wanting to offend them, to attack them. And you joke—but in an affectionate way—say something, the person accepts it, but you see that you are not insulting or belittling or humiliating [him]. So we always played around like that.

Angela's comments reflect how the terms of inclusion into a white family in Brazil can include being the butt of racial jokes. Similar to studies showing that US interracial couples downplay racist elements of family acceptance,[19] Angela accepts these jokes at face value. Angela understands these jokes as affectionate and without malicious intent, softening the family's interaction. At the same time, the jokes reveal the maintenance of a racial hierarchy that devalues blackness. Donato's integration into a white family comes with a reminder of his lower status on the racial hierarchy, allowing him (and his daughter) to be seen as subhuman. These incidents show how the inclusion of blacks into white families does not necessarily include acceptance as a racial equal or the dissolution of ethnoracial boundaries.

Although outright resistance was less common, a few black women mentioned the discomfort they experienced in the presence of their husbands' families. For example, Tatiana is a black woman who lives with her husband, Gaspar, in a multiracial neighborhood in the working-class North Zone of Rio de Janeiro. Tatiana stated that Gaspar's family had no problem with her being black, but she described one of Gaspar's family members making her feel uncomfortable at a family gathering.

> This relative came from far away; he came from the Northeast, and he saw me, right? He has known Gaspar since he was a baby. When he saw me with him, he started coming with this story of "Wow! She is *black woman!*" [her emphasis] "Of course I am!" I said to him, "So you were the only one to notice it up till now?" [*laughs*] I had to say it. [He said,] "Wow, the baby is so cute! Look at how the blood has mixed, huh!" . . . He said it a little shocked. . . . He wanted to be nice, but he was discriminatory. . . . I didn't like it. So then he said, "I, too, once had a *preta*, you know? There in Paraíba, a sly *preta*, you know?" [I said,] "I can't take it anymore!" So I left.

Tatiana was offended by Gaspar's uncle's comments ranging from her phenotype, the surprise at her child's appearance, and his off-color remarks about his prior liaison with a black woman. Unlike many US blacks, who openly stand up to stigmatization by using them as "teaching moments,"[20] Tatiana indirectly challenged the uncle's comments through her own joke. But then she chose to leave with her husband

and child instead of continuing to confront the uncle's racial comments, whether directly or in the form of another joke. Her comments illustrate how humor can be used both as a way to diffuse a racially charged conversation ("you were the only one to notice it") as well as to denigrate blacks who marry interracially. Black-white couples in Los Angeles did not remark on using humor in this way.

This use of humor is a way of highlighting the ethnoracial boundary that exists between Tatiana and Gaspar's white family. The uncle's use of humor called attention to the difference that exists between them and Tatiana. Tatiana's initial response also reifies the boundary between them yet tries to trivialize it. The uncle's later response to Tatiana sexualizes the ethnoracial boundary, creating an even more hostile environment for Tatiana. This incident shows not only how race-based humor can be used to negotiate black entrance into white families in Rio de Janeiro but also how it creates uncomfortable, even hostile, social spaces for black spouses.

Griselda, like Tatiana, experienced discrimination at the hands of her husband's relative. She is a thin, college-educated black woman in her late fifties, with light-brown skin and hair cropped close to her head. She inherited a condo in a wealthy area of the city where they live. Her husband, Teófilo, is a white man who never went to college but runs a small business that Griselda purchased for him. Despite Griselda's higher socioeconomic status, she said that her husband's aunt openly referred to her as her husband's "housekeeper," a low-status occupation commonly occupied by black women in Brazil. The comment suggests the intersection of race and gender in understandings of the role of black women in interracial relationships.

Humor was one way for white families to acknowledge the penetration of black spouses into white social spaces without coming across as racist. It showed that whites, even in Rio de Janeiro, where race mixing is supposedly historically prevalent, found it out of the ordinary and even problematic. Using humor was one way to redraw boundaries by reifying the existence of an "us" and a "them" without seeming racist. These jokes told in these families also suggest how blacks are constructed in Brazilian society: ugly, stupid, hypersexual, inappropriate life partners, and best suited to low-status occupations. These incidents suggest that when white families in Brazil are uncomfortable with blacks entering their families, they may use racialized language that can also be seen as not offensive in the Brazilian context. The fact that I rarely heard such stories among Angelinos suggests the families of my respondents in Los Angeles might recognize their implications as racist, even if white families experience similar discomfort.

Irony of Opposition

A cultural repertoire that emerged among Carioca respondents was the notion of what I call an *irony of opposition*. In the irony of opposition, the white partner's family members could be opposed to their relationship despite their own ancestry of race mixture or their romantic career involving people of a different color. This theme especially emerged among couples involving black men with white women. This was different from Los Angeles, where an irony of opposition did not emerge as a theme among black-white couples.

Ana María was one Rio respondent who experienced this form of opposition. She is a white woman and high-school dropout who is married to Cândido, a black man who entered the Brazilian armed forces after he graduated from high school. They met at a dance party in the south of Brazil, where he teased her about stealing her away. Ana María had a close friend who was so close to her growing up that she referred to her as her "sister." Her sister had dated Cândido before Ana María. Expectedly, she reacted negatively when, after they split up, Ana Maria started dating Cândido. Ana María described how her sister expressed her opposition in ethnoracial terms: "I was like 'I'm going to go out with him.' Then she comes with: 'A black man? With a black man?' 'Big-lipped' this, 'hair' that. These types of comments . . . : 'Ana Maria, really, that black man? . . . You're going to go out with that black man?" and I don't know what. "Really, with all the guys that you've gone out with, this black man? No. Oh, I know he works hard; I know he is a good person, but he is black.'"

Her sister's opposition to the relationship was likely based in jealousy or tension due to Ana Maria's dating a man she had gone out with first. But the terms she used clearly reflected an ethnoracial hierarchy that made Cândido undesirable. Ana Maria made it clear that her sister saw him as an outsider despite his other qualities, which she saw in a more positive light, but that did not make up for his lower status as a black man.

In another example, Idália is a white woman who is a high-school dropout, while her black husband, Róbinson, went to college. They met when she became his client at his workplace. Idália's mother is the daughter of a black-white couple herself and is married to a white man of German descent. Idália referred to him as "really white" (*brancão*) with blue eyes. According to the US racial logic, Idália would be multiracial, biracial, or black; however, in Brazil—with her light hair, skin, and eyes—she is white.

In both of their interviews, the couple described how Idália's mother was against their relationship despite her own black father (Idália's grandfather) and because of her own marriage to a white man. In his interview, he discusses "our color," likely referring to how both he and I were unambiguous, dark-skinned black people as well as his strong sense of groupness with blacks, both in Brazil and around the world. Róbinson understood his mother-in-law as engaged in the process of whitening through Idália's father, whom Róbinson refers to as "the Aryan" (*o ariano*).

> Her mother is mixed [*miscigenada*], you know? She is more towards our color; her father is the one that is a real Aryan. . . . So [her mother] did not like [our relationship] at all because she is more towards our color. [Idália's] father is the one that was a real Aryan. . . . She didn't like it because . . . when she married an Aryan, she thought that she was climbing [socially]. When Idália married a *black* man, she thought that she was descending. . . . [Idália's mother] would not even talk to me. . . . She ignored me. And when I was in Idália's house, when I saw her with her color like ours, I said, "Great! I'm safe." I was afraid of the Aryan. And the Aryan was the one who was the most fine [with it].

As Róbinson later summarized, "So you can see that, you know, sometimes you think the enemy is one person when it's really another." Róbinson found it ironic that his father-in-law, a very white man, accepted him while his mother-in-law, the child of a black-white couple who married across color herself, did not. The logic of whitening means that Idália was undoing this process.

Idália also described her mother's initial rejection of Róbinson: "He would come to a party at my house, and she would not greet him. . . . She would serve everyone else but him, you know?" Idália also described her father as accepting of Róbinson but said that he had died after they started dating. Idália observed, and Róbinson concurred, that her father's death had made her mother more accepting of their relationship. Her mother began speaking to Róbinson soon after and today accepts him as part of the family:

"My mother today likes him. [But] she continues being prejudiced. She says that she sees him as [a] white man. . . . She no longer sees him as a black man, got it? So she still has this prejudice inside of her. She likes him, but she still looks at him like an alien, you know?"

While her mother no longer engages in overt racial discrimination against Róbinson, she has had to undergo a cognitive shift, changing her perception of Róbinson's race in order to accept him. In spite of her mother's acceptance, Idália still understands her as treating her husband differently from white members of the family, as though he were from outer space instead of a black person whom she could not accept. For Idália's mother, Róbinson has crossed an ethnoracial boundary by changing how she categorizes him. However, Idália shows how this honorary white status is not entirely stable, since her mother still engages him as though he is different from Idália and "alien" to her own whitening attempts.

Los Angeles couples did not describe this irony of opposition. This may be due in part to the different racial logics operating in the two societies. Still, none of the Los Angeles respondents referenced white parents' or family members' prior relationships with nonwhites in making sense of opposition to their relationship. If anything, they referenced prior race mixing in their own lives or the lives of their family members as part of their understanding of family *acceptance* of their relationships. The irony of opposition also did not emerge as a theme among couples involving black women with white men in Rio de Janeiro.

The irony of opposition reveals how there is a double standard for negotiating ethnoracial boundaries in romantic relationships. Even as people engage in or are the products of race mixing, they can be against it for contemporary couples, especially white female family members. They can redraw ethnoracial boundaries in ways that socially exclude black partners. For Cariocas, when it came to race mixture, what was good for the goose was not good for the gander.

Los Angeles: Black Integration into White Families

White Male Autonomy

Just as in Rio de Janeiro, white male autonomy vis-à-vis their white families was a theme in the lives of Los Angeles couples. This was seen at the beginning of this chapter with Neil's story in which no one in his family had a problem with his black wife, Jennifer. Previous work has shown that white men face no issues in these relationships.[21] Rather than being a question of a division of gender roles in romantic relationships, I find that autonomy was a factor for white men. Unlike any other group in the study, several white men left their families in the dark about their relationships with black women. Black wives in Los Angeles expressed concern about not meeting their white husbands' families after what they thought was an appropriate amount of time dating, while white wives did not mention this as a concern with their black husbands. Nevertheless, white husbands seemed unconcerned about this distance. As I mentioned earlier, this situation was very different in Rio de Janeiro, where spouses had more regular contact with extended families and were often a part of their everyday lives. Yet even there, white men discussed the autonomy they experienced in their relationships despite greater familial integration. As a result, white husbands hardly experienced ethnoracial boundaries the way that respondents of other less privileged intersections of gender and race, including their black wives, did.

Black Women and Racial Ambiguity

Just as the black women in my Brazilian sample, the majority of black women in Los Angeles revealed that others either expressed confusion over their ethnic background or viewed them as multiracial. For example, Lana is a black woman with a college degree and has been living with Larry, a white man, for several years. She described the racial ambiguity that she experiences.

> LANA: I often get asked if I'm biracial, which I'm not. But I do think some of that sometimes has to do with how I talk or that I went to college. I definitely think that without realizing that, that's why people think that I'm biracial instead of just black.
>
> ME: Really?
>
> LANA: Yeah. It's really—obviously, I'm not an expert. I'm just speaking from my own experiences but, obviously, I can see it. Like pheno-typically, I am taller and slimmer like. . . . I guess what black women look like, I don't necessarily look that way. I look different than other black women they know, which is kind of, like, silly because every-body looks different, but I can see why [when] looking at me some people might think—you know I'm a little more light-skinned or whatever. It's definitely possible. I get confused for Hispanic some-times. I get all kinds of things. But I do think—there are people that have known me for years that just assumed that I was biracial and never asked me. . . . And it doesn't help that my mother is actually very light-skinned, so sometimes people see her and they can't tell that she's black at all . . . and then it kind of gets to a point, I think, in a friendship where people are kind of afraid to ask, and they feel stupid, like, "Oh, I've known you for six months, and I don't know what ethnicity you are."

Lana's comment illustrates how, similar to several black wives that I interviewed, her lighter skin and taller, slender frame that she references shows that she often navigates the world as a black woman who looks racially ambiguous. Similar to studies of skin tone in the United States,[22] outsiders' perceptions of these women's physical appearances may affect the extent to which they are seen as authentically black. An ambiguous physical appearance can make it harder for outsiders, including white in-laws, to draw an ethnoracial boundary against these black women since it is not clear to what category they belong.

Very few Angelino black men mentioned experiencing ambiguous racial identification by others. At the same time, the men who were the darkest in the Los Angeles sample were the ones who experienced the most hostility from white extended family members. This suggests an intersection between phenotype and gender to make ethnoracial boundaries more or less salient despite all of them sharing a black identity.

Opposition with Social Desirability

Echoing previous studies of US black-white couples,[23] the majority of the Los Angeles couples involving black men with white women experienced some degree of opposition to their relationship. This was despite the prevalence of color-blind ideology, political correctness, and multiculturalism in US society. The majority of the couples perceived negative reactions from white family members, particularly parents. The few white wives who did not experience opposition from their families often referenced their past interracial relationships as making their parents more accustomed to seeing them with nonwhite partners. For those couples that experienced opposition from white families, unlike in previous studies of US black-white couples, they not only relied on color-blind interpretations to understand it but alternated between color-blind and more overt race-based explanations.

Elizabeth is a white woman who lives in Los Angeles with her black husband, Trevor. Both have postbaccalaureate degrees and enjoy running in their spare time. They got to know each other through the church that they both attended. During their joint interview (one of the ten couple interviews that I conducted in addition to their separate individual interviews), they described going to Tennessee, where Elizabeth grew up, to seek her parents' blessing and permission to wed. Elizabeth reported she had told her parents about Trevor more than a year earlier, when they visited her in Los Angeles. She recalled what her father said to her at the time: "Well, you know, Elizabeth, all marriages have their idiosyncrasies. It really doesn't matter what color you are." By de-emphasizing difference, Elizabeth and Trevor understood this erasure of ethnoracial boundaries as acceptance of their relationship. However, her father's later reaction to their engagement surprised them.

TREVOR: It was a very hesitant reaction. It was just a hesitant reaction, and she was not expecting that, and I was not expecting that, I guess, and—

ELIZABETH: They were full of cautious advice.

TREVOR: "Have you considered this?"

ELIZABETH: "Have you thought about this? Have you thought about that?" . . . I think the general flair of the conversation—which was really not a conversation, it was really a one-way dialogue from my dad to us—was "Have you thought about how hard it's going to be?" And he was just really worried about all I potentially have to go through.

On what should have been a happy occasion, Elizabeth said that she became unhappy about her parents' reaction. She had understood her father as initially being open to her marrying a black man. However, they perceived his later reaction as showing that their interracial marriage was more than just another "idiosyncrasy." Elizabeth and Trevor perceived a shift in her parents' reaction from a more socially desirable response to expressing grave reservations about the potential problems of being a black-white couple.

However, in discussing Elizabeth's father's reaction further, both Elizabeth and Trevor minimized the role of race:

TREVOR: I was going to say, there are two sides to this. One is the racial dimension, but then there's also the religious dimension. And he did not know my family. . . . With me, all he knew was basically what Elizabeth has said. So for him, there were two things going on. One was the kind of racial dimension, which is not just something that you see every day in Tennessee. Okay, so that's something that's like . . . "Are you really, really sure [*laughs*] you want to do this?" 'Cause from, if you're in Tennessee, that's just something you don't see very often . . .

ELIZABETH: As a parent, I can understand. I can totally relate to that even though my kids are really young right now. I would not want them marrying somebody that I didn't know. You know, to have to give up one of your babies to a stranger. That'd be very hard.

TREVOR: And this is a tight-knit family, so those two dimensions come together and meet on that night [*laughs*] in June. And so, it was, it was, so you had this one-way conversation because we were both silent. . . . I mean, they were just, they're thinking out loud . . . [*laughs*], and so there was this hesitancy and all of this caution.

Elizabeth and Trevor's story shows how they reframe what could be interpreted as a racially motivated reaction on the part of her father. Although how they presented her father's previous comments suggests that he was thinking along racial lines, Elizabeth and Trevor emphasize the fact that he did not know Trevor or his family, despite their dating for many years. They argue that race was just one of the many motivations for her father's opposition. Elizabeth and Trevor try to overcome her father's redrawing of ethnoracial boundaries by emphasizing how Trevor was a stranger to the family. By doing so, they attempt to blur the ethnoracial boundary that Elizabeth's father had delineated between them.

In a few extreme cases, Angelino white women were ostracized by their families because of their interracial partnerships. Other studies of black-white couples in the United States and Great Britain have found similar patterns of family estrangement.[24] This was something Carioca couples did not experience. Stella, a white woman, is married to Edward, a black man, whom she met while pursuing a postbaccalaureate degree. She is originally from a small town in Indiana where her family still lives. When she decided to move to Los Angeles with Edward, her boyfriend at the time, her parents fought with her about the relationship, and then her sister and parents refused to speak with her for two years. Although her family is now accepting of her relationship with Edward, especially now that she was pregnant, Stella said, "At first, they tried to pretend like race wasn't the issue. They tried to pretend like that, you know, 'He's moving you across the country. . . .' For a while, it seemed like they were dancing around the issue when we all knew what the issue was. And then eventually, I was like 'Why won't you just admit, like, this is why.' And they eventually were like 'Yeah,' because, this is their famous line, like, 'I don't have a problem with black people, but I have a problem with my daughter dating one.'"

Stella recognized that her parents were trying to avoid acknowledging their opposition to her relationship with Edward based on his being black. Similar to Elizabeth's parents, her parents talked *around* disapproval of a romantic relationship with a black man. Both sets of parents expressed "concern"—a means of using a color-blind perspective to evaluate the relationship. Stella considered this color blindness as false, while Elizabeth and Trevor did not.

According to Stella, her paternal aunts and uncles (who lived away from the small town) disapproved of her parents' behavior when they found out. She said,

> Actually, to this day, my dad doesn't really get along with his family very well because [of] the time when all this was happening. Basically, my family blames me. They said that I was the one that called my dad's sister and told her, but I was like "I didn't tell anybody," like, "I did not talk to any of them." Well, they found out about kind of what was going on, and [my aunts and uncles] were really upset with my family . . . and they actually called them and kind of were like "You shouldn't—this is your daughter." And so basically, my family got so mad about that, and so even to this day, they're still, they don't have a very good relationship with them. . . . I know they still blame that on me. But yeah, they just don't have a very good relationship with them because, at the time, they stood up for me, and they didn't agree with [my parents].

Stella describes her parents and siblings as uncomfortable with extended family members knowing about their racist reactions to her relationship with Edward and as blaming her for exposing those reactions. This situation shows how, unlike decades ago, sharing overt antiblack sentiments and openly judging a person's worth based on their race is frowned upon in many white social circles. At the same time, it echoes studies showing how whites approve of interracial marriage as long as it is not a close relative.[25]

Elizabeth perceives her family as trying to provide a politically correct reaction to her intermarriage with a black man. Family members' attempts at socially desirable responses were not a theme that emerged in any of the interviews in Rio de Janeiro or with any of the couples involving white men and black women in Los Angeles.

Despite the actions of Stella's parents, Edward had a striking response when I asked him directly if his wife's parents were racists. He said that there were different definitions of being racist:

"I think kind of a conventional definition of it would be to treat a person differently because of race or ethnicity or because of how they look. I think that might be a conventional definition of being racist. If I define it that way, then I would say yes. I would say they are racist."

However, Edward continued, saying, "In their minds, I don't believe that they feel they're racist." He compared them to white supremacists on "Storm Front," a white supremacist website, and said that in comparison to white supremacists, they are not racists.

> I don't believe that when they see black people that they think . . . anything less of those people. . . . But I think that they just did not want her to marry a black guy or to be involved with a black guy. . . . [I]f you are a staunch racist and you really believe that people of another race are inferior in some sense, then you could never get to the point that they are at in terms of actually trying. So that's why I think there's kind of a gray area with them because . . . if you look at it in the sense of a person who is truly sort of an acknowledged racist and truly believes in racial inequalities, then I don't believe that kind of person could ever get to the point where Stella's family's at. I don't think they could ever welcome me into their home. . . . I do see them making the effort. And if a person makes a conscious decision to be racist . . . I don't think a person like that could ever get to the point of accepting their son or daughter being married to a black person or trying to accept it.

Arguably, Stella's parents' initial reaction clearly reveals that they consider blacks inferior to whites. However, Edward distinguishes Stella's family from people who see him as inferior. He draws on a color-blind approach to make sense of Stella's parents' response, comparing it to a more immutable, overt racism. This issue of expressing disapproval in politically correct terms was not a theme that emerged in any of the interviews in Rio de Janeiro. Brazilian couples did not describe the white parents that were against the relationships as being concerned with social desirability. However, no one in either research site considered white family members who expressed disapproval to be racist. Despite white family members redrawing ethnoracial boundaries by seeing blacks as undesirable outsiders, black-white couples did not draw a moral boundary against them by labeling them as racist.

Conclusion

As seen in table 5.1, there were a number of discursive tactics and cultural repertoires that black-white couples and their families drew on to navigate the integration of black spouses into white extended families. According to my Rio de Janeiro respondents, white family members engaged in more openly racist opposition to their relationships, particularly when they involved black men. Some families, while apparently accepting the relationship, would use racist humor as well as indirect insults to express discomfort with blacks marrying into the family. This included cultural tropes and stereotypes of black people. Couples also described an irony of opposition in which the fact that race mixing had already occurred in white extended families did not shield them from opposition to the relationship. These discursive strategies were characteristic of an inclusionary discrimination emblematic of Brazilian—and possibly more broadly, Latin American—race relations. They also ran counter to the myth of racial democracy in which race is not an impediment for interpersonal relationships. However, Rio de Janeiro respondents were less likely to report open or covert resistance among their families than the Los Angeles respondents. I attribute this to the closeness of extended families in Brazilian society.

In my Los Angeles data, couples understood white family members as using the discourse of "expressing concerns" about the relationship yet saw family members move to more overt discouragement of marrying black partners. Couples understood this "expressing concern" discourse as an attempt at social desirability on the part of white family members. This was emblematic of a US "laissez-faire" or "color-blind" racism. These couples experienced an exclusionary discrimination in which they were not fully integrated into the lives of white families. This led to them being seen as "other" for longer than with Carioca couples.

TABLE 5.1. White Families' Integration of Black Spouses

Discursive Strategies	Rio de Janeiro	Los Angeles
Redrawing	Overt	Covert
Form of integration	Inclusionary discrimination	Exclusionary discrimination

There was some overlap in how black partners were accepted (or not) by white families between the two sites. First, the greatest opposition to intermarriage was reserved for black men in both sites. Second, while US families were slower to learn acceptance, white family members had generally come to accept black partners, even if the terms of this acceptance were sometimes questionable. Third, white men experienced a great deal of autonomy in their relationships in both sites, whereas white women described experiences of racial boundary-policing by white extended family members. While historic constructions of race and gender are a part of these gender differences in both societies, the racial ambiguity of black wives was also a potential factor. Yet both humor and hypersexuality were used to stigmatize the black women in these relationships.

This chapter also illuminates how other social categories, such as gender, intersect to influence the negotiation of ethnoracial boundaries. White masculinity facilitated the lack of hostility toward—if not acceptance of—intermarriage by white family members. White husbands' negotiations of ethnoracial boundaries were the most facile, even in comparison to their black wives.

Families can redraw and highlight ethnoracial boundaries despite mixture. Even in a society like Brazil, known for its blurred boundaries, inclusionary discrimination can allow racism and blurred ethnoracial boundaries to coexist. Interaction across these boundaries through integration of black spouses into white families does not mean that they disappear or cease to be important. In fact, they reveal how white supremacy and antiblackness can remain intact despite similarities and differences in the nature of race and racism in both societies.

Furthermore, drawing ethnoracial boundaries was not the only social practice occurring with white families. There was an implicit understanding of hierarchy involved in the boundary redrawing that is often ignored by scholars of ethnoracial boundaries. These boundaries were not only about difference but also about hierarchy. We who are people of color in white supremacist societies are aware of the boundary-drawing that occurs that places people on the other side in a *higher* rank, occasionally doing it ourselves: "*They* take better care of their streets; they don't leave trash lying around." "*They* are good at math." "*They* are hard workers." However, as people with greater socioeconomic resources, it is far more perilous when dominant group members say and act on these perspectives. The role of hierarchies in boundary-drawing, so evident in white family reactions, has been undertheorized, particularly in the context of the New World. Future scholars would do well to make these dynamics explicit in their studies of social life.

6

Policing the Boundary

Interacting with Strangers in Public

Natalie is a white woman in her twenties who lives with Jerry, her black husband, in a predominantly white neighborhood in Los Angeles. They became friends while working the same late-night shift on the job. What started out as a hookup turned into a blossoming relationship. When they decided to marry, they started attending Jerry's church. Natalie explained to me why they are no longer members of this predominantly black church: "Some of the older sisters were conversing about how they didn't understand why he couldn't have found a sister at his [church] to have a relationship with. . . . I understand; he was considered quite a catch. . . . A lot of the little girlies had crushes on him, so it was like—I can kind of understand."

Natalie sees herself as having acquired a man who was highly desired in their religious community. While she might be projecting her own feelings when she assumes others also find him desirable, she probably understood the racial implications of these comments. Prior studies have shown that some black women understand intermarriage as abandoning and betraying the black community; others see it as a preference for white femininity in a tight dating and marriage market.[1] As a consequence of the discomfort, Natalie and Jerry now attend a more racially diverse church. Natalie mentioned that they see other interracial couples there and that she's never heard any disparaging comments from other parishioners about their interracial marriage.

As seen in the previous chapter, when people interact across ethnoracial boundaries, they do not cease to exist. In fact, outsiders can police and redraw them as a reminder of the ethnoracial difference between "us" and "them." Doing so can allow people to hoard resources, such as supposedly "marriageable" black men,[2] in an unequal marriage market. Those who find themselves policed may avoid particular social spaces, such as predominantly black or white social settings, maintaining pre-existing ethnoracial boundaries.

In this chapter, I examine how couples perceive outsiders who police ethnoracial boundaries. I show the different ways that people understand this process in Los Angeles and Rio de Janeiro. In a change of pace, I begin with Los Angeles couples, who experienced more racial boundary-policing than Carioca couples. I show how race, gender, class, and region can intersect to produce different themes that are salient for black-white couples when in public in these two settings.[3]

Boundary-Policing in Los Angeles

"Mixtures of People" and Racial Ambiguity

When we imagine the lives of black-white couples, we often characterize them as being rife with tension due to animosity toward their relationships. As discussed in previous chapters, this was not the case for the people that I interviewed. In Los Angeles, when I asked why this was so, couples often cited the racial diversity of the city and their diverse social circles. For instance, Elizabeth and Trevor live in a predominantly white neighborhood, and they both have postbaccalaureate degrees. They socialize primarily in church and university settings, which Elizabeth, a white woman, sees as very multiracial. When I asked her about the hostility from strangers, she said, "We haven't experienced that. It's been amazing. We go back to where our circle of friends are, and where we live too, 'cause in Los Angeles, we're surrounded by mixtures of people [of different races], and [interracial marriage] is common."

When Elizabeth said "mixtures of people," she was referring to the presence of people of different ethnic and racial backgrounds. She mentioned how Los Angeles is a city with racial and ethnic diversity. This, along with a significant presence of other interracial couples, prevented her from being seen as an oddity. Elizabeth's comments reflected how most interracial couples living in the United States live in multiracial, multiethnic, and multicultural cities.[4] This provides both opportunities for entering these relationships as well as environments that make them feel welcome. Such environments, when in public, have been referred to as "cosmopolitan canopies" where islands of civility across racial lines exist in racially segregated cities.[5] However, several couples described "archipelagos of conviviality" in which they inhabited a multitude of intimate spaces of ethnically and racially diverse friends that were available to them in a city like Los Angeles. Like Natalie, mentioned earlier, they understood multiracial social settings as sites for visibility management that prevented the policing of ethnoracial boundaries. By contrast, they sometimes referred to how they encountered more hostile looks in other areas of the country—such as the South and Midwest—in comparison to where they currently live. Couples in Rio de Janeiro occasionally described mixtures of people as a reason for their lack of experiences of hostility with strangers in public. However, it was more in reference to the various ancestries, degrees of race mixture, and variety of colors present in the individuals around them.

Interracial couples in general, and Los Angeles couples specifically, live in cities where a binary black-white racial system usually ceased to exist decades ago. Due to immigration from Asia and Latin America, Los Angeles and other major cities often have large populations of non-blacks. This is something that was important for Roxanne's experiences of being in a black-white couple. Roxanne is a black woman who lives in a predominantly white neighborhood with her white husband, Fred, and their two children. She said, "I never had issues. And I don't know if it had to do with maybe I don't look like I'm fully African American. . . . [B]ecause a lot of people, I think they assume that I'm Hispanic or South American or something because I'm not that dark, dark. . . . That's my only reason."

Due in part to the one-drop rule, African Americans in the United States have a wide range of physical traits, including skin tones ranging from very light to very dark. Roxanne, like other blacks in my sample, self-identifies as black or African American and was identified by one of my contacts as well as another respondent as the black person in the black-white couple. She was raised in a black family with a black identity but believes outsiders do not perceive her as black and thus are unlikely to police the boundary between blacks and whites. Several black women that I interviewed referred to sometimes being seen as racially ambiguous despite self-identifying as black. They often commented on their lighter skin color leading others to believe that they were not

African American. This seemed to decrease their experiences of hostility; without being certain their relationships were interracial, strangers did not feel the need to comment. Only one of the black men that I interviewed discussed being perceived as racially ambiguous; this was a very gendered phenomenon. In addition, couples who experienced the most hostility toward their relationships involved men and women who did not discuss racial ambiguity—those whom I perceived to be dark-skinned, even though we did not discuss their color. Categorization by outsiders is a necessary precursor to ethnoracial boundary-policing, and those who appear ambiguous make it difficult to do so. Ironically, despite the oft-discussed flexibility and ambiguity of racial boundaries in Brazil, none of the couples in Rio de Janeiro referenced their ethnoracial ambiguity to explain a lack of opposition from strangers.

Black Men with White Women: "White Girls Steal All the Good Black Guys"

Although blatant hostility was not salient for the black-white couples that I interviewed, further probing revealed that the majority of Los Angeles respondents had experienced overt, episodic hostility from strangers. When they discussed these experiences, they sometimes recalled incidents that had happened years ago and had stood out in their minds. These experiences, although rare, were more common in Los Angeles than in Rio de Janeiro, challenging widespread stereotypes of California's openness to race mixing. When asked about experiences with hostility in public, Los Angeles couples discussed experiences that they had with particular types of individuals that harassed them. Across race and gender combinations, Angelino couples described how both black and white strangers gave them strange looks. As a result of this experience, several husbands, both black and white, said that they stopped paying attention to how outsiders reacted to their being in public with their wives. This disruption in the looking-glass self (or "couple") allowed them to experience more ease when in public in comparison to their wives.

In their separate interviews, some wives, both black and white, complained about their husbands' not paying attention to these incidents. This was similar to couples in Rio de Janeiro, who also described experiencing stares and odd looks in public, despite its long history of race mixture. However, there was no discussion of the types of people who gave these looks. There was also a lack of gender differences in handling these looks.

In Los Angeles, white women often named black women as the main perpetrators of overt hostility to their relationships. For example, Allison and Yuri are a white female–black male young couple who live in a predominantly white neighborhood. When I asked her about opposition toward her relationship, Allison recounted an experience she had early in their relationship when Yuri lived in Inglewood, a predominantly black neighborhood. She said that she got on a bus headed toward Inglewood, and a group of black female adolescents began harassing her.

> One particular time, [three black girls] were on the bus. . . . They were making comments like "white people" this and "white people" that, and I didn't say nothing. . . . Then I went to pull my things [together], and they were like "Oh we scared her. Let's get off the bus with her." . . . Well, sure enough, they got off the bus with me. . . . They followed me to his house the entire way. . . . And the entire way, they were saying, "Oh you gonna walk through a black neighborhood . . ." you know, just going on and on and on about "Who could you possibly be coming to see? Look at you. . . . You don't know nothing about this neighborhood."

Allison perceived this incident as threatening and told Yuri to start meeting her at the bus stop when she came to visit him. Allison perceived statements like "Who could you possibly be coming to see?" as references to her interracial relationship, although Yuri was not present. She did not distinguish racial hostility toward her as a white woman in a black neighborhood from hostility toward her relationship. This incident revealed a clear demarcation of ethnoracial boundaries reminding Allison that she was not welcome in this black space to visit its black inhabitants.

Later in the interview, Allison admitted that it had been several years since she had been in a predominantly black social setting. This suggests that her strategy of avoiding the policing of ethnoracial boundaries was to avoid black social spaces altogether, stereotyping black women in general as hostile to her relationship.[6] For Allison, her marriage to a black man did not preclude her from using gender to redraw ethnoracial boundaries against black women and black spaces.

Allison echoed what several Angelino white wives told me during the course of their interviews: when they face opposition from strangers, it is from black women. A cognizance of the "marriage squeeze," in which black women outnumber "marriageable" black men, permeates Natalie's and Allison's interpretations of their social distancing. Racial and ethnic competition often emerge during struggles for scarce resources, including housing, jobs, and even marriage partners.[7] This supposed lack of marriageable black men means that black men with college experience (the exact men who are most likely to intermarry) and stable jobs, like those in my sample, become understood as a scarce resource. Natalie and Allison's comments seem to echo this notion that black women see them in competition for these marriageable black men.

On the other hand, group-position scholars argue that racial and ethnic competition is the result of collective understandings of what it means to be a part of a group as well as how group members rank alongside out-group members.[8] In this perspective, US antimiscegenation laws, the social norm of intraracial marriage, and interracial dating and marriage patterns excluding black women[9] all favor the notion that black men belong with black women. Since most black men marry black women, as a group, black men may have an intraracial preference or are excluded from members of other ethnoracial categories, notwithstanding structural impediments to intermarriage. For this reason, if marriage partners for black men were ranked in a queue, black women would be ranked at the top. However, white women who marry black men challenge this preference and this queue. The white wives who experience hostility from black women may be encountering situations in which black women seek to protect this marital and romantic queue.

Despite the supposed scarcity of marriageable black men in Brazil as well, the white wives whom I interviewed in Rio de Janeiro did not discuss black female hostility to their relationships. None of the Carioca spouses described incidents as hostile as Allison's nor revealed an avoidance of predominantly black neighborhoods. The closest sentiment would be that of the few black husbands in Rio de Janeiro who had been involved in black movement activities, they either ceased to participate in them or did not bring their white wives to such events. Overall, the lower levels of "groupness" in Brazil may explain why white women in Rio de Janeiro did not describe hostility from black women in public. As seen in chapters 2 and 3, there is less of a sense of "belonging together" among blacks and among whites in Brazil than in the United States. As a consequence, there is less of a sense of competition for scarce resources like "marriageable" black men among the Cariocas I interviewed.

She Said / He Said: Perceptions and Social Location

I was struck by how spouses did not always perceive incidents of policing ethnoracial boundaries in the same way. These differences were linked to intersecting social locations. For example, Stella is a white woman in her midtwenties and lives in a predominantly white neighborhood with her black husband, Edward. Stella described experiencing boundary-policing when she went out to a restaurant in Los Angeles with Edward and another black-white couple involving a white woman and a black man. They were all in another predominantly white neighborhood.

> We walked by a group of black girls, and . . . these two girls were looking right at us, and the one girl goes, "That's such a shame." And I was kind of like "Edward, did you guys hear that?" Maybe they're talking about something else, and so again, I don't know that they were particularly, I mean, they were looking right at us, and so maybe it was just—and I'm sure we probably stood out more because there was two of us. . . . But then I was kind of uncomfortable. . . . [A]nd I don't know if Edward feels the same way when we pass white guys—but sometimes when we do pass black girls or black guys or anybody, sometimes I do get a little self-conscious because I feel like, I wonder if they think I shouldn't be with him. Or if the black girl is thinking "Oh, I'm stealing a guy from [her]"—like stealing a good guy because, I mean, sometimes you hear that on TV shows or whatever the case is, black girls saying, "Oh, white girls steal all the good black guys." So sometimes I do have that in my head.

Some blacks see black men involved with white women as valuing whiteness (specifically white femininity) over blackness and black femininity, using romantic relationships to acquire greater resources and status and distancing themselves from black communities.[10] While it is impossible to know exactly what the woman meant when she said, "That's such a shame," Stella's reflections show how she sees black women policing her relationships through rude comments. Stella's unprompted remarks suggest that she pays a lot of attention to blacks and their reactions to her relationship with Edward. Whether or not black women are more likely to harass white women, by focusing on blacks, especially black women, white women may perceive more opposition from blacks than from whites.

Spontaneously, in his own interview, Edward recalled the same situation, but he did not describe it as part of a pattern. He said, "And I heard them say it, but it was kind of funny to me. So my initial reaction was to laugh. My friend's reaction was a little more confrontational." He followed his friend Sam, a former college football player, to the table where the women were sitting with some black men:

> [Sam] had some four-letter choice words with them. They—well, they didn't say anything. The guys they were with said something to Sam.... And so it kind of got a little serious, but at the same time, I'm 6'4", and he's a lot bigger than me, and they were at a table with these little guys, and so we calmly went over . . . and basically asked if we had a problem or something. And it was very clear that they didn't have a problem and that they were really wanting their women to sort of be quiet because I think that . . . I don't think that we were a problem that they wanted to have.

Like Stella, Edward recognized that the comments had originated from the black women at the table, but he attributes the gender divide to the threat he and Sam posed. As his comments illustrate, interpersonal interactions, including those involving people of different races, are shaped by the beliefs that people have of each other as well as how they think they will be perceived.[11] Edward's and his friend's physicality were factors in how he experienced their reaction to the situation, in which there was a subtext of potential physical violence. Psychologists have found that women perceive the same aggressive behaviors as more problematic and distressful than their male counterparts, especially when the aggressor is a woman.[12] Several husbands that I interviewed pointed out one explanation for this gender disparity in perceiving threat; many husbands, both black and white, discussed physical threats as explaining why they did not perceive opposition the way that their wives did. As one aspect of heteronormative masculinity, physicality and the potential for violence led Edward and Stella to have different perceptions of the same policing of racial boundaries.

Allison, Stella, and Natalie's comments demonstrate how white women's understanding of boundary-policing is one that is explicitly black and female. Part of this process involves highlighting incidents of overt opposition from black women as well as the strategy of avoiding future racial boundary-policing by not spending time in predominantly black spaces. Their black husbands, however, mentioned black women in specific incidents but did not describe them (or black men) as constant perpetrators of hostility toward their relationships. This gendered policing of ethnoracial boundaries led to distancing from the black social spaces by couples involving white women. Similar concerns did not emerge among black-white couples in Rio de Janeiro. This may be because of the lower levels of residential segregation where they lived in comparison to Los Angeles, such that even predominantly black neighborhoods are racially mixed.

Black Women with White Men in Los Angeles:
"Too Good for Black Men"

William and Betty are a white male–black female couple that live in a predominantly white neighborhood. Betty is a dark-skinned woman from Belize who came to the United States as a teenager. In their separate interviews, both mentioned incidents of harassment they experienced from black men in the San Francisco Bay Area. William said, "Let's see, there was one time where we were actually in Berkeley, and we were walking on Telegraph Avenue, and a man said—it was something along the lines of—'What do you think you're doing? You think you're too good that you have to be with a white boy?'" Betty recalled the same incident, as well as another: "We were just crossing the street from the university, and a guy started yelling. I don't remember what he was doing, and he was yelling at me; and then another time [we were] at a club, and this guy realized that we were together, and he said—he's Belizean—and he said, 'What are you doing with him?' . . . This was also in Berkeley. We got dirty looks. . . . We were scared."

Although these incidents did not happen in Los Angeles, they were striking because they occurred in a city known for its history of progressive leanings.[13] Betty was the main target of this opposition because she had broken a social norm by being romantically involved with a white man. Similar to other black female–white male couples, although she cites black men as perpetrators of hostility to her relationship, she did not perceive them as a constant threat. Nevertheless, the characteristics of the individual were salient, as they were for other Los Angeles respondents. This was different from Carioca respondents, who described other aspects of these incidents.

Born in the United States, Visola is a dark-skinned black woman of Kenyan descent. She lives in a predominantly black neighborhood with her white husband, Charles. Visola recounted hostility that she and Charles experienced when they were picking up their marriage license. She described a black man who was staring at her and Charles:

> I didn't think anything of it, and I just smiled back at him, and then his face turned. It went from kind of this bland look on his face—of just kind of staring at me—to this strange stare with some ugliness to it. . . . And then he was saying something to her, to the [black] woman he was with, and she was saying, "Oh, just be quiet, just be quiet. Leave it alone, leave it alone." Then he started getting louder in what he was saying, and then I was able to hear him after a while, and everyone in the room was able to hear him. Then I started hearing him say, "What does she think she's doing? What does she think she's doing sitting up here with some white man? She should be ashamed of herself. She should be ashamed of herself. She can't possibly be a real sister if she's up in here with this white man. . . ." And all of a sudden, I turned around, and I'm like "Are you talking to me?" And he was like "There's nobody else in the room that I would be talking to." And I looked at him, and then I got out of my seat, and Charles yanked my arm back. He was like "Babe, leave it alone."

The man's companion continued to try to soothe him, but the man began yelling at her. "No, no, no, no, I'm not leaving this alone." Security ultimately ejected him.

Visola describes how on what should have been a happy occasion, a black man who opposed her marriage to a white man targeted her. The few black female–white male couples who recounted incidents of overt hostility typically named black men as their perpetrators. Thus race and gender categories together also informed how black women and white men perceived the policing of racial boundaries in their lives. Nevertheless, they did not refer to being aware of constant policing by black people the way respondents like Stella did. In addition, their responses were unlike white female respondents, who revealed a fear of rejection because of their racial group membership.[14] This was very different from couples in Rio de Janeiro who did not discuss individual-level characteristics of perpetrators.

Surveys of attitudes toward black-white unions reveal blacks are more open to these relationships than whites,[15] with 16 percent of whites saying that they "strongly disapprove" of these relationships compared with 2 percent of blacks.[16] Yet the experiences of the couples I interviewed seem to suggest the opposite—that blacks are more opposed to these types of relationships. This may be related to what Patricia Hill Collins termed as *controlling images* in which blacks are seen as hostile in society.[17] This is similar to social psychological processes in which actions by blacks are perceived as more hostile than the same ones by whites.[18] These surveys may not reveal a distinction in whites' resistance—studies show they have little problem with intermarriage among strangers but would not engage in it themselves and would frown on it for their family members.[19] These explanations would result in fewer accounts of white strangers engaging in boundary-policing for these respondents. On the other hand, these surveys may reveal a discrepancy in black acceptance. It may be that they are more accepting of it when it involves family members than when it involves strangers. They may also be in favor of it in theory but less so in practice.

Angelino couples also suggested that whites act in a hostile way but are more covert in their animosity. Visola, for instance, perceived white hostility that never escalated the way the situation with the black man at the courthouse did: "White people tend to speak under their breath or things like that, and it's not as in your face as it is with African Americans. African Americans tend to want you to know what they're thinking when they're thinking it."

These comments reflect an awareness of "aversive"[20] or "color-blind"[21] racism that has become prevalent over the last fifty years. Couples in this study saw blacks as practicing more overt forms of racial boundary-policing, whereas whites were seen as acting covertly in showing their disdain for their relationships. In Rio de Janeiro, couples did not distinguish between how blacks and whites responded to them in public.

Mark is a white man who lives in a predominantly white neighborhood with his wife, Kelly, a black woman. Mark met a white man in New Orleans, where the man and his friends used racial epithets to describe blacks. Later, there was a family gathering, which this same acquaintance attended. Mark described an incident at the gathering in which he perceived the man expressing covert hostility to his relationship with Kelly. Mark said, "And I'm sitting there talking to him, and [Kelly] walked up, and he said, 'I got to go.' And he walked away, turned around and walked away. And of course, I knew why."

Afterward, he said that as far as hostility, "We've never had any, ever. Nothing." Mark's comments reflect that boundary-policing by whites may be very subtle, such that it is not always perceived as hostility. This covert nature in which many whites are seen to police racial boundaries for strangers may be one of the reasons couples perceive more hostility from blacks. Nevertheless, Mark's and Visola's different approaches to understanding whites' behaviors directed at their relationship may be grounded in differences in perceptions of aversive racism, forming more negative impressions when blacks engage in hostilities.[22] Along with previously mentioned factors such as heteronormative masculinity, this would explain why Mark did not count this as an instance of hostility toward his relationship.

"Here It's Not Declared Openly": Boundary-Policing in Rio de Janeiro

Perceptions of racial boundary-policing were very different in Rio de Janeiro than in Los Angeles. While sex-gender ratios put Afro-Brazilian women at a disadvantage in the marriage market,[23] none of the couples that I spoke to mentioned black women as a source of hostility to their relationships. In fact, none of the respondents used gender distinctions to describe racial boundary-policing. While many had never experienced outright hostility from strangers, unlike couples in Los Angeles, those who had did not consider gender a salient factor.

There were a variety of ways that Carioca black-white couples understood this lack of opposition in their lives. Many said that they do not pay attention to the reactions of outsiders to their relationships. For example, Bárbara is a white woman who recently moved with her husband, Brício, from a predominantly white neighborhood to a racially diverse one. She said, "I do not see [racism] in our relationship and do not see it in the eyes of the people who live among us." In other words, in Bárbara's case, as with other Brazilians I spoke with, either she did not pay attention to public reactions or the hostility simply does not exist.

Couples explained that racism is a covert problem in Brazil. Ursulina, a self-described brown woman (*parda*) who lives in a largely nonwhite, multiracial neighborhood, described this:

> People say, "Oh, here in Brazil, there is no discrimination, color issues, these things," but there is discrimination. There are people who still criticize those who marry whites. There are people who criticize those who marry blacks. This thing still exists, but it is very under the table. They don't openly say it like in other countries where it is said openly. People [there] say, "I don't like it; I don't like whites," isn't it like that? . . . No one yet has come up to me and said, "Oh, you married a white person," or whatever, or somebody . . . coming up to him and saying [this]—he never said this to me. That's why I say that here it's not declared openly.

Later, Ursulina explained that she has never experienced hostility to her relationship with her white husband in Rio de Janeiro. Her understanding is that in the abstract, there are people who are hostile to black-white unions, yet they do not openly state their opposition. Judging by how she rhetorically asks me for confirmation, she contrasts this to her understanding of the United States, where people are supposedly more vocal about their opposition to such couples. Given the previously mentioned experiences of couples in Los Angeles, she seems correct in her assessment. However, she says that this does not mean that there is no opposition to these relationships in Brazil. She understands this lack of hostility to her black-white relationship in terms of aversive racism in the Brazilian context with the subtle policing of racial boundaries in public in comparison to her notion of what happens in the United States.

Strategizing Black Movement Spaces

A few of the black spouses whom I interviewed in Rio de Janeiro had been involved in a variety of black movement activities over the course of their lives. In Brazil, there is a history of male black movement activists who married white women. For example, Abdias do Nascimento, the now-deceased black movement leader, was married to Elisa Larkin, a white woman of US origin who is a scholar of black cultural life and director of the Institute of Afro-Brazilian Studies and Research (IPEAFRO). Despite the presence of black-white couples in the black movement, several Carioca couples saw the black movement as hostile to interracial dating and marriage. Even some black Brazilians affiliated with the black movement understand black-white couples as problematic.[24]

However, black husbands engaged in several strategies of action that prevented them from experiencing the policing of ethnoracial boundaries in black movement spaces. One black husband, Wanderley, distanced himself from participating in black movement activities as he started dating his white wife for reasons that he said were unrelated to their relationship. This was despite being involved in other organizing efforts. Another black husband, Cândido, had prior experience with activists questioning him about his white partners. He had learned to ignore comments by outsiders when he attended events with his white wife, Ana María. Yet another black husband, Adão described how he had learned the hard way not to take his wife to such events. In chapter 2, Adão described his discomfort with being married to a wealthy white woman from the South Zone of Rio de Janeiro, where they both lived. During his interview, he was very uncomfortable, making it the most difficult interview to do. He stopped the interview several times to answer the phone, was initially very curt, sniffed continuously, and was in a hurry to finish the interview. He admitted that he had not introduced his wife, Marisa, to many of his black friends. In his interview, Adão described an event associated with the black movement.

ADÃO: I never take her to a place with lots of black people [lugar de negrão]. I never take her. . . . But there was one year when I felt bad, really bad! . . . It was the twentieth of November. . . . There was a concert in Lapa in homage of the Day of Black Consciousness, and it was many people playing and singing, and so I took Marisa. It was hard, but I took her.

ME: For you or for other people?

ADÃO: Because the others would . . . be able to see, you know? Really, there were friends from that phase of my life tied to the movement. Surely, I would go and run into people from that period. And so, I went with her, dude. And it was the first time, like, I was uncomfortable. And so afterwards, I became more relaxed and everything, but it was complicated, you see? But thank God it was the only experience I had. Afterwards, it never happened again.

Adão's comments show how avoiding events with many black people is one strategy to avoid potential opposition to the relationship. Not only does he avoid the ethnoracial policing of his friends, but also he does not have to experience the discomfort of being seen as a black man with a white wife in this space. This was different from black husbands in Los Angeles who did not openly admit to avoiding predominantly black social settings when with their white wives. However, it was similar to the experiences of white wives in Los Angeles who described staying in multiracial environments and avoided black social spaces.

"It Happens in the South": Region outside the City

Cariocas' few descriptions of racial boundary-policing focused on geography, rather than individual-level characteristics. Specifically, they regionalized hostility toward black-white couples by locating it generally in the southern region of Brazil or, specifically, inside of the city in the South Zone (*Zona Sul*). They consider these geographic areas to be white. They also implied that hostility was not related to the race of the harasser but to the whiteness of these areas. Residents of the South, composed of the Rio Grande do Sul, Paraná, and Santa Catarina, are largely descended from German, Italian, and Portuguese immigrants. Whereas Rio de Janeiro is 44 percent black and brown, in the South, it is only 20 percent.[25]

Like other countries in Latin America, in Brazil, region often maps onto norms and stereotypes of physical characteristics to a greater extent than in the United States.[26] For example, the state of Bahia is known as being predominantly black. People from the Northeast of Brazil (*nordestinos*) are understood to have an exclusive set of physical characteristics, notably a "flat head" (*cabeça chata*), which is also a derogatory slur for northeasterners. As mentioned in chapter 3, the South of the country is understood as predominantly white. Regionalism and race can play out at the metropolitan level as well, as seen in São Paulo, where middle-class whites avoid the downtown area due to its higher proportion of nonwhites and northeasterners.[27] In Rio de Janeiro, the South Zone is predominantly white. Given the segregation of many of Brazil's cities,[28] albeit moderate in comparison to the hypersegregated United States, region strongly informs ideas of race both within and outside of cities.

Couples said that opposition to their relationships was not a problem in their daily lives because the more potent form of racism is located in the South. Several individuals emphasized that Brazil is a racist country and that the South is particularly so. For example, Nicolas is a black man living in a racially mixed neighborhood near the center of Rio de Janeiro with his white wife, Laura.

It happens there in the South because that's where the first colonies [started]—the Dutch colony, the Portuguese, the Italians, all in the South. And I had a trip there; I was dating a blonde girl—she was blonde with blue eyes—and we went to a wine festival. If you had seen how the people looked at me, you know, even men, angry, mostly the men. . . . They were very angry, you know? . . . They think that mixing the races [is bad]. They still have this . . . some colonies still have this. And it was really funny because when we would pass by them, you know, the eyes followed us. She is very blonde, with blue eyes—and me, a *negão*.

Nicolas feels that men object to his interracial marriage more than women do, and his use of the term *negão*, which can imply virility and physical power, suggests that he considered the interaction gendered. However, he considers the fact that he was in the South more salient than gender, believing that race mixing in the South is not as valorized as it is in Rio. He understands region as central to the boundary-policing of black-white relationships. Strikingly, Angelinos also referenced hostility being more prevalent outside of Los Angeles, such as in the US South or the Midwest. When they did so, it was in reference to the South's history as the hotbed of Jim Crow and opposition to racial integration. However, among Angelino spouses, region was not as salient as a theme linked to policing racial boundaries as it was for Cariocas.

Deisy is a white woman living in a multiracial neighborhood in the West Zone (*Zona Oeste*) who described a similar experience of hostile glares in the South: "Once we were traveling to the South, and at that time, we weren't married yet, we were single, but people stared at us when we were together . . . because in the South, the majority is real white, you know? So they stared at us."

Deisy entered the South with Nicolas with some discomfort. She does not individualize the actions of the perpetrators but rather sees an entire region being hostile to her relationship due to their own whiteness. The idea that there is less race mixing in the South than in Rio informs both Deisy's and Nicolas's comments. They see the South as on the other side of an ethnoracial boundary, in which race mixture is not central to Brazilian southerners' sense of peoplehood like in the rest of Brazil.

"It's in the South Zone": Region inside the City

Many Carioca couples regionalized hostility to black-white couples within the city. They pointed to the predominantly white and wealthy South Zone of Rio de Janeiro as a site for experiencing hostility toward their relationships. The famous beaches of Copacabana, Ipanema, and Leblon are all in the South Zone. They also highlighted class as a factor in public hostility, reflecting the salience of class in Brazilian conceptions of race.[29] In Brazil, class has a long history of being understood as the sole source of racial inequality.[30] Afro-Brazilians are scarce in the Brazilian middle class and concentrated among the poor and working classes.[31] For these reasons, the elite areas of Rio are also predominantly white areas. Most couples did not live in the wealthy South Zone, but they had spent time there, and many pointed to that region of the city as a site for racism. This was different from black-white couples in Los Angeles, who emphasized the race of the perpetrators over the location of the hostility they experienced. This was true even for Angelino couples who avoided predominantly black spaces as a consequence.

In my interview with Sérgio, a black husband, I asked him about the last time that he had experienced opposition or discomfort due to being in his relationship with his white wife, Hilda. Despite living in a distant, multiracial, working-class suburb of Rio de Janeiro, he named a place in the South Zone.

> It was when we went to a mall in Gávea. . . . [T]he people stared at me kind of, in a weird way . . . because there it is a mall for white people. It's a place for white people. It's like this: due to Gávea being a locale where only rich people live, and here in Brazil, a majority of the rich people are white, you can make the association that who is rich is white. And in this place where only rich people live, the majority of the people who are around the mall are rich and are white. So they looked at me. We were walking; the people kept looking at me weirdly, you know? But they didn't get to saying anything. They just stared.

Sérgio understands the *Zona Sul* as a place where things like strange looks happen. His comments show how for him, and most couples, the policing of racial boundaries follows a territorial logic. Similar to other Cariocas who mentioned the South region of the country, he talked about a specific area of the city where hostility to his relationship is frequent. Furthermore, like several individuals who recounted instances of discomfort or hostility in their relationships while in public, he interpreted this as hostility toward him specifically, the black person in the couple.

In addition, black Brazilians intertwine race with class in their understandings of discrimination. Sérgio does just that in emphasizing class as a part of his understanding of the hostility he experienced. Unlike couples in Los Angeles, Sergio does not name types of individuals as perpetrators of hostility. This is because blacks in Brazil often understand racial discrimination as occurring in public spaces such as shopping malls, streets, and restaurants.[32] They see this as the outgrowth of policies that do not identify blacks as potential consumers or as equal citizens, not simply due to the prejudice or interpersonal discrimination of individual receptionists or salespeople.

However, this perspective was not limited to only black spouses in Rio de Janeiro. Bárbara is the white woman introduced earlier who described how she did not see hostility in the people who live around her. As mentioned before, she now lives with her black husband, Brício, in the North Zone, which is racially mixed with working-class and lower-middle-class families. In her interview, Bárbara spoke about her experiences of hostility toward her relationship with Brício.

> In the South Zone, we encounter discrimination . . . absolutely. When we moved to Laranjeiras [a neighborhood in the South Zone], a woman was very rude to Brício . . . saying that he did not live there, that he was there working for someone, you know? To serve someone. She ordered him to move his car quickly from where it was because it was disturbing her. But she said it in a tone like "I am above you." . . . He stuck his nose up at her because he is stuck up. He stuck his chest out and said that he was going to move the car when he could move the car, you know? I had gone up with the groceries, and he was waiting for me to come down to move the car. There was another episode also. This same woman was in the elevator, and we were about to take the elevator, and she waited until we had gone up before she would go up. . . . We entered the elevator, and she walked out. . . . Brício stuck his nose up, inflated his chest, and entered and did not even give her a glance.

Bárbara interpreted this woman's hostility toward her husband as opposition to their relationship. This instance with this woman in their apartment building framed her understanding of the South Zone as a region of the city that is hostile to blacks in general. Yet in this space, Brício, a black with several degrees, becomes read as a laborer "working for someone." Unlike Angelinos, Bárbara does not categorize the woman as white, although it is likely implied by the neighborhood being in the South Zone. Now that they live in the North Zone, they can avoid such incidents in the future.

Eloíza is a college-educated black woman living with her white husband, Vitor (also college educated), in a multiracial, bohemian neighborhood in the center of town: "One day, me and Vitor . . . I don't know if it was Copacabana or Ipanema. There was a beggar . . . [and] she was lying down [on the street] . . . [and] she saw that we were passing by. So we were not going to walk over her. She stared at us, and then she turns and says, 'What a beautiful man! With this horribly ugly woman—and black too!'"

Eloíza interpreted the situation, which took place in a South Zone neighborhood near the beach, as an example of public hostility to her relationship. Following the same patterns as other Rio respondents, she describes the incident occurring in a public place in the South Zone. As a beggar, the perpetrator's class status was apparent; in addition, since race and class are so intertwined, it is likely that the beggar was another woman of African descent. However, unlike the respondents in Los Angeles who also recounted incidents of overt hostility, Eloíza did not mention the race and color nor emphasize the gender of the beggar.

This incident illustrates how the beggar's comments pin Eloíza and Vitor as opposites based on their levels of attractiveness and that Eloíza's race (not Vitor's) makes them incompatible in her eyes. In her interview, Eloíza later discussed the woman's comments as rooted in racialized understandings of beauty in which whites, especially those with light-colored eyes like her husband, are considered attractive and blacks are seen as ugly, with undesirable physical features. Physical attractiveness was the basis for a symbolic boundary that overlapped with the social boundaries of ethnoracial distinction. Black spouses in Los Angeles did not reference being seen as less attractive in comparison to their white spouses. Furthermore, none of the black people that I interviewed in either site referred to being seen as too attractive for their white partners, whether by strangers or otherwise.

"One of Your Whores": Couples and Sex Tourism in Rio's South Zone

Sexuality is a core element of racial and moral boundaries.[33] For black Brazilian women, race and gender intersected to affect perceptions of hostility to their relationships in the South Zone. Several black women expressed concern over being mistaken for prostitutes when venturing into that region of the city. None of the white women I interviewed nor the men of either color reported this fear of being mistaken for a sex worker or a customer. Copacabana, Ipanema, and other areas of the South Zone are known for sexual tourism between white foreigners and Afro-Brazilian women. The meaning of black female–white male pairings in Rio de Janeiro is imbued with stereotypes about sex tourism and influenced the experiences of couples who have nothing to do with the industry. Despite the South Zone being only a small part of the city, it sexualized understandings of hostility to relationships involving black women married to white men. This was not an issue for any of the Angelino spouses whom I interviewed.

Silvia is college-educated woman who identifies herself as both a black woman and a mixed woman (*mestiça*) due to her racially mixed ancestry. Her husband, Harry, is a college-educated white man from the United States, and they live in a racially mixed neighborhood in the North Zone. In her interview, she said, "For the black woman, when she ends up with a white man, she is seen as a whore" and that it is even worse when the white man is a foreigner. I asked her if she has ever felt that way, and she described something that happened early in their relationship.

> SILVIA: We were in a mall in the South Zone, in the Ipanema shopping mall. A man came and followed us, a security guard. I was wearing flip-flops, dressing freely, so he thought that I was one of those . . . "friends of the beach" [*amigas, lá da praia*]. So then I left. That's all.
> ME: Did he say anything to you guys?
> SILVIA: No, he just followed us.

Silvia describes a reason for the discomfort that many blacks feel when in wealthy, predominantly white public spaces—she and her now-husband, Harry, were harassed by a security guard. While this is an institutional practice within the mall, it is also part of a larger moral panic surrounding targeting sex tourism and sex trafficking in Brazil.[34] The institutional nature of being harassed by security guards may be why, like other Cariocas, Silvia does not emphasize the color of the guard. Being followed in stores and shopping centers is an experience common to people of African descent across the diaspora. However, because of the Brazilian hypersexualization of the pairing of Afro-Brazilian women with white men, especially *gringos*, this experience takes on a sexualized tone. Being policed in a public space reminded them of their ethnoracial difference despite race mixture supposedly being in the norm. It also serves as a reminder that this pairing is not respectable for wealthy, white areas. In Los Angeles, Allison, who earlier described being followed by a group of black girls, was the only Angelino who described having her presence questioned and being followed in segregated areas. This was also not a concern for the Carioca white husbands of black wives.

To negotiate the perception that they were sex workers when they were in the South Zone, black wives described engaging in particular strategies. Delfina is one such woman and is a college-educated black woman who lives in the South Zone. Her husband, Auguste, is French, potentially making them the typical sex worker–tourist pairing in the eyes of those in the South Zone: "I have to go out looking really nice. . . . When we go out, I can't wear tops that stop [midriff] or really short shorts because then everyone will think that I'm his prostitute."

As a response to stigmatization,[35] Delfina's comments show how she negotiates her presentation of self to others to avoid being mistaken for a prostitute. Since she lives in the South Zone, it is difficult to use avoidance as a tactic in dealing with these incidents, like some of the couples in Los Angeles who had avoided black-dominated spaces. Being cognizant of the clothes that she wears is much easier than moving to another area of the city.

Eloíza was also conscious of being perceived as a prostitute in the South Zone:

"I'm loving, but I'm not that cheesy. I hate that; I never liked cheesy boyfriends, and [my husband's] like that. . . . So when we're walking on the street, he tries to take my hand . . . this makes me uncomfortable, walking hand in hand, so I give him my [index] finger to hold. So I told him one day, 'Vitor, when they see you and me holding hands, people will think I'm one of your whores.' He said, 'That's absurd. Really!'"

Black women in my study like Eloíza make light of their perceived involvement in sexual tourism through jokes. Humor allows her to approach an uncomfortable subject in a way that is not disparaging to her. Nevertheless, not engaging in public displays of affection with her husband while in the South Zone, including something as innocuous as hand-holding, allows her to avoid the stigmatization of being seen as a participant in the sex industry. In Los Angeles, couples of either race-gender combination in Los Angeles did not describe negotiating being seen as participants in the sex industry when in public with their spouses.

The experiences of these black women demonstrate how despite being married to white men, they are not able to navigate certain spaces in Rio de Janeiro the same way that white women or black men are. Despite never facing overt hostility to their relationships the way the Los Angeles couples had, black women in Rio de Janeiro were impacted by the prevalence of the sex industry in the city. For this reason, the South Zone takes on a different type of hostile meaning for these black female–white male couples, in which racial boundaries are not only spatialized and classed but also sexualized.

Conclusions

Table 6.1 summarizes the differences and similarities in perceptions of racial boundary-policing in the two sites. I find that unlike common understandings about the lives of black-white couples, couples in both sites do not experience great deals of hostility toward their relationships regularly. This is particularly the case in Rio de Janeiro, where there were lower levels of experiences of boundary-policing. Nevertheless, in both places, race mixture was an explanation for the lack of public opposition. In Los Angeles, it was race mixture in terms of the diverse types of people, whereas in Rio de Janeiro, it was a race mixture in terms of the ancestries of the people there.

Most couples had perceived hostility toward their relationships by strangers when in public. Los Angeles couples point to blacks as perpetrators of overt boundary-policing, with white women perceiving black women as their main harassers. Black husbands saw their masculinity as protecting them from seeing black women as a threat in the same way that their white wives did. On the other hand, couples with black wives and white husbands largely reported incidents involving black men; however, they did not see black men as an ongoing source of hostility. Since color-blind racism is less prevalent among blacks,[36] it is

---

TABLE 6.1. Boundary-Policing in Los Angeles and Rio de Janeiro

Discourse	Los Angeles	Rio de Janeiro
Type of perpetrator	Individual	Region
Race of perpetrator	Black	White (and wealthy)
Strategy of action	Avoid black communities	Occasional visits to white communities Presentation of self

possible that they are more vocal in revealing their opposition to black-white couples. At the same time, gendered and racialized perceptions of threat and aggression may mean that actions by blacks and women (and especially, black women) stand out more. Also, covert forms of hostility from whites mean that they are identified less often as perpetrators of boundary-policing. For these couples, particularly those involving black men with white women, avoiding black social spaces was a strategy that they employed to avoid boundary-policing. After incidents of boundary-policing, some US white wives avoided predominantly black spaces with their black husbands. These small decisions reify already existing ethnoracial boundaries.

Black-white couples in Rio de Janeiro mostly perceived a lack of overt hostility to their relationships. Nevertheless, when it occurred, couples demonstrated a regionalized understanding of boundary-policing occurring outside of the city in the country's southern region and within the city in its wealthy, predominantly white South Zone. The South Zone was a site of hypersexualization for black women married to white men, demonstrating how race and gender intersections matter for understandings of racial boundary-policing. For Carioca couples, ethnoracial boundaries were regionalized and could even be sexualized. Similar to Angelino couples, they unknowingly reproduced and reinforced those boundaries through their avoidance of those spaces. In both sites, couples drew on preexisting discourses of race and strategies of action in their social construction of ethnoracial boundaries, whether avoiding black communities or engaging in different tactics of respectability in their presentations of self. Overall, this chapter reveals how other social categories and symbolic and moral boundaries overlapped and aided in the construction of ethnoracial boundaries.

Conclusion

"Can Interracial Love Save Us?"

In the twenty-first century, no one ever says that a man marrying a woman should bring about gender equality. In fact, feminist scholars have alerted us to the myriad ways that patriarchy is perpetuated in marriage and family life. Yet many in the United States have the assumption that interracial marriage should automatically lead to racial equality. In the United States, 2017 marked the fiftieth anniversary of the landmark 1967 *Loving v. Virginia* Supreme Court decision outlawing state antimiscegenation laws. Strikingly, it was also the year that Prince Harry of the British royal family and Meghan Markle, a biracial American woman, announced their engagement. To celebrate interracial love, the *New York Times* ran an editorial titled "How Interracial Love Is Saving America" by Sheryll Cashin. The author cited research by the Pew Research Center on how 17 percent of newlyweds and 20 percent of cohabiting relationships are either interracial or interethnic, many times higher than in 1967. Cashin saw the enlightened whites who had married across color lines as being at the forefront of a "New Reconstruction" in the Trump era.

To my knowledge, interracial couples are not currently leading nor associated with activism for Reconstruction-like policies or to improve the well-being of Americans across ethnoracial boundaries. Examining the actual lives of interracial couples, this should come as no surprise. *Boundaries of Love* overtly challenges this sanguine picture of interracial marriage being the solution to white supremacy. Adopting a "critical constructionist" perspective, this book reveals how black-white couples—whether in a society where they are flexible or one in which they are more rigid—often reproduced ethnoracial boundaries. *Boundaries of Love* reveals how couples do this in a variety of ways: through ethnoracial preferences in romance, making sense of their own and their spouses' racial identities, categorizing their children, understanding white extended family reactions, and making sense of how to spend time in public as a couple. On occasion, husbands relied on patriarchal notions of marriage to bridge over the distance between blackness and whiteness. In addition, some spouses pushed against or changed the meaning of ethnoracial boundaries. Nevertheless, none of the couples in either society revealed a disintegration or blurring of racial boundaries that many, including academics, have come to expect. Spouses understood their partners as different from them in ethnoracial terms, whether or not they used creative beer metaphors (chapter 2). No one referenced boundary-blurring, all-encompassing identities—such as being children of God or being avid sports fans—to challenge ethnoracial boundaries. In fact, as I talk about in chapter 5, the way Los Angeles couples categorized their children suggested the social construction of a new category.

On its face, the assertion that race mixing does not erase racism appears to be a straw-man argument. However, race mixture as a solution to racism has been a potent racial ideology in both Brazil and the United States. The ideology of Brazil as a "racial democracy" has characterized the society as having harmonious race relations, integration, and high proportions of interracial mating. This ideology obscured how centuries of race mixing have coexisted alongside a white socioeconomic and political elite, despite more than half of Brazilians being people of color. The notion that "interracial love saves America" can gloss over ethnoracial preferences based in antiblackness, whether for whites who choose partners closer to European standards of beauty or blacks who conform to ideas of blacks as less desirable romantic partners in comparison to nonblacks. Of course, not all the couples that I interviewed subscribed to either of these notions. However, enough of them did in both societies to call into question the blanket statement that all interracial love is antiracist.

Love and the Social Construction of Race

A year before the fiftieth anniversary of *Loving v. Virginia*, the Hollywood film *Loving* depicted how the couple lived in Virginia, went to Washington, DC, to get married, and were arrested multiple times in their home state for violating antimiscegenation laws. In the film, while the lawsuits against the state of Virginia went to the Supreme Court, Mildred and Richard Loving spent their lives in isolation with little interest in the details of the court proceedings. *Loving* shows the happy ending of Virginia finally recognizing their marriage, allowing them to move closer to the community they came from.

Like the Lovings, the couples whom I interviewed largely lived quiet lives, going to work and school, raising their children (if they had them), and dealing with the responsibilities of daily life. Despite their love for each other, decades after *Loving v. Virginia* and in very different locales, black-white couples were still forced to navigate white supremacist societies that value white lives over black ones. Adopting a critical constructionist approach, *Boundaries of Love* reveals how these couples chose love and family as they used other social categories like gender, socioeconomic status, and even region to give meaning to ethnoracial boundaries in their respective societies. It reveals the subtle and overt nuances of race mixing in societies with persisting racial hierarchies. This book challenges the assumption that ethnoracial boundaries, a particular type of "us" versus "them," become erased or blurred through intermarriage and the children born to these couples.

Critical Constructionism and Ethnoracial Boundaries

Critical constructionism draws on ethnicity and nationalism's concern with ethnoracial boundaries but applies them outside of the realm of the state to how nonelites and members of marginalized communities negotiate them. It builds on race and ethnicity scholarship to reveal interactions across ethnoracial boundaries while challenging the essentialism of ethnoracial categories. Building on traditional critical race theory (CRT), a critical constructionist approach focuses on how race is reproduced in important institutions such as the family, paying attention to how race intersects with a variety of other social categories, such as gender and educational status, to produce disadvantage. Yet critical constructionism draws on the tools of social science to provide an empirically driven perspective on how ethnoracial boundaries are constructed through social interaction. What is gained through a critical constructionist approach is being able to unpack the nuanced ways that the residue of white supremacy affects the meanings that people give to their lives across societies.

In the first chapter, I introduced the concept of the "romantic career" in which people negotiate ethnoracial boundaries in their partnering preferences. In Rio de Janeiro, I found white spouses experiencing a "privilege of preferences," with white wives often discussing their adoration for *negão*, "big black men." Black husbands in Rio de Janeiro often understood themselves as willing objects of white women's pursuit, a technique of neutralization for managing the stigma of interracial intimacies. On the other hand, black wives married to white husbands understood themselves as seeking revenge on black men, especially with foreign *gringos*. This was different for white husbands, who often had patterns of dating stigmatized women of varying types. This played out differently in Los Angeles, with white women being largely silent about ethnoracial preferences in their romantic careers. Unlike their Carioca counterparts, black husbands said there were few black women in their opportunity structures, such as schools and neighborhoods, as explanations for why they had dated nonblacks throughout their romantic careers. White men in Los Angeles were also drawn to difference, and their black wives described openness to dating men across colors, including both black and white men, without a discussion of opportunity structures or revenge. For most couples in both societies, ethnoracial boundaries were central to how they made sense of their romantic careers.

Next, in chapter 2, I unpacked the "black" in the black-white couple, showing how both self-identification and partner-identification of the black spouse function in the two societies. I find that white spouses in Rio de Janeiro have a shallower understanding of their black spouses' blackness, often not recognizing the importance of family, ancestry, or racial discrimination. In Los Angeles, there was more congruence within couples surrounding what blackness comprised for their partners. Yet white spouses were more concerned with labels and multiracial ancestry than their black spouses. In addition, black spouses saw themselves as close to the ethnoracial boundaries of blackness. This chapter reveals how both black and white spouses engage in the social construction of ethnoracial boundaries of blackness.

Chapter 3 analyzed what it meant to be "white" for white spouses and for their black partners in both societies. I showed how white spouses in Rio de Janeiro employed ethnoracial reflexivity in their understandings of their whiteness, with education level influencing this process. Due to their racially mixed ancestry, Carioca white spouses often saw themselves as having lower degrees of whiteness than imagined "Aryans," with gender modulating this process. In Los Angeles, white spouses completely changed the meanings of whiteness from a racial category to one of "ethnic options" rooted in discrete European categories. In both societies, patriarchy allowed husbands to engage in bridging discourse across ethnoracial boundaries, mitigating the distance between them and their wives. Ethnoracial boundaries were far more flexible and pliable for white spouses in general, albeit more so for Carioca white spouses.

Chapter 4 discussed how parents categorized their children and its implications for affirmative action policy. In Rio de Janeiro, the flexibility of ethnoracial boundaries allowed parents to move from black to white when expectations did not match the realities of a child's appearance. This is in contrast to parents in Los Angeles who constructed a stable "biracial" category in their racial identification of their children. When questions of their child's eligibility for affirmative action emerged, Los Angeles parents engaged in boundary-work to harden the boundary between white and "biracial" while increasing its fluidity with blackness.

The next chapter revealed the process of black spousal integration into white extended families. Kind, well-meaning white families often recognized black spouses as ethnoracial outsiders and used different ways in the two societies to highlight these ethnoracial boundaries, whether through being overt or humorous in Rio de Janeiro or through moving between covert and overt strategies to avoid the racist label in Los Angeles. This chapter showed how white supremacy can continue to operate in interracial marriages and integrated families, with blackness continuing to be devalued vis-à-vis whiteness. This occurs through both inclusionary and exclusionary forms of discrimination.

In chapter 6, I compared how Angelino and Carioca spouses perceived ethnoracial boundary-policing by strangers in public. I found that while most couples had experienced it, none experienced it frequently.

In Los Angeles, respondents perceive boundary-policing as mainly the actions of black individuals, with gender playing an important role. In Rio de Janeiro, white regions and class were central factors, with hyper-sexualization of black women affecting strategies for being in public. This chapter reveals how differing understandings of ethnoracial boundaries in the two societies influence how black-white couples make sense of public hostility to their marriages.

Critical constructionism reveals how distinctions of "us" versus "them" do not become erased in these marriages. As seen in the cases of spouses in Rio de Janeiro and Los Angeles, these ethnoracial boundaries can be part of the appeal of entering a relationship with a person of a different color. In addition, membership in ethnoracial categories is still a part of how people identify themselves, are identified by their partners, categorize their children, and adjudicate their eligibility for affirmative action. In addition, ethnoracial boundaries are salient in how black spouses become incorporated into white families. They are certainly a part of how the outside world sees them. Furthermore, as social actors, many black-white couples structure their lives around race and ethnicity. This can be in terms of only spending time in diverse social spaces in which they do not stand out as well as avoiding particular spaces where they are more apt to experience hostility. Strikingly, this is true even in a society like Brazil that is known around the world for centuries of race mixture and its relatively more flexible ethnoracial boundaries. Adopting a critical constructionist perspective reveals the importance of other social categories, such as gender, educational attainment, and region, as building blocks for these boundaries. Furthermore, contrary to those who claim racism is solely a structural phenomenon, this book has shown how nonelites can reproduce racial and ethnic boundaries in their understandings of their lives.

Moving Forward

Brazil and US Latin-Americanization

Among race scholars, Brazilianists often emphasize how much Brazil is unlike the United States in terms of its race relations, while US scholars often take for granted that racialization processes are the same everywhere. As one of the first studies to take a comparative and qualitative approach to how racial boundaries are lived in the twenty-first century in these two societies, this study complicates these simplistic under-standings of race relations in both sites of research. In addition, it decenters US race relations as representative of all societies.

Is the United States witnessing a black/nonblack divide? A triracial system with whites, honorary whites, and collective blacks?[1] Future studies of interracial couples can shed light on whether this is happen-ing through comparing the experiences of black-white, black-Latinx, black-Asian, and black-multiracial couples with other configurations of interracially married couples. Evidence for this divide could be dem-onstrated if the experiences of black-nonblack families are drastically different from other multiracials. In addition, as Asians and Latinxs occupy large proportions of intermarried spouses in the United States, comparative studies of interracial marriage *within* the United States can show the ways that different types of couples navigate racial boundaries as well as the characteristics of these boundaries that can become salient (e.g., language, religion, immigration status, nationality). With the Brit-ish royal family openly incorporating a woman who is the daughter of a black mother and a white father, it behooves us as scholars to think about these issues on a global scale.

The Family

As interracial marriages and multiracial families increase in number, the family may become a more salient site for racial discrimination than has been previously acknowledged, including families involving nonblacks who marry black partners. Beyond "rebound racism" from the outside world,[2] ethnoracial distinctions and discriminatory acts based on those boundaries in the family are important to consider in understanding social relations within as well as across given societies. For example, social psychologists have shown how US black parents and other par-ents of color challenge white supremacy as they raise their children.[3] However, little is known about the ways white parents communicate or reproduce notions of ethnoracial status among their children; the ways that silence and color blindness around race are disseminated within white families can illuminate an important mechanism of white supremacy. Scholars of Brazil have already examined differences in child outcomes by race and color, including racial classifications, investments in education, and differences in affective relations.[4] For US family scholars, issues of colorism and ethnoracial distinction are the next frontier for understanding inequality.[5]

The growth of same-sex couples in the United States and Brazil problematizes the heteronormativity of norms of race mixture. In addition, new forms of fertility technology such as surrogacy, artificial insemination, and in vitro fertilization all call into question new ways that families may be involved in the social construction of race as well as the role of intersectionality in these social processes. While these issues are beyond the scope of this book, future research should examine new understandings of race mixture for twenty-first-century realities.

Affirmative Action

In both societies, debates around who is eligible for affirmative action show that parent origin is important. A complete picture of parents' socioeconomic status would include not only their income but also their education and ethnoracial categorization. These should be considered in the tribunals that Brazilians have created to weed out "Afro-convenients" who are white for all intents and purposes except for when it comes to taking advantage of affirmative action quotas. In the United States, those who value diversity on university campuses should make a special effort to recruit students with both parents of US slave ancestry. While black immigrants and biracial students often suffer from the same racial discrimination as "monoracial" students without white parentage, they can experience many privileges that facilitate their college degree attainment. While descendants of black immigrants and white parentage contribute to the diversity of college campus life, their presence should come alongside and not displace native "all-black" counterparts. For this reason, we need to think beyond "affirmative action" to newer policies that create a diverse student body as well as address generations of exclusion of people of color from higher education.

Ideologies of Race Mixture

Race and ethnicity should not matter for whom we love. Unfortunately, in societies built on and structured around white supremacy, race can be front and central in who a person chooses to love. Interracial love can inadvertently reproduce racist notions about the type of people who are desirable partners. While in the past, this had led to discussions of status exchange, today, it seems that there is a socioeconomic threshold for people of color to marry whites that is less overt in white-white or black-black marriages. For this reason, it can be problematic to place interracial marriages as somehow intrinsically better than same-race love.

In the United States, many understand race mixing as a sign that racism is on the decline. This has often been accompanied by the fetishization of children with racially mixed ancestry, including positive stereotypes, as mentioned in chapter 4. Many US liberals have advocated the idea that "we will all be brown in the future" as a promise providing a false hope of a better racial tomorrow. However, this esteem for race mixture has been a red herring. Rather than advocating for public policy to repair injustices inflicted upon African Americans and other communities of color, interracial love has seemed to offer a remedy based in individual choice, something very appealing in a liberal democracy.

However, Brazil may have something to teach the United States in terms of the relationship between race mixing and racial inequality. These liberal sentiments are similar to arguments made half a century ago in Brazil, where race mixture would supposedly eradicate racism and racial inequality by essentially "diluting" the black population.[6] The *mulato* was the ideal person, someone who was brown enough to withstand the tropical climate, benefitted from the intellectual inheritance of European ancestors, yet also had an appreciation for Afro-Brazilian cultural styles and music, such as by knowing how to samba.[7] Assimilationist notions of using race mixture to promote a racially mixed national identity (democracy ideology) obscure and suppress discussion of racial inequality and deride very real cultural differences. This ideology of racial harmony through race mixing failed in a "racial democracy" like Brazil. The Brazilian case illuminates how generations of race mixing can leave racial inequality and white supremacy intact.

Collective Action

While there have never been more interracial marriages and multiracial families, the quality of life for African Americans has not improved
over the last several decades. Measures of residential segregation, levels of black incarceration, and black-white gaps in education, income,
and a host of other objective measures of racial inequality have either
increased or have not budged over the same time period. The increased
media coverage around police killings in recent years reminds us of the
continuing need for activism around the same issues of police violence
that have plagued the United States since the creation of the police in
this society. Seemingly, racial inequality and hierarchies can coexist
with race mixing in the US context as well. Similar to Brazil decades ago,
increasing race mixture has served as a red herring from the need for activism and social policy to address racial inequality in the United States.

Thinking about racial integration along two axes, in which interpersonal relations fall on the horizontal axis and socioeconomic equality
on the vertical axis,[8] can explain how growing rates of intermarriage in
both the United States and Brazil can exist alongside racial inequality.
In addition, a celebration of race mixture as a sign of an end to racism echoes the black activist claim that race mixture is a form of black
genocide.[9] Furthermore, with the rise of Trump, a very vocal minority
understands the "browning" of the United States, whether through
immigration, race mixture, or both, as a form of white genocide.

Boundaries of Love shows that the burgeoning of black consciousness in Brazil has not ushered in a rejection of race mixture. As has
historically been the case, blackness and black pride can coincide with
both nonblack racial ancestry as well as interracial marriage. In fact,
many leaders in the black Brazilian movement have been interracially
married. Yet those respondents with experience in black movement
circles described rejection and hostility. The salience of race mixture in
the Brazilian racial consciousness and the upswing in cross-color marriages means that the movement should do a better job of destigmatiz-
ing these relationships. In fact, nonblack allies, such as white spouses
or children of Afro-descendants, may provide an untapped source of
solidarity for the movement. The racist, historical practice of whitening Afro-descendants through race mixture may have been intended as

nonviolent genocide, but there is a middle ground between embracing it and rejecting anyone who happens to marry across color. The gender imbalances of contemporary race mixture are a likely reason for hostility toward those relationships. Nevertheless, disparaging it can isolate potential allies in the fight for racial equality for Afro-Brazilians.

In the United States, thus far, there has been no social movement led by interracially married couples as Cashin suggested. If anything, before the Trump presidency, the rise in intermarriage dampened the desire of white liberals to fight for racial equality, lazily leaving it up to individual choice and (marriage) market forces, all the while placing the burden on multiracial children to solve the race problem. With the dawning of the Trump era, white spouses married to people of color have not yet collectively mobilized under this particular identity to fight for racial justice for their spouses and their children. While time will tell if this will become a reality, the rise in white supremacist violence in the Trump era would make such organizing a dangerous endeavor. In addition, trying to usher in a "New Reconstruction" might lead to the same increase in "whitelash" that occurred during the first one, when the rise of the Ku Klux Klan first emerged.

Melting-pot ideology has fallen out of favor in the United States for its racist, whitening overtones as well as the cultural pluralism at the heart of US society. However, a new metaphor that unites all Americans across the racial, color, and immigrant-origin spectrum is sorely needed. Brazilian racial democracy as well as the US's *e pluribus unum* are goals that are remade with every generation. In the United States, the Trump presidency has threatened the national motto of uniting disparate peoples. Social movement activists have an opportunity to craft a new US narrative that celebrates the nation's diversity while striving to make it a more perfect union. Thinking explicitly about bridging across and truly blurring ethnoracial boundaries with a multicultural, class-conscious, and gender-sensitive new American identity can aid in this endeavor. We cannot leave it up to multiracial families to carry the load for all of us.

ACKNOWLEDGMENTS

The Lord works in mysterious ways. If it had not been for a misunderstanding with Anne Peplau at the University of California, Los Angles (UCLA), this book would have never been comparative. I am grateful for her intellectual support and the National Science Foundation Interdisciplinary Graduate Education and Research Traineeship (IGERT) in Interdisciplinary Relationship Sciences funding that helped me get this research under way. For their support, I also thank the UCLA Department of Sociology, the UCLA Center for Brazilian Studies, the UCLA Latin American Institute, the UCLA Bunche Center for African American Studies, the Institute of American Cultures, and the University of Pennsylvania Center for Africana Studies.

I am grateful for Edward Telles's guidance in understanding how racial dynamics work in the Brazilian context. Stefan Timmermans's advice on balancing academic projects, both new and old, still remains very helpful. Mignon Moore has offered important guidance in all facets of my research project and has been a wonderful mentor, gently challenging my own biases while training me to be successful as a sociologist. Belinda Tucker also provided useful perspectives on interracial marriages and helped me find couples to interview.

I am especially indebted to the University of Pennsylvania Center for Africana Studies for two years of writing and research as a postdoctoral fellow. Their support allowed me to go back to Brazil to carry out more interviews with black-white couples as well as have them transcribed. Tukufu Zuberi read several papers that formed the bases of journal articles and chapters, providing new insight and direction. Deborah Thomas, Cord Whitaker, and the other scholars in the University of Pennsylvania Race and Empire Working Group provided useful feedback in a rigorous academic space. Camille Charles and Grace Kao provided great mentoring during my time there. My time at Penn was enriched by insights from the sociology department, who provided multiple venues for me to present my research, especially in preparation for job talks. Eduardo Bonilla-Silva was visiting Penn while I was there and tasked me with unabashedly challenging reigning sociological ideas of race and ethnicity both in the United States and in Brazil, for which I am appreciative.

I am grateful to France Winddance Twine, Tanya Golash-Boza, Gladys Mitchell-Walthour, and Elizabeth Hordge-Freeman for helping me develop many ideas that formed the basis for many book chapters and sections. Vilna Bashi-Treitler offered great advice on how to handle writing the first book as well as reminding me that sometimes it is good not to be hardheaded. I am also grateful to Mary Patillo, Howard Winant, and Rose Brewer for their useful conversations.

I am thankful to all the people who read and gave feedback on early versions of my chapters. Crystal Fleming and Onoso Imoagene helped me hash out new ideas as well as refine old ones. I am grateful to Tanya Katerí Hernández for her "quick and dirty" read of the entire manuscript as well as providing opportunities to discuss my research at Fordham Law's Center on Race, Law, and Justice. Nancy Yuen also provided valuable insight on early drafts of my work.

The anonymous reviewers who read my work were very helpful and offered great feedback. Thank you for your behind the scenes contributions!

In Brazil, Graziella Silva helped me find couples to interview, as did Rolf Malungo de Souza. Juliana and Maria Cristina Freire helped a lot with Portuguese translations, especially involving Carioca *giria*, or slang. Angela Paiva and Jose Luis Petriccelli were extremely helpful for thinking through white Brazilian taboos against intermarriage. Izabella Lacerda Pimento, a fellow social scientist, was a godsend. My Brazilian "buppies" Ana and Marina Meirelles and dear friends Ana Rosa and Patrick Swan allowed me to get my foodie life while helping me find couples to interview. Fabiana Erramo and Marize Rocha got me to stop being a snob and drink *chopp* like a proper Carioca. Marize's father, Senhor Rocha, made *feijoadas* for me that were so good, they almost made me cry. Barbecues at the Rocha's reminded me that despite the beaches, urban rainforests, breathtaking views, and samba, the best part of the Marvelous City is its people.

I have to thank my Rutgers colleagues for their support as I navigated health difficulties alongside the stress of writing my first book.

Drew Humphries and Jane Siegel were excellent chairs who protected us junior faculty as we got our first projects as faculty on the tenure track under way. Drew knew what my book was about before I even had the (deviance) language for it. Sherry Pisacano, Cati Coe, Michelle Meloy, and our dean, Kris Lindenmeyer, all had a part in making life on the tenure track manageable. When I thought the book needed "just a few tweaks" before I sent it to the editors, Joanie Mazelis was not having it and marched me off to my office to "send it to Ilene now! Send it now! Go!" If it had not been for Joanie, I would not have had the guts to take action. Oscar Holmes, Keith Green, and Stacy Hawkins have helped me establish a sense of a Rutgers "Blackademic" writing community. I am also appreciative of my amazing undergraduate research assistants Tamara Boles and Ashley Flores. As women of color, I am excited for what the future holds for them.

Stacia Gilliard-Matthews was a great colleague, prayerful sister in Christ, and dear friend. Even as she battled her own travails, I am glad that she was a sister on so many levels, from our shared black female academic "fabulosity" to our shared desire to do God's will in the world.

I am grateful to Goretti Gonzalez, who kindly humored my 2 a.m. calls when I would tell her that I was sure that I was dying. She reminded me that I tended to do that when I'm stressed out and would help me figure out where those fears came from. David Cort, Jenny Oshen, Ana Misic, Elizabeth Joniak, Kobie, Oscar Holmes, Keith Green, Marie Kanu, and Kim Comerford were all a regular part of my support system. Thanks are also deserved for Mireya Loza, who is a hero of mine. Kinohi Nishikawa and Neetu Khanna were my Faculty Success Program writing accountability group for several years. We shared joys, setbacks, and triumphs and saw each other get our respective book contracts. I am also thankful to the numerous friends who edified me as I had awkward conversations with strangers in public; Carolyn Gonzalez, Portia Jackson, Natasha Rivers, Fabiana Erramo, and Marize Rocha had my back as I gathered up the nerve for those encounters.

I appreciate Ryan Mulligan for pointing to salient themes that needed greater fleshing out in a later version of the manuscript. I would especially like to thank Ilene Kalish for her help navigating the book review and publishing process. Maryam Alim, Kate Epstein, and Ulli Ryder all also helped make this book possible, and for this I am indebted.

The couples with whom I spent so much time and who were kind enough to take hours out of their days to allow me to interview them were so gracious. I especially appreciate the couples who were not put off by a stranger (particularly a black woman) asking them about their relationships that seemed interracial on the outside. They shared their triumphs, travails, and banalities with me, and I feel honored to be able to share their different perspectives.

Clifford and Lillian Osuji have always made excellence a taken-for-granted standard. The rest of the "Osuji Five" have offered so much support; thank you Chidi, my dear sister; Ndidi; OJ "Jeffrey"; and Obinna Osuji. God knew what He was doing when He blessed me with family members who are related by both blood and Spirit. You all have reminded me to pray when I was overcome by the blows of life and to remember how I am more than a conqueror.

All of you have decreased the *wahala* in my life while helping me move *pa'lante y con alegria*.

APPENDIX A

Tables

APPENDIX TABLE 1. Rio de Janeiro Respondents' Names, Educational Statuses, and Ages

Wife	Husband	Wife College	Husband College	Status Exchange	Wife Age	Husband Age
Ana Maria	Cândido				50	44
Bárbara	Brício	x	x		31	36
Carlota	Adair	x	x		50	49
Deisy	Wanderley	x	x		53	52
Eloíza	Vitor	x	x		41	42
Flávia	Ulises	x		x	27	26
Griselda	Teófilo	x		x	51	58
Hilda	Sérgio	x	x		37	34
Idália	Róbinson		x	x	49	43
Juliana	Patrício	x			52	49
Katarina	Otávio				37	44
Laura	Nicolas				36	45
Marisa	Adão	x	x		50	39
Nádia	Leandro	x	x		45	28
Ofélia	Konrad		x	x	45	44
Priscila	Jorge	x		x	38	34
Raquel	Isidoro	x	x		31	34
Silvia	Harry	x	x		27	24
Tatiana	Gaspar	x	x		40	40
Ursulina	Fabrício				50	65
Verônica	Edvaldo				24	24
Angela	Donato				21	27
Brígida	Caetano				47	43
Carol	Benjamin	x	x		35	34
Delfina	Auguste	x	x		48	48

(continued)

APPENDIX TABLE 1. Rio de Janeiro Respondents' Names, Educational Statuses, and Ages (*cont.*)

Wife	Husband	Wife College	Husband College	Status Exchange	Wife Age	Husband Age
Edite	Bartolomeu				33	38
Fernanda	Claúdio				28	35
Gabriela	Danilo		x	x	50	47

Shaded rows indicate black husband–white wife couples. Nonshaded rows indicate black wife–white husband couples.

APPENDIX TABLE 2. Los Angeles Respondents' Names, Educational Statuses, and Ages

Wife	Husband	Wife College	Husband College	EAM*	Wife Age	Husband Age
Allison	Yuri	x	x	x	30	29
Betty	William	x	x	x	35	42
Charlotte	Vincent	x	x	x	33	35
Elizabeth	Trevor	x	x	x	46	50
Felicity	Ronald	x	x	x	31	33
Gloria	Quentin	x			30	31
Helen	Perry	x	x	x	57	54
Indira	Orion	x			50	51
Jennifer	Neil	x	x	x	34	33
Kelly	Mark	x	x	x	53	53
Lana	Larry	x	x	x	35	53
Madison	Kevin	x	x	x	29	35
Natalie	Jerry	x			28	27
Pavla	Gary	x	x	x	24	26
Roxanne	Fred	x	x	x	50	54
Stella	Edward	x	x	x	29	54
Taiwo	Daniel	x	x	x	34	34
Visola	Charles	x	x	x	33	39
Yvonne	Aaron	x	x	x	38	35

Shaded rows indicate black husband–white wife couples. Nonshaded rows indicate black wife–white husband couples.
* EAM refers to marriages involving educational assortative mating in which partners match on their levels of education.

APPENDIX TABLE 3. Couples with Children in Both Sites

Rio de Janeiro		Los Angeles	
Wife	Husband	Wife	Husband
Deisy	Wanderley	Allison	Yuri
Eloíza	Vitor	Betty	William
Katarina	Otávio	Elizabeth	Trevor
Laura	Nicolas	Gloria	Quentin
Ofélia	Konrad	Kelly	Mark
Priscila	Jorge	Madison	Kevin
Tatiana	Gaspar	Pavla	Gary
Angela	Donato	Roxanne	Fred
Brígida	Caetano	Visola	Charles
Carol	Benjamin	Yvonne	Aaron
Delfina	Auguste		

Shaded rows indicate black husband–white wife couples. Nonshaded rows indicate black wife–white husband couples.

APPENDIX B

Methods and Fieldwork

I studied abroad as an undergraduate in Granada, Spain, where the centuries-old Moorish castle, the Alhambra, still stands. I remember having a discussion with my host sister, Raquel, in which she took for granted that North Africans look very different from Spaniards. I was confused. "How can you tell who is Maghrebi?" I asked. Raquel was shocked but had a glimmer in her eye and smirked as she asked me, "You mean you can't tell us apart?"

That was a very awkward moment for me. My North American eyes could not read the ways that Spaniards distinguished themselves from North Africans. As olive-toned people, they honestly all looked alike to me. Partly, it was my assumption that generations of Moorish rule meant that Spaniards and North Africans were indistinguishable. To complicate matters, I could not tell Spanish Roma apart from their non-Roma *payo* counterparts or newly arrived foreigners from the Maghreb. The majority of people I saw around me would have a difficult time identifying as white back home. I remember eyeing Raquel suspiciously, with her long, thick curls and tanned skin and thinking that she looked like any of the women we would have called "mixed" in Chicago. The phenotypic norms of Spaniards, whose whiteness was implicit, were completely lost on me.

However, living for months in Spain, I started to see people with different eyes. Of course, for the women it was much easier, since clothing such as headscarves were often dead giveaways for religious distinctions. I assimilated to the notion that being white in Spain ranged from having characteristically Nordic features with light-colored hair and eyes to having a toasty "olive" complexion. I learned that small noses, small lips, and hair without tight curls were synonymous with their side of the ethnoracial boundary. Apart from clothing, larger noses, fuller lips, and paying attention to "baby hair" and the "kitchen" or nape of the neck were signs Spaniards used to distinguish between themselves and recent Moroccan immigrants. *Gitanos*, as the Spanish Roma were called, stereotypically had light-colored, green eyes alongside skin no darker than olive. These stereotypes often led to intriguing moments in which some US Latinxs and white Americans whom I studied abroad with were pleased to blend in with Spaniards until they opened their mouths and spoke a New World Spanish.

As an unambiguous black woman, I found these stereotypes fascinating as I went to Spain again, this time to Barcelona as a Fulbright fellow. I interviewed many second-generation immigrants from Equatorial Guinea, the only Spanish colony in Africa. Like me, they physically stood out with dark-brown skin and West African physical features. I overheard a Catalan woman musing on how odd it was that there were more people with light-colored eyes in southern Spain than in Catalonia. The physical feature that *granadinos* (people from Granada) associated with gitanos had become a Catalonian way to stereotype the people of southern Spain. People in Catalonia were closer to Europe, Catalonians often told me, implicitly noting less Moorish ancestry and, hence, a less-contested whiteness.

The reason I mention this is that in Brazil, there was a similar code of whiteness. Being white meant being able to pass for someone who looks like they are from Spain, Italy, or Portugal, places with a lower color threshold for whiteness than the United States. However, in Rio de Janeiro, I found that having a flat nose or very curly hair—namely, looking like Raquel—disqualified you from whiteness. For Brazilians, the hair did not lie. Many Carioca men, especially those who looked more racially ambiguous, cut their hair extremely short and were thus able to pass as white. They reminded me of the nappy "kitchens" of North Africans in Spain.

My eyes once more started acclimating, but this time to Brazilian standards of whiteness, blackness, and everything in between. However, I did not trust them. In the name of social science, I did not want to be accused of imposing a North American perspective on respondents. For this reason, I only asked native Brazilians for black-white couples to interview. I did not have this problem when I returned to Los Angeles to recruit more couples. Yet I realized that my eyes could still lie to me. I will never forget attending UCLA's Jazzfest and walking up to a dark-skinned black man and his white wife, asking if they were married. When they said that they were, I asked if they would be interested in participating in my study and proceeded to explain it to them. The woman immediately became irate: "I'm not white. I'm black!" She explained that she was Creole, part of a racially mixed group of people from Louisiana who come in a variety of colors, many whom had settled in California. Accidentally, I had offended her in the name of social science research.

Through the process of finding respondents in Los Angeles, I learned that mine were not the only eyes that could lie. I soon became aware that when white friends and colleagues nominated black-white couples for me to interview, the black person often did not identify him or herself as black. In the opposite of my situation with the Creole woman, whites often applied the one-drop rule to identifying black spouses, whereas they did not always see themselves as "just black." On two separate occasions, whites had recommended black-white couples for me to interview, only to find, upon arriving at the couples' homes, that the "black" person identified herself (usually it was a woman) as multiracial, not black. On one occasion, the woman had not seen her Afro-Caribbean father since she was a child. After those two incidents, I became better at screening Los Angeles respondents for black or white identities among the potential respondents before potential interviews.

Interviewer Effects

Most scholars who have examined race and color in Brazil to date have generally been white researchers visiting from North America and Europe. In Brazil, there is a negative relationship between the interviewer's color and respondent's color,[1] such that with white interviewers, Brazilian respondents tend to darken themselves, and with darker interviewers, they lighten themselves. This may have led Brazilians in previous studies to exaggerate their nonwhiteness vis-à-vis "Aryan" interviewers. There has not been an equivalent phenomenon for blacks or whites in the United States.

As a dark-skinned black woman, my respondents may have claimed stronger white identities than they would have otherwise. On the other hand, black spouses may have emphasized their ambiguity or their black identities, depending on whether I was lighter or darker in skin tone than them. As mentioned before, eligibility for participation was based on fellow Cariocas' assessment of whether they were a black-white couple. In addition, screening couples for their identities over the phone likely minimized potential "interviewer effects" since they could not see my own skin color to let it influence their responses. In addition, I unpack outsiders' perceptions versus self-identification by gaining part-ners' perspectives on their own colors, as I discussed in chapters 3 and 4.

An "Angry" or "Available" Black Woman in the Field

My own "ethnoracial reflexivity" was fraught with complications over my ability to discern how others saw me in the two settings.[2] In the United States, the "angry black woman" (ABW) is supposed to be hostile to black men romantically involved with white women.[3] In Los Angeles, I was supposed to be the ABW trying to understand why white women "are trying to take all the good black men." For example, my first US interviewee, Allison, was a white woman who revealed that she was "scared" about my interviewing her but could not identify why. In my many years of conducting qualitative interviews for different projects, that was the first time I had ever had such a response. In addition, since most studies of interracial couples involve white women (whether talk-ing alongside their black husbands or alone), prior scholarship on this topic had not adequately prepared me for this image in the looking glass.

To overcompensate for this stereotype, when recruiting in public spaces in Los Angeles, I often had another person, often, though not always, white, with me. On one occasion, I remember being at a restau-rant with a multiracial group of friends in Little Tokyo and spotting a black man with a white woman. Seeing potential respondents, I forced my male friend from Portugal to accompany me out of the restaurant to try to interview them. I was attempting to look like someone who had no problem with interracial dating and marriage. This tactic failed on this occasion but was successful on another. I mainly used the recommen-dations of friends, acquaintances, and couples themselves as recruiters.

When interviewing couples in Los Angeles, building rapport with couples, especially with the white women in the relationships, was important because of the ABW stereotype. As I would be interviewing husbands and wives separately, I was careful not to appear as though I were driving a wedge between them or troubled by their relationship. I often approached wives first as a way of avoiding these tensions. I also let interviewees decide where they wanted to be interviewed. I noticed that three pairs of highly educated couples, all involving black women with white men, preferred to be interviewed outside of their homes. However, the overwhelming majority of couples allowed me into their homes to interview them.

To manage my ethnoracial reflexivity and the ABW stereotype, I smiled more often to cultivate a nonthreatening, cheery persona. I also began interviews by asking respondents about their childhood, their experiences in school, and their parents' occupations while their children were growing up. This built rapport with the respondents before asking them harder questions about their dating histories or their racial preferences in dating and marriage. I was very conscious of smiling and nodding during uncomfortable moments to make respondents feel comfortable revealing taboo sentiments.

In Brazil, I had a harder time understanding how other people saw me as a black woman studying black-white couples. Like other scholars before me, I saw myself as an inquisitive social scientist of color concerned with the condition of racialized minorities. As a result of this prior scholarship, I was mostly prepared to negotiate my identification as an African American, a US citizen, and a woman. However, I was not prepared to be seen as a black woman who was sexually available, particularly to white men. On one occasion, while I was waiting for a bus, a white man dressed as an Orthodox Jew asked me in heavily accented English, "Sex? For money?" As a Christ-follower, it was startling to be approached by a seemingly religious man. Intellectually, I knew that religious people have been participants in the sex trade for centuries. Yet spiritually, it hurt more since we were supposedly both religious people.

Navigating Africanness

As a dark-skinned black woman sporting short dreadlocks, I could blend in as a Brazilian, even a Bahian (*baiana*), as long as I did not speak. *Bahian* is a term that not only is exclusive to people from the state of Bahia but is also used to refer to people of dark skin and of African ancestry. However, after two years in Spain, my use of Iberian cognates, speaking with an accent, and lack of Carioca slang often led Brazilians to read me as a native of Angola or Mozambique, both Portuguese-speaking countries in Africa. On one occasion, I was chastised for not expressing pride in Angola's beautiful capital, Luanda. I was proud that I did not have a strong American accent and that I could pass as a native speaker. Yet as a second-generation immigrant with roots in the most populous country in Africa, with the highest GDP, my Naija pride was stung. This mislabeling left me uncomfortable and would often result in me clarifying how my parents were immigrants from Nigeria to the United States. For Brazilians with cultural affinities for the Yoruba, this again was uncomfortable since I grew up with parents who drew sharp ethnic lines against Yoruba and Hausa peoples. At the same time, the appreciation for Africa was refreshing and especially helped me bond with *negras frustradas* and their black husbands as well as, of course, black women with strong *negra* identities.

For several American interviewees, I had a sense that my Nigerian heritage was an asset. It helped build camaraderie with the several respondents who were first- or second-generation black immigrants, had (surprisingly) spent time in Nigeria, or were whites married to these people. From a psychological perspective, it allowed me to place some distance between myself and my black American sisters to withstand yet capture the negative things that I heard about black women. (This was similar to the ethnic boundary that I drew on to hear yet distance myself from the negative things said about Afro-Brazilian women in Rio de Janeiro.) This dance between being an insider versus an outsider means that I may have missed some of the nuances of African American life that respondents alluded to. At the same time, I suspect that it also helped Angelinos suspend their disbelief when discussing the social construction of blackness in the United States.

NOTES

PREFACE

1 Gilberto Freyre, *The Masters and the Slaves: A Study in the Development of Brazilian Civilization* (Berkeley: University of California Press, 1933).

INTRODUCTION. RACE MIXING AND ETHNORACIAL BOUNDARIES

1 Charles Tilly, "Social Boundary Mechanisms," *Philosophy of the Social Sciences* 34, no. 2 (2004); Michéle Lamont and Virag Molnar, "The Study of Boundaries in the Social Sciences," *Annual Review of Sociology* (2002).

2 Stephen Cornell and Douglas Hartmann, *Ethnicity and Race: Making Identities in a Changing World* (Thousand Oaks, CA: Pine Forge Press, 1998); Richard Jenkins, *Social Identity* (New York: Routledge, 2008).

3 Fredrik Barth, *Ethnic Groups and Boundaries: The Social Origin of Culture Difference* (Prospect Heights, IL: Waveland Press, 1969).

4 Donna M. Goldstein, *Laughter Out of Place: Race, Class, Violence, and Sexuality in a Rio Shantytown* (Berkeley: University of California Press, 2003); Chinyere K. Osuji, "Confronting Whitening in an Era of Black-Consciousness: Racial Ideology and Black-White Marriages in Brazil," *Ethnic and Racial Studies* (2013).

5 Barth, *Ethnic Groups and Boundaries*.

6 Rogers Brubaker, *Ethnicity without Groups* (Cambridge, MA: Harvard University Press, 2004).

7 Stanley Bailey, *Legacies of Race: Identities, Attitudes, and Politics in Brazil* (Palo Alto, CA: Stanford University Press, 2009); Livio Sansone, *Blackness without Ethnicity: Constructing Race in Brazil* (New York: Palgrave Macmillan, 2003).

8 Mara Loveman, *National Colors: Racial Classification and the State in Latin America* (New York: Oxford University Press, 2014).

9 Aaron Gullickson and Ann Morning, "Choosing Race: Multiracial Ancestry and Identification," *Social Science Research* 40 (2014); Stanley Bailey and Michelle Peria, "Racial Quotas and the Culture War in Brazilian Academia," *Sociology Compass* 4 (2010).

10 Andreas Wimmer, "Beyond and Below Racial Homophily: Erg Models of a Friendship Network Documented on Facebook," *American Journal of Sociology* 116, no. 2 (2010).

11 Andreas Wimmer, *Ethnic Boundary Making: Institutions, Power, Networks* (New York: Oxford University Press, 2013).

12 Edward E. Telles, *Race in Another America: The Significance of Skin Color in Brazil* (Princeton, NJ: Princeton University Press, 2004); Graziella Morães da Silva and Marcelo Paixão, "Mixed and Unequal: New Perspectives on Brazilian Ethnoracial Relations," in *Pigmentocracies: Ethnicity, Race and Color in Latin America,* ed. Edward Telles and PERLA (Chapel Hill: University of North Carolina Press, 2014).

13 Douglas S. Massey and Nancy A. Denton, *American Apartheid: Segregation and the Making of the Underclass* (Cambridge, MA: Harvard University Press, 1993); Patrick Sharkey, *Stuck in Place: Urban Neighborhoods and the End Process toward Racial Equality* (Chicago, IL: University of Chicago Press, 2013).

14 Rachel F. Moran, *Interracial Intimacy: The Regulation of Race and Romance* (Chicago, IL: University of Chicago Press, 2001); Randall Kennedy, *Interracial Intimacies: Sex, Marriage, Identity, and Adoption,* 1st ed. (New York: Pantheon, 2003).

15 S. E. Gaither and S. R. Sommers, "Living with an Other-Race Roommate Shapes Whites' Behavior in Subsequent Diverse Settings," *Journal of Experimental Social Psychology* 49, no. 2 (2013); S. E. Gaither et al., "Examining the Effects of I-Sharing for Future White-Black Interactions," *Social Psychology* 47, no. 3 (2016).

16 Massey and Denton, *American Apartheid.*

17 Karyn R. Lacy, *Blue-Chip Black: Race, Class, and Status in the New Black Middle Class* (Berkeley: University of California Press, 2007).

18 Prudence L. Carter, *Keepin' It Real: School Success beyond Black and White* (Oxford: Oxford University Press, 2005); Amy C. Wilkins, *Wannabes, Goths, and Christians: The Boundaries of Sex, Style, and Status* (Chicago, IL: University of Chicago Press, 2008); Sandra S. Smith and Mignon R. Moore, "Intraracial Diversity and Relations among African-Americans: Closeness among Black Students at a Predominantly White University," *American Journal of Sociology* 106, no. 1 (2000).

19 France Winddance Twine, *A White Side of Black Britain: Interracial Intimacy and Racial Literacy* (Durham, NC: Duke University Press, 2010); Jessica Vasquez-Tokos, *Marriage Vows and Racial Choices* (New York: Russell Sage Foundation, 2017).

20 Kimberly McClain DaCosta, *Making Multiracials: State, Family, and Market in the Redrawing of the Color Line* (Stanford, CA: Stanford University Press, 2007); K. A. Rockquemore and D. L. Brunsma, *Beyond Black: Biracial Identity in America* (Rowman and Littlefield, 2007); David L. Brunsma, "Interracial Families and the Racial Identification of Mixed-Race Children: Evidence from the Early Childhood Longitudinal Study," *Social Forces* 84 (2005).

21 Rather than using Latino/a or choosing one gendered term over the other, I use the gender-neutral term *Latinx* unless gender is specified.

22 Clara Rodriguez, *Changing Race: Latinos, the Census, and the History of Ethnicity in the United States* (New York: New York University Press, 2000); G. Cristina Mora, *Making Hispanics: How Activists, Bureaucrats, and Media Constructed a New American* (Chicago, IL: University of Chicago Press, 2014).

23 Signithia Fordham and John Ogbu, "Black Students' School Success: Coping with the 'Burden of Acting White,'" *Urban Review* 18 (1986); but see Carter, *Keepin' It Real*, for a contrasting perspective.

24 Jennifer Hochschild, Vesla Weaver, and Traci Burch, *Transforming the American Racial Order* (Princeton, NJ: Princeton University Press, 2012).

25 Sylvia Zamora, "Racial Remittances: The Effect of Migration on Racial Ideologies in Mexico and the United States," *Sociology of Race and Ethnicity* 2, no. 4 (2016).

26 Tiffany Joseph, *Race on the Move: Brazilian Migrants and the Global Reconstruction of Race* (Palo Alto, CA: Stanford University Press, 2015).

27 Richard Delgado and Jean Stefancic, *Critical Race Theory: The Cutting Edge*, 2nd ed. (Philadelphia, PA: Temple University Press, 2000).

28 Kimberlé Crenshaw, "Mapping the Margins: Intersectionality, Identity, Politics, and Violence against Women of Color," in *The Public Nature of Private Violence: The Discovery of Domestic Abuse*, ed. M. Fineman and R. Mykitiuk (New York: Routledge, 1994); and "Demarginalizing the Intersection of Race and Sex: A Black Feminist Critique of Antidiscrimination Doctrine, Feminist Theory and Antiracist Politics," *University of Chicago Legal Forum* 189, no. 1 (1989).

29 Tanya Golash-Boza, "A Critical and Comprehensive Sociological Theory of Race and Racism," *Sociology of Race and Ethnicity* 2, no. 2 (2016).

30 Michael Omi and Howard Winant, *Racial Formation in the United States: From the 1960s to the 1990s*, 3rd ed. (New York: Routledge, 2015).

31 See Joseph, *Race on the Move*; and Helen Marrow, "To Be or Not to Be (Hispanic or Latino): Brazilian Racial and Ethnic Identity in the United States," *Ethnicities* 3, no. 4 (2003): 427–64; for discussions of how Brazilians identify with the term *Latino* but not *Hispanic*.

32 Kennedy, *Interracial Intimacies*.

33 Thomas E. Skidmore, "Bi-racial U.S.A. vs. Multi-racial Brazil: Is the Contrast Still Valid?," *Journal of Latin American Studies* 25, no. 2 (1993); Telles, *Race in Another America*.

34 Jeffrey Lesser, *Negotiating National Identity: Immigrants, Minorities, and the Struggle for Ethnicity in Brazil* (Durham, NC: Duke University Press, 1999).

35 Oracy Nogueira, *Tanto Preto Quanto Branco: Estudos de Relações Raciais*, vol. 9 (São Paulo: T. A. Queiroz, 1985); Antônio Sérgio Alfredo Guimarães, *Racismo E Anti-Racismo No Brasil* (São Paulo: FUSP [Fundação de Apoio à Universidade de São Paulo], 2005).

36 Amy C. Steinbugler, *Beyond Loving: Intimate Racework in Lesbian, Gay, and Straight Interracial Relationships* (New York: Oxford University Press, 2012).

37 Michéle Lamont, *Money, Morals, and Manners: The Culture of the French and American Upper-Middle Class* (Chicago, IL: University of Chicago Press, 1992); *The Dignity of Working Men: Morality and the Boundaries of Race, Class, and Immigration* (Cambridge, MA: Harvard University Press, 2000); Michèle Lamont et al., *Getting Respect: Responding to Stigma and Discrimination in the United States, Brazil, and Israel* (Princeton, NJ: Princeton University Press, 2016).

38 Kennedy, *Interracial Intimacies*.

39 Jennifer Lee and Frank D. Bean, *The Diversity Paradox: Immigration and the Color Line in Twenty-First Century America* (New York: Russell Sage Foundation, 2010); Nogueira, *Tanto Preto Quanto Branco*, 9.

40 Moran, *Interracial Intimacy*.

41 Kennedy, *Interracial Intimacies*.

42 Joane Nagel, *Race, Ethnicity, and Sexuality: Intimate Intersections, Forbidden Frontiers* (New York: Oxford University Press, 2003).

43 Hortense Powdermaker, *After Freedom: A Cultural Study in the Deep South* (New York: Viking Press, 1939).

44 John St. Clair Drake and H. R. Cayton, *Black Metropolis* (New York: Harcourt, Brace, and World, 1945), 181.

45 Kennedy, *Interracial Intimacies*.

46 Ida B. Wells-Barnett, Frederick Douglass, and the Society for the Furtherance of the Brotherhood of Man, *Southern Horrors: Lynch Law in All Its Phases* (New York: *New York Age*, 1892); Ida B. Wells-Barnett and Alfreda M. Duster, *Crusade for Justice: The Autobiography of Ida B. Wells* (Chicago, IL: University of Chicago Press, 1970), 64.

47 Gunnar Myrdal, *An American Dilemma: The Negro Problem and American Democracy, New York* (New York: Harper Brothers, 1944).

48 Myrdal, *American Dilemma*.

49 Drake and Cayton, *Black Metropolis*, 181.

50 Lawrence Bobo, James R. Kluegel, and Ryan A. Smith, "Laissez-Faire Racism: The Crystallization of a Kinder, Gentler, Anti-Black Ideology," *Racial Attitudes in the 1990s: Continuity and Change*, ed. Steven Tuch and Jack Martin (Westport, CT: Praeger, 1997).

51 These ideas were first discussed in Eduardo Bonilla-Silva's *White Supremacy and Racism in the Post–Civil Rights Era* (New York: Lynne Rienner, 2001) and later developed in his *Racism without Racists: Color-Blind Racism and the Persistence of Racial Inequality in the United States* (Lanham, MD: Rowman and Littlefield, 2006).

52 Zhenchao Qian and Daniel T. Lichter, "Changing Patterns of Interracial Marriage in a Multiracial Society," *Journal of Marriage and Family* 73, no. 5 (2011); US Census Bureau, "Interracial and Interethnic Coupled Households Appendix Tables," *Households and Families: 2010 Census Brief*, 2012, http://www.census.gov.

53 Dan Rodríguez-García, "Intermarriage and Integration Revisited: International Experiences and Cross-Disciplinary Approaches," *Annals of the American Academy of Political and Social Science* 662, no. 1 (2015); Miri Song, "Is Intermarriage a Good Indicator of Integration?," *Journal of Ethnic and Migration Studies* 35, no. 2 (2009); Erica Chito Childs, *Navigating Interracial Borders: Black-White Couples and Their Social Worlds* (New Brunswick, NJ: Rutgers University Press, 2005); Vasquez-Tokos, *Marriage Vows*; Kumiko Nemoto, *Racing Romance: Love, Power, and Desire among Asian American / White Couples* (New Brunswick, NJ: Rutgers University Press, 2009); Heather M. Dalmage, *Tripping on the Color Line:*

Black-White Multiracial Families in a Racially Divided World (New Brunswick, NJ: Rutgers University Press, 2000); Steinbugler, *Beyond Loving.*

54 Kim M. Williams, *Mark One or More: Civil Rights in Multiracial America* (Ann Arbor: University of Michigan Press, 2006).

55 Lee and Bean, *Diversity Paradox.*

56 Karen R. Humes, Nicholas A. Jones, and Roberto R. Ramirez, "Overview of Race and Hispanic Origin: 2010," US Census Bureau, March 2011, https://www.census .gov/content/dam/Census/library/publications/2011/dec/c2010br-02.pdf.

57 Eduardo Bonilla-Silva, "We Are All Americans!: The Latin Americanization of Racial Stratification in the USA," *Race and Society* 5, no. 1 (2002); G. Reginald Daniel, *Race and Multiraciality in Brazil and the United States: Converging Paths?* (University Park: Pennsylvania State University Press, 2006); Carl N. Degler, *Neither Black nor White: Slavery and Race Relations in Brazil and the United States* (Madison: University of Wisconsin Press, 1986); Skidmore, "Bi-racial U.S.A."

58 E. A. Golebiowska, "The Contours and Etiology of Whites' Attitudes toward Black-White Interracial Marriage," *Journal of Black Studies* 38, no. 2 (2007); M. J. Rosenfeld, "Racial, Educational and Religious Endogamy in the United States: A Comparative Historical Perspective," *Social Forces* 87, no. 1 (2008); Qian and Lichter, "Changing Patterns."

59 Matthijs Kalmijn, "Trends in Black/White Intermarriage," *Social Forces* 72 (1993).

60 M. Belinda Tucker and Claudia Mitchell-Kernan, "New Trends in Black American Interracial Marriage: The Social Structural Context," *Journal of Marriage and the Family* 52, no. 1 (1990).

61 Magnus Morner, *Race Mixture in the History of Latin America* (Boston, MA: Little Brown, 1967).

62 Telles, *Race in Another America.*

63 Muriel Nazzari, "Concubinage in Colonial Brazil: The Inequalities of Race, Class, and Gender," *Journal of Family History* 21, no. 2 (1996).

64 Anthony Marx, *Making Race and Nation: A Comparison of the United States, South Africa, and Brazil* (New York: Cambridge University Press, 1998); Degler, *Neither Black nor White.*

65 Herbert Klein and Francisco Vidal Luna, *Slavery in Brazil* (New York: Cambridge University Press, 2010).

66 Oliveira Vianna, *Populações Meridionaes Do Brasil* (Brasilia: Senado Federal, 1952), 181; Daniel, *Race and Multiraciality*; William Edward Burghardt Du Bois, "The Future of Africa in America (April 1942)," in *Against Racism: Unpublished Essays, Papers, Addresses, 1887–1961*, ed. Herbert Aptheker (Amherst: University of Massachusetts Press, 1985), 181.

67 Thomas E. Skidmore, *Black into White: Race and Nationality in Brazilian Thought* (New York: Oxford University Press, 1974); Nancy Stepan, *The Hour of Eugenics: Race, Gender, and Nation in Latin America* (Ithaca, NY: Cornell University Press, 1991); Marisol De la Cadena, Indigenous Mestizos: The Politics of Race and Culture in Cuzco, Peru, 1919–1991 (Durham, NC: Duke University Press, 2000).

68 D. J. Hellwig, ed. *African-American Reflections on Brazil's Racial Paradise* (Philadelphia, PA: Temple University Press, 1992), 52; Du Bois, "Future of Africa," 181.

69 Abdias Do Nascimento, *Brazil, Mixture or Massacre? Essays in the Genocide of a Black People* (Dover, MA: Majority Press, 1989).

70 Gilberto Freyre, *The Masters and the Slaves: A Study in the Development of Brazilian Civilization* (Berkeley: University of California Press, 1933); Guimarães, *Racismo E Anti-Racismo*; Guimarães, "Racial Democracy," in *Imagining Brazil (Global Encounters)*, ed. Jessé Souza and Valter Sinder (Lanham, MD: Lexington, 2005).

71 Freyre, *Masters and the Slaves.*

72 Guimarães, "Racial Democracy."

73 Telles, *Race in Another America.*

74 Degler, *Neither Black nor White.*

75 Edward E. Telles and Christina A. Sue, "Race Mixture: Boundary Crossing in Comparative Perspective," *Annual Review of Sociology* 35 (2009).

76 My translation of Thales de Azevedo, *As Elites De Côr: Um Estudo Da Ascensão Social* (São Paulo: Companhia Editora Nacional, 1955), 79.

77 Michael G. Hanchard, *Orpheus and Power: The Movimento Negro of Rio De Janeiro and São Paulo, Brazil, 1945–1988* (Princeton, NJ: Princeton University Press, 1993); Marx, *Making Race and Nation.*

78 Melissa Nobles, *Shades of Citizenship: Race and the Census in Modern Politics* (Stanford, CA: Stanford University Press, 2000).

79 Mala Htun, "From 'Racial Democracy' to Affirmative Action: Changing State Policy on Race in Brazil," *Latin American Research Review* 39, no. 1 (2004); Tianna S. Paschel and Mark Sawyer, "Contesting Politics as Usual: Black Social Movements, Globalization, and Race Policy in Latin America," *Souls* 10, no. 3 (2008).

80 Graziella Moraes da Silva, "Ações Afirmativas No Brasil E Na África Do Sul," *Tempo Social, Revista de Sociologia da USP* 18, no. 2 (2006); Seth Racusen, "Fictions of Identity and Brazilian Affirmative Action," *National Black Law Journal* 21, no. 3 (2010).

81 Graziella Moraes da Silva and Elisa P. Reis, "Perceptions of Racial Discrimination among Black Professionals in Rio De Janeiro," *Latin American Research Review* 46, no. 2 (2011).

82 Bailey, *Legacies of Race*; Telles, *Race in Another America.*

83 Silva and Paixão, "Mixed and Unequal"; Marcelo Paixão and Luiz M. Carvano, *Relatório Anual Das Desigualdades Raciais No Brasil, 2007–2008* (Rio de Janeiro: Garamond Universitária, 2008); Telles, *Race in Another America*; Carlos Hasenbalg, *Discriminação E Desigualdades Raciais No Brasil* (Rio de Janeiro: Graal, 1979); Nelson do Valle Silva and Carlos Hasenbalg, "Relações Raciais No Brasil Contemporâneo" (Rio de Janeiro: Rio Fundo Editora, 1992).

84 Robin E. Sheriff, *Dreaming Equality: Color, Race, and Racism in Urban Brazil* (New Brunswick, NJ: Rutgers University Press, 2001); Laura Moutinho, *Razão, "Cor" E Desejo* (São Paulo: UNESP, 2004).

85 Carlos Antonio Costa Ribeiro and Nelson do Valle Silva, "Cor, Educação E Casamento: Tendências Da Seletividade Marital No Brasil, 1960 a 2000," *DADOS* 52, no. 1 (2009); José Luis Petruccelli, "Seletividade Por Cor E Escolhas Conjugais No Brasil Dos 90," *Estudos Afro-Asiaticos* 23, no. 1 (2001); Telles, *Race in Another America*.

86 Telles, *Race in Another America*; Petruccelli, "Seletividade Por Cor."

87 Osagie Obasogie, *Blinded by Sight: Seeing Race through the Eyes of the Blind* (Stanford, CA: Stanford University Press, 2014).

88 Robert J. Wuthnow, "Taking Talk Seriously: Religious Discourse as Social Practice," *Journal for the Scientific Study of Religion* 50, no. 1 (2011).

89 Jessie Bernard, *The Future of Marriage* (New Haven, CT: Yale University Press, 1982).

90 Telles, *Race in Another America*.

91 Christie D. Batson, Zhenchao Qian, and Daniel T. Lichter, "Interracial and Intraracial Patterns of Mate Selection among America's Diverse Black Populations," *Journal of Marriage and Family* 68, no. 3 (2006).

92 Guimarães, "Racial Democracy."

93 Nogueira, *Tanto Preto Quanto Branco*, 9.

94 Guimarães, *Racismo E Anti-Racismo*; Graziella Moraes da Silva and Elisa P. Reis, "The Multiple Dimensions of Racial Mixture in Rio de Janeiro, Brazil: From Whitening to Brazilian Negritude," *Ethnic and Racial Studies* 35, no. 3 (2011): 382–99; Telles and Sue, "Race Mixture."

95 Instituto Brasileiro de Geografía e Estadística (IBGE), "Pesquisa Nacional por Amostra de Domicílios (PNAD) 2005–2006," accessed January 5, 2008, https://ww2.ibge.gov.br/home/estatistica/pesquisas/pesquisa_resultados.php?id_pesquisa =40.

96 Silva and Reis, "Perceptions of Racial Discrimination."

97 Edward E. Telles, "Racial Ambiguity among the Brazilian Population," *Ethnic and Racial Studies* 25, no. 3 (2002); Rodolfo Espino and Michael M. Franz, "Latino Phenotypic Discrimination Revisited: The Impact of Skin Color on Occupational Status," *Social Science Quarterly* 83, no. 2 (2002); Telles, *Race in Another America*.

98 Lee and Bean, *Diversity Paradox*.

99 Robert S. Weiss, *Learning from Strangers: The Art and Method of Qualitative Interview Studies* (New York: Free Press, 1995).

100 See Christine Schwartz and Robert D. Mare, "Trends in Educational Assortative Marriage from 1940 to 2003," *Demography* 43 (2005).

101 Margaret E. Greene and Vijayendra Rao, "The Marriage Squeeze and the Rise in Informal Marriage in Brazil," *Social Biology* 42, no. 1–2 (1995).

102 Marcos A. Rangel, "Marriage, Cohabitation, and Intrahousehold Bargaining: Evidence from Brazilian Couples," in *Working Paper* (2003).

103 Brazilian Federal Constitution, article 226, paragraph 3 (1988).

104 Larry L. Bumpass, James A. Sweet, and Andrew Cherlin, "The Role of Cohabitation in Declining Rates of Marriage," *Journal of Marriage and the Family* 53, no. 4 (1991).

105 Wendy D. Manning and Pamela J. Smock, "Why Marry? Race and the Transition to Marriage among Cohabitors," *Demography* (1995); Pamela J. Smock, "Cohabitation in the United States: An Appraisal of Research Themes, Findings, and Implications," *Annual Review of Sociology* 26, no. 1 (2000).

106 Erica Chito Childs, "Looking behind the Stereotypes of the 'Angry Black Woman': An Exploration of Black Women's Responses to Interracial Relationships," *Gender & Society* 19, no. 4 (2005).

107 Rogers Brubaker, *Ethnicity without Groups* (Cambridge, MA: Harvard University Press, 2004).

108 Benedict Anderson, *Imagined Communities: Reflections on the Origin and Spread of Nationalism*, rev. and extended ed. (New York: Verso, 1991).

109 Mary Waters, *Ethnic Options: Choosing Identities in America* (Berkeley: University of California Press, 1990).

110 Dalmage, *Tripping on the Color Line*; Chito Childs, *Navigating Interracial Borders*.

111 Daniel, *Race and Multiraciality*; Skidmore, *Black into White*; Hellwig, *African-American Reflections*.

112 Daniel, *Race and Multiraciality*; Marx, *Making Race and Nation*; Skidmore, "Bi-racial U.S.A."

113 Telles, *Race in Another America*; Bailey, *Legacies of Race*.

114 Joseph, *Race on the Move*; Silva and Reis, "Perceptions of Racial Discrimination"; Helen Marrow, "To Be or Not to Be (Hispanic or Latino): Brazilian Racial and Ethnic Identity in the United States," *Ethnicities* 3, no. 4 (2003).

115 Michèle Lamont et al., *Getting Respect*.

116 Chito Childs, *Navigating Interracial Borders*; Vasquez-Tokos, *Marriage Vows*; Nemoto, *Racing Romance*; Dalmage, *Tripping on the Color Line*; Steinbugler, *Beyond Loving*.

117 Austin J. Staley, "Racial Democracy in Brazilian Marriage: Toward a Typology of Negro-White Intermarriage in Five Brazilian Communities," *American Catholic Sociological Review* 21, no. 2 (1960); Zelinda dos Santos Barros, "Casais Inter-Raciais E Suas Representações Acerca De Raça" (Bahia, Brazil: Universidade Federal da Bahia, 2003); Moutinho, *Razão, "Cor" E Desejo*.

CHAPTER 1. PREFERENCES AND THE ROMANTIC CAREER

1 Erica Chito Childs, *Navigating Interracial Borders: Black-White Couples and Their Social Worlds* (New Brunswick, NJ: Rutgers University Press, 2005), 118.

2 Rosalind King and Jenifer Bratter, "A Path toward Interracial Marriage: Women's First Partners and Husbands across Racial Lines," *Sociological Quarterly* 48 (2007); Richard Lewis and George Yancey, "Biracial Marriages in the United States: An Analysis of Variation in Family Member Support," *Sociological Spectrum* 15, no. 4 (1995).

3 George Yancey, "Who Interracially Dates: An Examination of the Characteristics of Those Who Have Interracially Dated," *Journal of Comparative Family Studies* 33, no. 2 (2002); K. M. Kouri and M. Lasswell, "Black-White Marriages: Social

Change and Intergenerational Mobility," *Marriage and Family Review* 19, no. 3–4 (1993).

4 Peter Blau, Terry Blum, and Joseph E. Schwartz, "Heterogeneity and Intermarriage," *American Sociological Review* 47 (1982).

5 Howard S. Becker, "Becoming a Marihuana User," *American Journal of Sociology* 59, no. 3 (1953).

6 Anselm Strauss, *Mirrors and Masks: The Search for Identity* (London: Martin Robertson, 1969).

7 Patricia Hill Collins, *Black Sexual Politics* (New York: Routledge, 2004).

8 Chito Childs, *Navigating Interracial Borders*, 68, 176.

9 Amy C. Wilkins, *Wannabes, Goths, and Christians: The Boundaries of Sex, Style, and Status* (Chicago, IL: University of Chicago Press, 2008).

10 Mara Viveros Vigoya, "Más Que Una Cuestión De Piel: Determinantes Sociales Y Orientaciones Subjetivas En Los Encuentros Y Desencuentros Heterosexuales Interraciales En Bogotá," in *Raza, Etnicidad Y Sexualidades: Ciudadanía Y Multiculturalismo En América Latina*, ed. Peter Wade, Fernando Urrea, and Mara Viveros (Bogotá: Universidad Nacional de Colombia, Facultad de Ciencias Humanas, Centro de Estudios Sociales [CES], 2008).

11 Tanya Katerí Hernández, "Sexual Harassment and Racial Disparity: The Mutual Construction of Gender and Race," *Gender, Race, and Justice* 4 (2001); Tanya Katerí Hernández, "Sex in the [Foreign] City: Commodification and the Female Sex Tourist," in *Rethinking Commodification: Cases and Readings in Law and Culture*, ed. Joan Williams and Martha Ertman (New York: New York University Press, 2005); Erica Lorraine Williams, *Sex Tourism in Bahia: Ambiguous Entanglements* (Urbana: University of Illinois Press, 2013).

12 Laura Moutinho, *Razão, "Cor" E Desejo* (São Paulo: UNESP, 2004).

13 Kumiko Nemoto, *Racing Romance: Love, Power, and Desire among Asian American / White Couples* (New Brunswick, NJ: Rutgers University Press, 2009).

14 Amy C. Steinbugler, *Beyond Loving: Intimate Racework in Lesbian, Gay, and Straight Interracial Relationships* (New York: Oxford University Press, 2012).

15 Tomas Jimenez, "Affiliative Ethnic Identity: A More Elastic Link between Ethnic Ancestry and Culture," *Ethnic and Racial Studies* 33 (2010); C. Yodanis, S. R. Lauer, and Risako Ota, "Inter-ethnic Romantic Relationships: Enacting Affiliative Ethnic Identities," *Journal of Marriage and Family* 74 (2012).

16 Erica Chito Childs, "Looking behind the Stereotypes of the 'Angry Black Woman': An Exploration of Black Women's Responses to Interracial Relationships," *Gender & Society* 19, no. 4 (2005).

17 For a discussion of *morena* as a census category, see Harris et al. (1993) and Telles (1995).

18 Marvin Scott and Stanford Lyman, "Accounts," *American Sociological Review* 33 (1968).

19 Gresham M. Sykes and David Matza, "Techniques of Neutralization: A Theory of Delinquency," *Sociological Review* 22, no. 6 (1957).

20 Chito Childs, "Looking behind the Stereotypes."

21 Aaron Gullickson and Florencia Torche, "Patterns of Racial and Educational Assortative Mating in Brazil," *Demography* 51, no. 3 (2014); Edward E. Telles, *Race in Another America: The Significance of Skin Color in Brazil* (Princeton, NJ: Princeton University Press, 2004).

22 Thales de Azevedo, *As Elites De Côr: Um Estudo Da Ascensão Social* (São Paulo: Companhia Editora Nacional, 1955).

23 Chinyere K. Osuji, "Difference or Convergence: Black-White Couples and Race Relations in the US and Brazil," *Qualitative Sociology* 37 (2014).

24 For this pattern in Afro-Brazilian families, see Elizabeth Hordge-Freeman, *The Color of Love: Racial Features, Stigma, and Socialization in Afro-Brazilian Families* (Austin: University of Texas Press, 2015).

25 France Winddance Twine, *Racism in a Racial Democracy: The Maintenance of White Supremacy in Brazil* (New Brunswick, NJ: Rutgers University Press, 1998); Robin E. Sheriff, *Dreaming Equality: Color, Race, and Racism in Urban Brazil* (New Brunswick, NJ: Rutgers University Press, 2001).

26 Stanley Bailey, *Legacies of Race: Identities, Attitudes, and Politics in Brazil* (Palo Alto, CA: Stanford University Press, 2009); Livio Sansone, *Blackness without Ethnicity: Constructing Race in Brazil* (New York: Palgrave Macmillan, 2003).

27 Michael O. Emerson, Rachel Tolbert Kimbro, and George Yancey, "Contact Theory Extended: The Effects of Prior Racial Contact on Current Social Ties," *Social Science Quarterly* 83, no. 3 (2002).

28 Cynthia Feliciano, Belinda Robnett, and Golnaz Komaie, "Gendered Racial Exclusion among White Internet Daters," *Social Science Research* 38 (2009).

29 Nemoto, *Racing Romance*.

30 Collins, *Black Sexual Politics*.

31 Charles Horton Cooley, *Human Nature and the Social Order* (New York: Scribners, 1902).

32 Hortense Powdermaker, *After Freedom: A Cultural Study in the Deep South* (New York: Viking Press, 1939), 41.

33 Margaret L. Hunter, *Race, Gender, and the Politics of Skin Tone* (New York: Routledge, 2005).

34 Nemoto, *Racing Romance*.

35 Denise Brennan, *What's Love Got to Do with It? Transnational Desires and Sex Tourism in the Dominican Republic* (Durham, NC: Duke University Press, 2004); Kamala Kempadoo and Jo Doezema, *Global Sex Workers: Rights, Resist, Redefinition* (New York: Routledge, 1998); Hernández, "Sexual Harassment and Racial Disparity."

36 Hernández, "Sexual Harassment and Racial Disparity"; Joane Nagel, *Race, Ethnicity, and Sexuality: Intimate Intersections, Forbidden Frontiers* (New York: Oxford University Press, 2003); Nemoto, *Racing Romance*; Williams, *Sex Tourism in Bahia*.

37 Chito Childs, "Looking behind the Stereotypes," 85, 86; Averil Y. Clarke, *Inequalities of Love: College-Educated Black Women and the Barriers to Romance and*

Family (Durham, NC: Duke University Press, 2011); Mark Sawyer, "Don't Even Try to Blame It on Rio," *The Root*, July 3, 2008, http://www.theroot.com/dont -even-try-to-blame-it-on-rio-1790899983.

38 Mary Waters, *Ethnic Options: Choosing Identities in America* (Berkeley: University of California Press, 1990).

39 Chito Childs, "Looking behind the Stereotypes"; Chito Childs, *Navigating Interracial Borders*. Also see Hernández, "Sexual Harassment and Racial Disparity," for a discussion of white women finding desirability through sex tourism.

40 A. D. Powell and A. S. Kahn, "Racial Differences in Women's Desires to Be Thin," *International Journal of Eating Disorders* 17 (1995); S. M. Desmond et al., "Black and White Adolescents' Perceptions of Their Weight," *Journal of School Health* 59 (1989).

41 C. L. Glasser, B. Robnett, and C. Feliciano, "Internet Daters' Body Type Preferences: Race-Ethnic and Gender Differences," *Sex Roles* 61, no. 14 (2009).

42 Chinyere K. Osuji, "An African/Nigerian-American Studying Black-White Couples in Los Angeles and Rio De Janeiro," in *Race and the Politics of Knowledge Production: Diaspora and Black Transnational Scholarship in the United States and Brazil*, ed. Gladys Mitchell-Walthour and Elizabeth Hordge-Freeman (New York: Palgrave MacMillan, 2016).

43 Daniella Dorneles de Andrade, "On Norms and Bodies: Findings from Field Research on Cosmetic Surgery in Rio de Janeiro, Brazil," *Reproductive Health Matters* 18, no. 35 (2010).

44 Blau, Blum, and Schwartz, "Heterogeneity and Intermarriage."

45 Osuji, "Difference or Convergence."

46 Clarke, *Inequalities of Love*.

47 Tonya Mosley, "Finding a Black Man: Dating Woes for Seattle's Black Women," Kuow.org, October 31, 2013, http://kuow.org/post/finding-black-man-dating-woes -seattles-black-women; Charlie Penn, "Why Is It So Hard for Black Women to Find the Love They Deserve," *Essence*, November 5, 2015, http://www.essence.com; Zahra Barnes, "The Ugly Truth about Dating Online as a Woman of Color," *Self*, June 6, 2016, http://www.self.com.

CHAPTER 2. BOUNDARIES OF BLACKNESS

1 Ann Swidler, "Culture in Action: Symbols and Strategies," *American Sociological Review* (1986); Michele Lamont and Jonathan H. Turner, "Culture and Identity," in *Handbook of Sociological Theory* (New York: Plenum, 2001).

2 Edward E. Telles, *Race in Another America: The Significance of Skin Color in Brazil* (Princeton, NJ: Princeton University Press, 2004).

3 Charles Horton Cooley, *Human Nature and the Social Order* (New York: Scribners, 1902).

4 William Edward Burghardt Du Bois, *The Souls of Black Folk: Essays and Sketches* (Chicago, IL: A. C. McClurg and Co., 1903).

5 See the following for discussions of these issues among multiracial Americans: Nikki Khanna, "The Role of Reflected Appraisals in Racial Identity: The Case of

Multiracial Asians," *Social Psychology Quarterly* 67, no. 2 (2004); Nikki Khanna, "If You're Half Black, You're Just Black: Reflected Appraisals and the Persistence of the One-Drop Rule," *Sociological Quarterly* 51, no. 1 (2010); Miri Song and Peter Aspinall, "Is Racial Mismatch a Problem for Young 'Mixed Race' People in Britain? The Findings of Qualitative Research," *Ethnicities* 12, no. 6 (2012).

6 Telles, *Race in Another America*; Graziella Morães da Silva and Marcelo Paixão, "Mixed and Unequal: New Perspectives on Brazilian Ethnoracial Relations," in *Pigmentocracies: Ethnicity, Race and Color in Latin America*, ed. Edward Telles and PERLA (Chapel Hill: University of North Carolina Press, 2014).

7 Melissa Herman, "Do You See Me as I Am? How Observers' Backgrounds Affect Their Perceptions of Multiracial Faces," *Social Psychology Quarterly* 73, no. 1 (2010).

8 Rogers Brubaker, *Ethnicity without Groups* (Cambridge, MA: Harvard University Press, 2004).

9 Stanley Bailey, *Legacies of Race: Identities, Attitudes, and Politics in Brazil* (Palo Alto, CA: Stanford University Press, 2009); Mara Loveman, *National Colors: Racial Classification and the State in Latin America* (New York: Oxford University Press, 2014); Livio Sansone, *Blackness without Ethnicity: Constructing Race in Brazil* (New York: Palgrave Macmillan, 2003).

10 Gladys Mitchell-Walthour, "Racism in a Racialized Democracy and Support for Affirmative Action Policy in Salvador and São Paulo, Brazil," in *Re-examining the Black Atlantic: Afro-Descendants and Development* (Lansing: Michigan State University Press, 2012).

11 Benedict Anderson, *Imagined Communities: Reflections on the Origin and Spread of Nationalism*, rev. and extended ed. (New York: Verso, 1991).

12 Michael Dawson, *Black Visions* (Chicago, IL: University of Chicago Press, 2001).

13 See Tatum (2003) for a discussion of black students' tactics in predominantly white spaces.

14 Graziella Moraes da Silva and Elisa P. Reis, "Perceptions of Racial Discrimination among Black Professionals in Rio De Janeiro," *Latin American Research Review* 46, no. 2 (2011).

15 Edward Telles and PERLA (Project on Ethnicity and Race in Latin America), ed., *Pigmentocracies: Ethnicity, Race and Color in Latin America* (Chapel Hill: University of North Carolina Press, 2014).

16 Silva and Paixão, "Mixed and Unequal."

17 Oracy Nogueira, *Tanto Preto Quanto Branco: Estudos de Relações Raciais*, vol. 9 (São Paulo: T. A. Queiroz, 1985), 9.

18 Alondra Nelson, *The Social Life of DNA: Race, Reparations, and Reconciliation after the Genome* (Boston, MA: Beacon Press, 2016).

19 Telles, *Race in Another America*.

20 Silva and Reis, "Perceptions of Racial Discrimination."

21 Silva and Paixão, "Mixed and Unequal."

22 Marvin Harris et al., "Who Are the Whites? Imposed Census Categories and the Racial Demography of Brazil," *Social Forces* 72, no. 2 (1993): 451–62.

23 Telles, *Race in Another America.*

24 Silva and Reis, "Perceptions of Racial Discrimination"; Michèle Lamont et al., *Getting Respect: Responding to Stigma and Discrimination in the United States, Brazil, and Israel* (Princeton, NJ: Princeton University Press, 2016).

25 Harris et al. "Who Are the Whites?"

26 Telles, *Race in Another America.*

27 Erica Lorraine Williams, *Sex Tourism in Bahia: Ambiguous Entanglements* (Urbana: University of Illinois Press, 2013); Kia Lily Caldwell, *Negras in Brazil: Re-envisioning Black Women, Citizenship, and the Politics of Identity* (New Brunswick, NJ: Rutgers University Press, 2007).

28 Kia Lily Caldwell, "'Look at Her Hair': The Body Politics of Black Womanhood in Brazil," *Transforming Anthropology* 11 (2003).

29 Telles, *Race in Another America.*

30 Elizabeth Hordge-Freeman, *The Color of Love: Racial Features, Stigma, and Socialization in Afro-Brazilian Families* (Austin: University of Texas Press, 2015).

31 Osagie Obasogie, *Blinded by Sight: Seeing Race through the Eyes of the Blind* (Stanford, CA: Stanford University Press, 2014).

32 Telles, *Race in Another America.*

33 Edward Telles and Stanley Bailey, "Understanding Latin American Beliefs about Racial Inequality," *American Journal of Sociology* 118, no. 6 (2013); Peter Fry and Yvonne Maggie, "Cotas Raciais: Construindo Um País Dividido?," *Econômica: Revista da Pós-Graduação em Economia da UFF* 6, no. 1 (2004).

34 See France Winddance Twine, *Racism in a Racial Democracy: The Maintenance of White Supremacy in Brazil* (New Brunswick, NJ: Rutgers University Press, 1998), for a discussion of a small town that used to have plantation slavery yet where many Afro-Brazilians denied it had operated.

35 Obasogie, *Blinded by Sight*; Tanya Golash-Boza, *Yo Soy Negro: Blackness in Peru* (Gainesville: University Press of Florida, 2012).

36 George Reid Andrews, *Afro-Latin America, 1800–2000* (New York: Oxford University Press, 2004).

37 Michael G. Hanchard, *Orpheus and Power: The Movimento Negro of Rio De Janeiro and São Paulo, Brazil, 1945–1988* (Princeton, NJ: Princeton University Press, 1993); Sansone, *Blackness without Ethnicity.*

38 Herbert Klein and Francisco Vidal Luna, *Slavery in Brazil* (New York: Cambridge University Press, 2010).

39 Sandra S. Smith and Mignon R. Moore, "Intraracial Diversity and Relations among African-Americans: Closeness among Black Students at a Predominantly White University," *American Journal of Sociology* 106, no. 1 (2000). For a similar dynamic in a different subsection of the black community, black lesbians, see Mignon Moore, *Invisible Families: Gay Identities, Relationships, and Motherhood among Black Women* (Berkeley: University of California Press, 2011).

40 Zhenchao Qian and Daniel T. Lichter, "Changing Patterns of Interracial Marriage in a Multiracial Society," *Journal of Marriage and Family* 73, no. 5 (2011)

41 Telles and PERLA, *Pigmentocracies.*

42 Richard A. Peterson and Roger M. Kern, "Changing Highbrow Taste: From Snob to Omnivore," *American Sociological Review* 61, no. 5 (1996).

43 Suzanne Macartney, Alemayehu Bishaw, and Kayla Fontenot, "Poverty Rates for Selected Detailed Race and Hispanic Groups by State and Place: 2007–2011," *American Community Survey Briefs*, 2013, https://www2.census.gov/library/publications/2013/acs/acsbr11-17.pdf.

44 Darnell M. Hunt and Ana-Christina Ramon, *Black Los Angeles: American Dreams and Racial Realities* (New York: New York University Press, 2010).

45 Darién J. Davis, *Avoiding the Dark: Race and the Forging of National Culture in Modern Brazil* (Brookfield, VT: Ashgate, 1999); and "Racial Parity and National Humor: Exploring Brazilian Samba from Noel Rosa to Carmen Miranda," in *Latin American Popular Culture: An Introduction*, ed. William H. Beezley and Linda A. Curcio-Nagy (Wilmington, DE: Scholarly Resources, 2000).

46 Erika V. Hall, Katherine W. Phillips, and Sarah S. Townsend, "A Rose by Another Name? The Consequences of Sub-typing 'African Americans' from 'Blacks,'" *Journal of Experimental Social Psychology* 56 (2015).

47 Cheryl Y. Judice, *Interracial Marriages between Black Women and White Men* (Amherst, NY: Cambria Press, 2008).

48 Randall Kennedy, *Interracial Intimacies: Sex, Marriage, Identity, and Adoption*, 1st ed. (New York: Pantheon, 2003), 74.

49 M. P. P. Root, *Love's Revolution: Interracial Marriage* (Philadelphia, PA: Temple University Press, 2001).

50 Randall Kennedy, *Sellout: The Politics of Racial Betrayal* (New York: Pantheon, 2008).

51 Chinyere K. Osuji, "An African/Nigerian-American Studying Black-White Couples in Los Angeles and Rio De Janeiro," in *Race and the Politics of Knowledge Production: Diaspora and Black Transnational Scholarship in the United States and Brazil*, ed. Gladys Mitchell-Walthour and Elizabeth Hordge-Freeman (New York: Palgrave MacMillan, 2016).

52 Cathy Cohen, *Boundaries of Blackness: AIDS and the Breakdown of Black Politics* (Chicago, IL: University of Chicago Press, 1999).

CHAPTER 3. BOUNDARIES OF WHITENESS

1 Kirk Johnson, Richard Pérez-Peña, and John Eligon, "Rachel Dolezal, in Center of Storm, Is Defiant: 'I Identify as Black,'" *New York Times*, June 16, 2015, http://www.nytimes.com; KXLY, "Raw Interview with Rachel Dolezal," *YouTube*, video, 8:55, June 11, 2015. https://www.youtube.com/watch?v=0KRj_h7vmMM.

2 Rachel Dolezal, "Rachel Dolezal on Her Connection with the 'Black Experience,'" *MSNBC*, video, 2:06, June 16, 2015, http://www.msnbc.com.

3 John Hartigan, *Racial Situations: Class Predicaments of Whiteness in Detroit* (Princeton, NJ: Princeton University Press, 1999); J. R. Feagin and H. Vera, *White Racism: The Basics* (New York: Routledge, 1995); David Roediger, *The Wages*

of Whiteness: Race and the Making of the American Working Class (New York: Verso, 1999); Ruth Frankenberg, *The Social Construction of Whiteness: White Women, Race Matters* (Minneapolis: University of Minnesota Press, 1993); France Winddance Twine, *A White Side of Black Britain: Interracial Intimacy and Racial Literacy* (Durham, NC: Duke University Press, 2010).

4 Monica McDermott, *Working-Class White: The Making and Unmaking of Race Relations* (Berkeley: University of California Press, 2006); Matthew W. Hughey, *White Bound: Nationalists, Antiracists, and the Shared Meanings of Race* (Stanford, CA: Stanford University Press, 2012); Amy C. Wilkins, *Wannabes, Goths, and Christians: The Boundaries of Sex, Style, and Status* (Chicago, IL: University of Chicago Press, 2008).

5 Liv Sovik, "We Are Family: Whiteness in the Brazilian Media," *Journal of Latin American Cultural Studies* 13 (2004); Stephanie Dennison, "Blonde Bombshell: Xuxa and Notions of Whiteness in Brazil," *Journal of Latin American Cultural Studies* 22 (2013); Amelia Simpson, *Xuxa: The Mega-marketing of Gender, Race, and Modernity* (Philadelphia, PA: Temple University Press, 1993).

6 Thomas E. Skidmore, *Black into White: Race and Nationality in Brazilian Thought* (New York: Oxford University Press, 1974).

7 D. J. Hellwig, ed. *African-American Reflections on Brazil's Racial Paradise* (Philadelphia, PA: Temple University Press, 1992), 52; William Edward Burghardt Du Bois, "The Future of Africa in America (April 1942)," in *Against Racism: Unpublished Essays, Papers, Addresses, 1887–1961*, ed. Herbert Aptheker (Amherst: University of Massachusetts Press, 1985), 181.

8 Christina A. Sue, *Land of the Cosmic Race: Race Mixture, Racism, and Blackness in Mexico* (Oxford: Oxford University Press, 2013).

9 Carlos Alberto Figueiredo da Silva and Jorge França Motta, "Relendo O Significado De RaçA," *Revista Augustus* 14 (2009).

10 Edward E. Telles, *Race in Another America: The Significance of Skin Color in Brazil* (Princeton, NJ: Princeton University Press, 2004); Edward Telles and PERLA (Project on Ethnicity and Race in Latin America), ed., *Pigmentocracies: Ethnicity, Race and Color in Latin America* (Chapel Hill: University of North Carolina Press, 2014).

11 Andreas Wimmer, *Ethnic Boundary Making: Institutions, Power, Networks* (New York: Oxford University Press, 2013).

12 Telles, *Race in Another America*; Telles and PERLA, *Pigmentocracies*.

13 Edward E. Telles and René Flores, "Not Just Color: Whiteness, Nation, and Status in Latin America," *Hispanic American Historical Review* 93, no. 3 (2013).

14 Tiffany Joseph, *Race on the Move: Brazilian Migrants and the Global Reconstruction of Race* (Palo Alto, CA: Stanford University Press, 2015); Robin E. Sheriff, *Dreaming Equality: Color, Race, and Racism in Urban Brazil* (New Brunswick, NJ: Rutgers University Press, 2001).

15 For more on Xuxa and whiteness, see Dennison, "Blonde Bombshell"; and Amelia Simpson (1999).

16 Graziella Moraes da Silva and Elisa P. Reis, "Perceptions of Racial Discrimination among Black Professionals in Rio De Janeiro," *Latin American Research Review* 46, no. 2 (2011).

17 J. Feagin and E. O'Brien, *White Men on Race: Power, Privilege, and the Shaping of Cultural Consciousness* (Boston, MA: Beacon Press, 2013).

18 Telles and Flores, "Not Just Color."

19 Telles, *Race in Another America.*

20 Antônio Sérgio Alfredo Guimarães, *Racismo E Anti-Racismo No Brasil* (São Paulo: FUSP [Fundação de Apoio à Universidade de São Paulo], 2005), 185; Oracy Nogueira, *Tanto Preto Quanto Branco: Estudos de Relações Raciais*, vol. 9 (São Paulo: T. A. Queiroz, 1985), 9.

21 C. Yodanis, S. R. Lauer, and Risako Ota, "Inter-ethnic Romantic Relationships: Enacting Affiliative Ethnic Identities," *Journal of Marriage and Family* 74 (2012); Tomas Jimenez, "Affiliative Ethnic Identity: A More Elastic Link between Ethnic Ancestry and Culture," *Ethnic and Racial Studies* 33 (2010).

22 J. Crocker, B. Major, and C. Steele, "Social Stigma," in *The Handbook of Social Psychology*, ed. D. T. Gilbert, S. T. Fiske, and G. Lindzey (Boston, MA: McGraw-Hill, 1998); Michéle Lamont and Nissim Mizrachi, "Ordinary People Doing Extraordinary Things: Responses to Stigmatization in Comparative Perspective," *Ethnic and Racial Studies* 35, no. 3 (2011).

23 Camille Zubrinsky Charles, *Won't You Be My Neighbor? Race, Class, and Residence in Los Angeles* (New York: Russell Sage Foundation, 2009).

24 A diminutive of the word *branco.*

25 Edward E. Telles and Tianna Paschel, "Who Is Black, White, or Mixed Race? How Skin Color, Status, and Nation Shape Racial Classification in Latin America," *American Journal of Sociology* 120, no. 3 (2014).

26 Ellis Monk, "The Consequences of 'Race and Color' in Brazil," *Social Problems* 63 (2016).

27 Stanley Bailey, *Legacies of Race: Identities, Attitudes, and Politics in Brazil* (Palo Alto, CA: Stanford University Press, 2009).

28 Livio Sansone, *Blackness without Ethnicity: Constructing Race in Brazil* (New York: Palgrave Macmillan, 2003).

29 Anthony Marx, *Making Race and Nation: A Comparison of the United States, South Africa, and Brazil* (New York: Cambridge University Press, 1998).

30 Frankenberg, *Social Construction of Whiteness.*

31 Wimmer, *Ethnic Boundary Making.*

32 Frankenberg, *Social Construction of Whiteness*; Feagin and Vera, *White Racism*; Roediger, *Wages of Whiteness.*

33 Herbert Gans, "Symbolic Ethnicity: The Future of Ethnic Groups and Cultures in America," *Ethnic and Racial Studies* 2 (1979).

34 Mary Waters, *Ethnic Options: Choosing Identities in America* (Berkeley: University of California Press, 1990).

35 Stephen Cornell and Douglas Hartmann, *Ethnicity and Race: Making Identities in a Changing World* (Thousand Oaks, CA: Pine Forge Press, 1998).

36 Michael Omi and Howard Winant, *Racial Formation in the United States: From the 1960s to the 1990s*, 3rd ed. (New York: Routledge, 2015).

37 D'Vera Cohn, "American Indian and White, but Not 'Multiracial,'" *Pew Research Center*, June 11, 2015, http://www.pewresearch.org.

38 Randall Kennedy, *Interracial Intimacies: Sex, Marriage, Identity, and Adoption*, 1st ed. (New York: Pantheon, 2003); John Burma, "The Measurement of Negro 'Passing,'" *American Journal of Sociology* 52, no. 1 (1946); E. W. Eckard, "How Many Negroes 'Pass'?," *American Journal of Sociology* 52, no. 6 (1947).

39 Wimmer, *Ethnic Boundary Making*.

40 Wilkins, *Wannabes, Goths, and Christians*.

41 Twine, *White Side of Black Britain*.

42 Erica Chito Childs, "Looking behind the Stereotypes of the 'Angry Black Woman': An Exploration of Black Women's Responses to Interracial Relationships," *Gender & Society* 19, no. 4 (2005); and *Navigating Interracial Borders: Black-White Couples and Their Social Worlds* (New Brunswick, NJ: Rutgers University Press, 2005).

43 Frankenberg, *Social Construction of Whiteness*.

44 France Winddance Twine and Amy C. Steinbugler, "The Gap between Whites and Whiteness: Interracial Intimacy and Racial Literacy," *Du Bois Review* 3, no. 2 (2006).

45 Cornell and Hartmann, *Ethnicity and Race*; Richard Jenkins, *Social Identity* (New York: Routledge, 2008).

CHAPTER 4. BLACK, WHITE, MIXED OR BIRACIAL

1 Wendy Roth, *Race Migrations: Latinos and the Cultural Transformation of Race* (Stanford, CA: Stanford University Press, 2012).

2 Peter Fry et al., *Divisões Perigosas: Políticas Raciais No Brasil Contemporâneo* (Rio de Janeiro: Civilização Brasileira, 2007).

3 Pâmela Oliveira, "MP Investiga Universitários por Fraude no Sistema de Cotas," *Veja*, March 17, 2014, http://veja2.abril.com.br/; Alan Tiago Alves, "Uesb Apura Fraude em Matrículas de 7 Estudantes Declarados Quilombolas," *Globo*, October 19, 2016, http://g1.globo.com.

4 Ruben Berto and Lauro Neta, "Filho de Aposentado da Petrobras Declarou Renda de R$ 450 para Burlar Sistema de Cotas na Uerj," *Globo*, March 17, 2014, https://oglobo.globo.com.

5 Machado Da Costa, Paulo Saldaña, and Felipe Maia, "Comissão Federal para Avaliar Negros Cotistas é Questionada por Advogados," *Folha De São Paulo*, March 8, 2016, http://www1.folha.uol.com.br.

6 Camille Z. Charles et al., *Taming the River: Negotiating the Academic, Financial, and Social Currents in Selective Colleges and Universities* (Princeton, NJ: Princeton University Press, 2009).

7 Herbert Klein and Francisco Vidal Luna, *Slavery in Brazil* (New York: Cambridge University Press, 2010).

8 Thomas E. Skidmore, "Bi-racial U.S.A. vs. Multi-racial Brazil: Is the Contrast Still Valid?," *Journal of Latin American Studies* 25, no. 2 (1993).

9 Edward E. Telles, *Race in Another America: The Significance of Skin Color in Brazil* (Princeton, NJ: Princeton University Press, 2004).

10 Luisa Farah Schwartzman, "Does Money Whiten? Intergenerational Changes in Racial Classification in Brazil," *American Sociological Review* 72, no. 6 (2007).

11 Erica Lorraine Williams, *Sex Tourism in Bahia: Ambiguous Entanglements* (Urbana: University of Illinois Press, 2013).

12 Williams, *Sex Tourism in Bahia*.

13 Kim M. Williams, *Mark One or More: Civil Rights in Multiracial America* (Ann Arbor: University of Michigan Press, 2006).

14 "Virginia Parents Outraged after Walmart Security Allegedly Suspected Father of Kidnapping Biracial Daughters," *Huffington Post*, May 23, 2013, http://www.huffingtonpost.com.

15 Amy C. Steinbugler, *Beyond Loving: Intimate Racework in Lesbian, Gay, and Straight Interracial Relationships* (New York: Oxford University Press, 2012).

16 France Winddance Twine, *A White Side of Black Britain: Interracial Intimacy and Racial Literacy* (Durham, NC: Duke University Press, 2010).

17 DaCosta, *Making Multiracials*; Williams, *Mark One or More*.

18 Tanya Katerí Hernández, *Racial Subordination in Latin America: The Role of the State, Customary Law and the New Civil Rights Response* (Cambridge: Cambridge University Press, 2014).

19 Telles, *Race in Another America*; Stanley Bailey, *Legacies of Race: Identities, Attitudes, and Politics in Brazil* (Palo Alto, CA: Stanford University Press, 2009).

20 João Feres Júnior, Luiz Augusto Campos, and Veronica Toste Daflon, "Fora De Quadro: A Ação Afirmativa Nas Páginas D'o Globo," *Contemporânea* 2 (2011); Verônica Toste Daflon and João Feres Júnior, "Ação Afirmativa Na Revista Veja: Estratégias Editoriais E O Enquadramento Do Debate Público," *Revista Compolítica* 2 (2012).

21 G. Rhodes et al., "Attractiveness of Own-Race, Other-Race, and Mixed-Race Faces," *Perception* 34, no. 3 (2005); Robert L. Reece, "'What Are You Mixed With?': The Effect of Multiracial Identification on Perceived Attractiveness," *Review of Black Political Economy* 43 (2016); J. P. Sims, "Beautiful Stereotypes: The Relationship between Physical Attractiveness and Mixed-Race Identity," *Identities* 19, no. 1 (2012).

22 Cheryl Y. Judice, *Interracial Marriages between Black Women and White Men* (Amherst, NY: Cambria Press, 2008).

23 Williams, *Mark One or More*.

24 Kerry-Ann Rockquemore and David L. Brunsma, *Beyond Black: Biracial Identity in America* (Rowman and Littlefield, 2007).

CHAPTER 5. "A FLY IN THE BUTTERMILK"

1 France Winddance Twine, *A White Side of Black Britain: Interracial Intimacy and Racial Literacy* (Durham, NC: Duke University Press, 2010).

2 These findings were initially published in Chinyere Osuji, "Divergence or Convergence: Black-White Interracial Couples and White Family Reactions in the U.S. and Brazil," Qualitative Sociology 37 (2014).

3 M. P. P. Root, *Love's Revolution: Interracial Marriage* (Philadelphia, PA: Temple University Press, 2001); Erica Chito Childs, *Navigating Interracial Borders: Black-White Couples and Their Social Worlds* (New Brunswick, NJ: Rutgers University Press, 2005); Laura Moutinho, *Razão, "Cor" E Desejo* (São Paulo: UNESP, 2004).

4 Edward E. Telles, *Race in Another America: The Significance of Skin Color in Brazil* (Princeton, NJ: Princeton University Press, 2004).

5 M. J. Rosenfeld, "Racial, Educational and Religious Endogamy in the United States: A Comparative Historical Perspective," Social Forces 87, no. 1 (2008).

6 Patricia Hill Collins, *Black Sexual Politics* (New York: Routledge, 2004), 255.

7 Joel Zito Araújo, *A Negação Do Brasil: O Negro Na Telenovela Brasileira* (São Paulo: Editora SENAC São Paulo, 2000); Jaime do Amparo Alves, "Narratives of Violence: The White Imagination and the Making of Black Masculinity in *City of God*," Sociedade e Cultura 12, no. 2 (2009); Rolf Ribeiro de Souza, "As Representações Do Homem Negro E Suas Consequências," Revista Fórum Identidades 6 (2009).

8 Kia Lily Caldwell, *Negras in Brazil: Re-envisioning Black Women, Citizenship, and the Politics of Identity* (New Brunswick, NJ: Rutgers University Press, 2007); J. D. Hall, *Revolt against Chivalry: Jessie Daniel Ames and the Women's Campaign against Lynching* (New York: Columbia University Press, 1993).

9 A. L. Ferber, *White Man Falling: Race, Gender, and White Supremacy* (Rowman and Littlefield, 1998).

10 Luisa Farah Schwartzman, "Does Money Whiten? Intergenerational Changes in Racial Classification in Brazil," American Sociological Review 72, no. 6 (2007); Carlos Antonio Costa Ribeiro and Nelson do Valle Silva, "Cor, Educação E Casamento: Tendências Da Seletividade Marital No Brasil, 1960 a 2000," DADOS 52, no. 1 (2009).

11 Rachel F. Moran, *Interracial Intimacy: The Regulation of Race and Romance* (Chicago, IL: University of Chicago Press, 2001).

12 Mara Viveros Vigoya, "Más Que Una Cuestión De Piel: Determinantes Sociales Y Orientaciones Subjetivas En Los Encuentros Y Desencuentros Heterosexuales Interraciales En Bogotá," in *Raza, Etnicidad Y Sexualidades: Ciudadanía Y Multiculturalismo En América Latina*, ed. Peter Wade, Fernando Urrea, and Mara Viveros (Bogotá: Universidad Nacional de Colombia, Facultad de Ciencias Humanas, Centro de Estudios Sociales [CES], 2008).

13 Nadine Fernandez, *Revolutionizing Romance: Interracial Couples in Contemporary Cuba* (New Brunswick, NJ: Rutgers University Press, 2010).

14 Lawrence D. Bobo et al., "The Real Record on Racial Attitudes," in *Social Trends in American Life: Findings from the General Social Survey since 1972*, ed. Peter V. Marsden (Princeton, NJ: Princeton University Press, 2012).

15 Mark Sawyer, *Racial Politics in Post-revolutionary Cuba* (Cambridge: Cambridge University Press, 2006).

16 A. R. Radcliffe-Brown, "On Joking Relationships," *Africa* 13, no. 3 (1940).

17 Donna Goldstein, "'Interracial' Sex and Racial Democracy in Brazil: Twin Concepts?," *American Anthropologist* 101, no. 3 (1999); Donna M. Goldstein, *Laughter Out of Place: Race, Class, Violence, and Sexuality in a Rio Shantytown* (Berkeley: University of California Press, 2003); Christina A. Sue and Tanya Golash-Boza, "'It Was Only a Joke': How Racial Humour Fuels Colour-Blind Ideologies in Mexico and Peru," *Ethnic and Racial Studies* 36, no. 10 (2013).

18 Elizabeth Hordge-Freeman, *The Color of Love: Racial Features, Stigma, and Socialization in Afro-Brazilian Families* (Austin: University of Texas Press, 2015); France Winddance Twine, *Racism in a Racial Democracy: The Maintenance of White Supremacy in Brazil* (New Brunswick, NJ: Rutgers University Press, 1998); Robin E. Sheriff, *Dreaming Equality: Color, Race, and Racism in Urban Brazil* (New Brunswick, NJ: Rutgers University Press, 2001); Mónica Moreno Figueroa, "Negociando La Pertenéncia: Família y Mestizaje en México," in *Raza, Etnicidad Y Sexualidades: Ciudadanía Y Multiculturalismo En América Latina*, ed. Peter Wade, Fernando Urrea, and Mara Viveros (Bogotá: Universidad Nacional de Colombia, Facultad de Ciencias Humanas, Centro de Estudios Sociales [CES], 2008); Christina A. Sue, *Land of the Cosmic Race: Race Mixture, Racism, and Blackness in Mexico* (Oxford: Oxford University Press, 2013).

19 Chito Childs, *Navigating Interracial Borders*.

20 Crystal M. Fleming, Michéle Lamont, and Jessica S. Welburn, "African Americans Respond to Stigmatization: The Meanings and Salience of Confronting, Deflecting Conflict, Educating the Ignorant and 'Managing the Self,'" *Ethnic and Racial Studies* 35 (2012); Michéle Lamont and C. M. Fleming, "Everyday Antiracism," *Du Bois Review* 2, no. 1 (2005).

21 Cheryl Y. Judice, *Interracial Marriages between Black Women and White Men* (Amherst, NY: Cambria Press, 2008).

22 Margaret L. Hunter, *Race, Gender, and the Politics of Skin Tone* (New York: Routledge, 2005).

23 Chito Childs, *Navigating Interracial Borders*.

24 Twine, *White Side of Black Britain*; Root, *Love's Revolution*.

25 Y. K. Djamba and S. R. Kimuna, "Are Americans Really in Favor of Interracial Marriage? A Closer Look at When They Are Asked about Black-White Marriage for Their Relatives," *Journal of Black Studies* 45, no. 6 (2014); Melissa R. Herman and Mary E. Campbell, "I Wouldn't but You Can: Attitudes toward Interracial Marriage," *Social Science Research* 41 (2010).

CHAPTER 6. POLICING THE BOUNDARY

1 Erica Chito Childs, "Looking behind the Stereotypes of the 'Angry Black Woman'": An Exploration of Black Women's Responses to Interracial Relationships," *Gender & Society* 19, no. 4 (2005); and *Navigating Interracial Borders: Black-White Couples and Their Social Worlds* (New Brunswick, NJ: Rutgers University Press, 2005).

2 Averil Y. Clarke, *Inequalities of Love: College-Educated Black Women and the Barriers to Romance and Family* (Durham, NC: Duke University Press, 2011); William Julius Wilson, *When Work Disappears: World of the New Urban Poor* (New York: Vintage Press, 1997).

3 Findings were initially published in Chinyere Osuji, "Racial 'Boundary-policing': Perceptions of Black-White Interracial Couples in Los Angeles and Rio de Janeiro," *Du Bois Review* 10 (2013).

4 "2010 Census Shows Interracial and Interethnic Married Couples Grew by 28 Percent over Decade," US Census Bureau, April 25, 2012, https://www.census.gov/newsroom/releases/archives/2010_census/cb12-68.html.

5 Elijah Anderson, *The Cosmopolitan Canopy: Race and Civility in Everyday Life* (New York: Norton, 2011).

6 For debates surrounding black women's reactions to couples involving white women and black men, see Chito Childs, "Looking behind the Stereotypes." But for a retort, see Michael Jeffries, "Right to Be Hostile? A Critique of Erica Chito Childs's 'Looking behind the Stereotypes of the "Angry Black Woman,"'" *Social Science Research on Race* 3 (2006). Also see Marcyliena Morgan and Dionne Bennett, "Getting off of Black Women's Backs: Love Her or Leave Her Alone," *Du Bois Review* 3, no. 2 (2007).

7 Susan Olzak, *The Dynamics of Ethnic Competition and Conflict* (Stanford, CA: Stanford University Press, 1992); Fredrik Barth, *Ethnic Groups and Boundaries: The Social Origin of Culture Difference* (Prospect Heights, IL: Waveland Press, 1969).

8 Herbert Blumer, "Race Prejudice as a Sense of Group Position," *Pacific Sociological Review* 1, no. 1 (1958); Lawrence Bobo and V. L. Hutchings, "Perceptions of Racial Group Competition: Extending Blumer's Theory of Group Position to a Multiracial Social Context," *American Sociological Review* 61, no. 6 (1996).

9 Cynthia Feliciano, Belinda Robnett, and Golnaz Komaie, "Gendered Racial Exclusion among White Internet Daters," *Social Science Research* 38 (2009); Clarke, *Inequalities of Love*; Zhenchao Qian and Daniel T. Lichter, "Changing Patterns of Interracial Marriage in a Multiracial Society," *Journal of Marriage and Family* 73, no. 5 (2011).

10 Amy C. Wilkins, "Stigma and Status: Interracial Intimacy and Intersectional Identities among Black College Men," *Gender & Society* (2012); Chito Childs, "Looking behind the Stereotypes."

11 Nicole J. Shelton and Jennifer A. Richeson, "Interracial Interactions: A Relational Approach," *Advances in Experimental Social Psychology* 38 (2006).

12 S. A. Basow et al., "Perceptions of Relational and Physical Aggression among College Students: Effects of Gender of Perpetrator, Target, and Perceiver," *Psychology of Women Quarterly* 31, no. 1 (2007); N. R. Crick, J. K. Grotpeter, and M. A. Bigbee, "Relationally and Physically Aggressive Children's Intent Attributions and Feelings of Distress for Relational and Instrumental Peer Provocations," *Child Development* 73, no. 4 (2002); N. R. Crick and D. A. Nelson, "Relational and Physical Victimization within Friendships: Nobody Told Me There'd Be Friends like These," *Journal of Abnormal Child Psychology* 30, no. 6 (2002); J. A. Paquette and M. K. Underwood, "Gender Differences in Young Adolescents' Experiences of Peer Victimization: Social and Physical Aggression," *Merrill Palmer-Quarterly* 45 (1999).

13 Seymour M. Lipset and Philip G. Altbach, "Student Politics and Higher Education in the United States," *Comparative Education Review* 10 (1966).

14 Shelton and Richeson, "Interracial Interactions."

15 Richard Lewis and George Yancey, "Biracial Marriages in the United States: An Analysis of Variation in Family Member Support," *Sociological Spectrum* 15, no. 4 (1995).

16 Lawrence Bobo, "Inequalities That Endure? Racial Ideology, American Politics, and the Peculiar Role of the Social Sciences," in *The Changing Terrain of Race and Ethnicity*, ed. Maria Krysan and Amanda E. Lewis (New York: Russell Sage Foundation, 2004).

17 Patricia Hill Collins, *Black Feminist Thought* (New York: Routledge, 2000).

18 J. Correll et al., "Across the Thin Blue Line: Police Officers and Racial Bias in the Decision to Shoot," *Journal of Personality and Social Psychology* 92, no. 6 (2007); E. A. Plant and B. M. Peruche, "The Consequences of Race for Police Officers' Responses to Criminal Suspects," *Psychological Science* 16, no. 3 (2005).

19 Eduardo Silva, *Racism without Racists: Color-Blind Racism and the Persistence of Racial Inequality in the United States* (Lanham, MD: Rowman and Littlefield, 2006). Melissa Herman and Mary E. Campbell, "I Wouldn't but You Can: Attitudes toward Interracial Marriage," *Social Science Research* 41 (2010).

20 Adam R. Pearson, John F. Dovidio, and Samuel L. Gaertner, "The Nature of Contemporary Prejudice: Insights from Aversive Racism," *Social and Personality Psychology Compass* 3 (2009); John F. Dovidio, Kerry Kawakami, and Samuel Gaertner, "Implicit and Explicit Prejudice and Interracial Interaction," *Journal of Personality and Social Psychology* 82, no. 1 (2002).

21 Bonilla-Silva, *Racism without Racists*.

22 Dovidio, Kawakami, and Gaertner, "Implicit and Explicit Prejudice."

23 Elza Berquó and Maria Andréa Loyola, "União Dos Sexos E Estratégias Reprodutivas No Brasil," *Revista Brasileira de Estudos de População* 1, no. 1/2 (1984); Ana María Goldani, "Racial Inequality in the Lives of Brazilian Women," in *Race in Contemporary Brazil: From Indifference to Inequality*, ed. Rebecca Reichmann (University Park: Pennsylvania State University Press, 1999).

24 Chinyere K. Osuji, "An African/Nigerian-American Studying Black-White Couples in Los Angeles and Rio De Janeiro," in *Race and the Politics of Knowledge Production: Diaspora and Black Transnational Scholarship in the United States and Brazil*, ed. Gladys Mitchell-Walthour and Elizabeth Hordge-Freeman (New York: Palgrave MacMillan, 2016); Marcia Contins, *Lideranças Negras* (Rio de Janeiro: Aeroplano, 2005).

25 Instituto Brasileiro de Geografía e Estadistica (IBGE), "Pesquisa Nacional por Amostra de Domicílios (PNAD) 2005–2006," accessed January 5, 2008, https://ww2.ibge.gov.br/home/estatistica/pesquisas/pesquisa_resultados.php?id_pesquisa=40.

26 Peter Wade, *Race and Ethnicity in Latin America* (Chicago, IL: Pluto Press, 1997).

27 Maureen O'Dougherty, *Consumption Intensified: The Politics of Middle-Class Daily Life in Brazil* (Durham, NC: Duke University Press, 2002).

28 Edward E. Telles, *Race in Another America: The Significance of Skin Color in Brazil* (Princeton, NJ: Princeton University Press, 2004).

29 Stanley Bailey, *Legacies of Race: Identities, Attitudes, and Politics in Brazil* (Palo Alto, CA: Stanford University Press, 2009).

30 Florestan Fernandes, *The Negro in Brazilian Society* (New York: Columbia University Press, 1969).

31 Telles, *Race in Another America*.

32 Graziella Moraes da Silva and Elisa P. Reis, "Perceptions of Racial Discrimination among Black Professionals in Rio De Janeiro," *Latin American Research Review* 46, no. 2 (2011); Angela Figueiredo, *Novas Elites De Cor: Estudo Sobre Os Profissionais Liberais Negros De Salvador* (São Paulo: Annablume, 2002).

33 Joane Nagel, *Race, Ethnicity, and Sexuality: Intimate Intersections, Forbidden Frontiers* (New York: Oxford University Press, 2003).

34 Erica Lorraine Williams, *Sex Tourism in Bahia: Ambiguous Entanglements* (Urbana: University of Illinois Press, 2013).

35 Nissim Mizrachi and Hanna Herzog, "Participatory Destigmatization Strategies among Palestinian Citizens, Ethiopian Jews and Mizrahi Jews in Israel," *Ethnic and Racial Studies* 35, no. 3 (2011); Crystal M. Fleming, Michéle Lamont, and Jessica S. Welburn, "African Americans Respond to Stigmatization: The Meanings and Salience of Confronting, Deflecting Conflict, Educating the Ignorant and 'Managing the Self,'" *Ethnic and Racial Studies* 35 (2012).

36 Bonilla-Silva, *Racism without Racists*.

CONCLUSION. "IS INTERRACIAL LOVE SAVING AMERICA?"

1 Eduardo Bonilla-Silva, *White Supremacy and Racism in the Post–Civil Rights Era* (New York: Lynne Rienner, 2001); Eduardo Bonilla-Silva, *Racism without Racists* (Lanham, MD: Rowman and Littlefield, 2006).

2 Heather M. Dalmage, *Tripping on the Color Line: Black-White Multiracial Families in a Racially Divided World* (New Brunswick, NJ: Rutgers University Press, 2000).

3 Diane Hughes et al., "Parents' Ethnic-Racial Socialization Practices: A Review of Research and Directions for Future Study," *Developmental Psychology* 42, no. 5 (2006).

4 Elizabeth Hordge-Freeman, *The Color of Love: Racial Features, Stigma, and Socialization in Afro-Brazilian Families* (Austin: University of Texas Press, 2015); Luisa Farah Schwartzman, "Does Money Whiten? Intergenerational Changes in Racial Classification in Brazil," *American Sociological Review* 72, no. 6 (2007); Edward E. Telles, *Race in Another America: The Significance of Skin Color in Brazil* (Princeton, NJ: Princeton University Press, 2004).

5 Linda M. Burton et al., "Critical Race Theories, Colorism, and the Decade's Research on Families of Color," *Journal of Marriage and Family* 72, no. 3 (2010).

6 Gilberto Freyre, *The Mansions and the Shanties: The Making of Modern Brazil* [*Sobrados e Mucambos*], trans. Harriet De Onís (Los Angeles: University of California Press, 1980); and *The Masters and the Slaves: A Study in the Development of Brazilian Civilization* (Berkeley: University of California Press, 1933).

7 Suzanne Bost, *Mulattas and Mestizas: Representing Mixed Identities in the Americas, 1850–2000* (Athens: University of Georgia Press, 2005); Daniel McNeil, *Sex and Race in the Black Atlantic: Mulatto Devils and Multiracial Messiahs* (New York: Routledge, 2010).

8 Telles, *Race in Another America.*

9 Abdias Do Nascimento, *Brazil, Mixture or Massacre? Essays in the Genocide of a Black People* (Majority Press, 1989).

APPENDIX B

1 Edward E. Telles and René Flores, "Not Just Color: Whiteness, Nation, and Status in Latin America," *Hispanic American Historical Review* 93, no. 3 (2013).

2 Chinyere K. Osuji, "An African/Nigerian-American Studying Black-White Couples in Los Angeles and Rio De Janeiro," in *Race and the Politics of Knowledge Production: Diaspora and Black Transnational Scholarship in the United States and Brazil,* ed. Gladys Mitchell-Walthour and Elizabeth Hordge-Freeman (New York: Palgrave MacMillan, 2016).

3 Erica Chito Childs, "Looking behind the Stereotypes of the 'Angry Black Woman': An Exploration of Black Women's Responses to Interracial Relationships," *Gender & Society* 19, no. 4 (2005).

REFERENCES

Alves, Jaime do Amparo. "Narratives of Violence: The White Imagination and the Making of Black Masculinity in *City of God*." *Sociedade e Cultura* 12, no. 2 (2009): 301–9.

Anderson, Benedict. *Imagined Communities: Reflections on the Origin and Spread of Nationalism*. Rev. and extended ed. New York: Verso, 1991.

Anderson, Elijah. *The Cosmopolitan Canopy: Race and Civility in Everyday Life*. New York: Norton, 2011.

Andrews, George Reid. *Afro-Latin America, 1800–2000*. New York: Oxford University Press, 2004.

Araújo, Joel Zito. *A Negação Do Brasil: O Negro Na Telenovela Brasileira*. São Paulo: Editora SENAC São Paulo, 2000.

Azevedo, Thales de. *As Elites De Côr: Um Estudo Da Ascensão Social*. São Paulo: Companhia Editora Nacional, 1955.

Bailey, Stanley R. *Legacies of Race: Identities, Attitudes, and Politics in Brazil*. Palo Alto, CA: Stanford University Press, 2009.

Bailey, Stanley, and Michelle Peria. "Racial Quotas and the Culture War in Brazilian Academia." *Sociology Compass* 4 (2010): 592–604.

Barros, Zelinda dos Santos. "Casais Inter-Raciais E Suas Representações Acerca De Raça." Salvador, Brazil: Universidade Federal da Bahia, 2003.

Barth, Fredrik. *Ethnic Groups and Boundaries: The Social Origin of Culture Difference*. Prospect Heights, IL: Waveland Press, 1969.

Basow, Susan A., Kristen F. Cahill, Julie E. Phelan, Kathryn Longshore, and Ann McGillicuddy-DeLisi. "Perceptions of Relational and Physical Aggression among College Students: Effects of Gender of Perpetrator, Target, and Perceiver." *Psychology of Women Quarterly* 31, no. 1 (2007): 85–95.

Batson, Christie D., Zhenchao Qian, and Daniel T. Lichter. "Interracial and Intraracial Patterns of Mate Selection among America's Diverse Black Populations." *Journal of Marriage and Family* 68, no. 3 (2006): 658–72.

Becker, Howard S. "Becoming a Marihuana User." *American Journal of Sociology* 59, no. 3 (1953): 235–42.

Bernard, Jessie. *The Future of Marriage*. New Haven, CT: Yale University Press, 1982.

Berquó, Elza, and Maria Andréa Loyola. "União Dos Sexos E Estratégias Reprodutivas No Brasil." *Revista Brasileira de Estudos de População* 1, no. 1/2 (1984): 35–99.

Blau, Peter, Terry Blum, and Joseph E. Schwartz. "Heterogeneity and Intermarriage." *American Sociological Review* 47 (1982): 45–62.

Blumer, Herbert. "Race Prejudice as a Sense of Group Position." *Pacific Sociological Review* 1, no. 1 (1958): 3–7.

Bobo, Lawrence. "Inequalities That Endure? Racial Ideology, American Politics, and the Peculiar Role of the Social Sciences." In *The Changing Terrain of Race and Ethnicity*, edited by Maria Krysan and Amanda E. Lewis, 13–42. New York: Russell Sage Foundation, 2004.

Bobo, Lawrence, and V. L. Hutchings. "Perceptions of Racial Group Competition: Extending Blumer's Theory of Group Position to a Multiracial Social Context." *American Sociological Review* 61, no. 6 (1996): 951–72.

Bobo, Lawrence D., Camille Z. Charles, Maria Krysan, and Alicia D. Simmons. "The Real Record on Racial Attitudes." In *Social Trends in American Life: Findings from the General Social Survey since 1972*, edited by Peter V. Marsden, 38–82. Princeton, NJ: Princeton University Press, 2012.

Bobo, Lawrence, James R. Kluegel, and Ryan A. Smith. "Laissez-Faire Racism: The Crystallization of a Kinder, Gentler, Anti-Black Ideology." *Racial Attitudes in the 1990s: Continuity and Change*. Westport, CT: Praeger, 1997.

Bonilla-Silva, Eduardo. *Racism without Racists: Color-Blind Racism and the Persistence of Racial Inequality in the United States*. Lanham, MD: Rowman and Littlefield, 2006.

Bost, Suzanne. *Mulattas and Mestizas: Representing Mixed Identities in the Americas, 1850–2000*. Athens: University of Georgia Press, 2005.

"Brazilian Federal Constitution." Article 226, paragraph 3. 1988.

Brennan, Denise. *What's Love Got to Do with It? Transnational Desires and Sex Tourism in the Dominican Republic*. Durham, NC: Duke University Press, 2004.

Brubaker, Rogers. *Ethnicity without Groups*. Cambridge, MA: Harvard University Press, 2004.

Brunsma, David L. "Interracial Families and the Racial Identification of Mixed-Race Children: Evidence from the Early Childhood Longitudinal Study." *Social Forces* 84 (2005): 1131.

Bumpass, Larry L., James A. Sweet, and Andrew Cherlin. "The Role of Cohabitation in Declining Rates of Marriage." *Journal of Marriage and the Family* 53, no. 4 (1991): 913–27.

Burma, John. "The Measurement of Negro 'Passing.'" *American Journal of Sociology* 52, no. 1 (1946): 18–22.

Burton, Linda M., Eduardo Bonilla-Silva, Victor Ray, Rose Buckelew, and Elizabeth Hordge-Freeman. "Critical Race Theories, Colorism, and the Decade's Research on Families of Color." *Journal of Marriage and Family* 72, no. 3 (2010): 440–59.

Caldwell, Kia Lily. "'Look at Her Hair': The Body Politics of Black Womanhood in Brazil." *Transforming Anthropology* 11 (2003): 18–29.

———. *Negras in Brazil: Re-envisioning Black Women, Citizenship, and the Politics of Identity*. New Brunswick, NJ: Rutgers University Press, 2007.

Carter, Prudence L. *Keepin' It Real: School Success beyond Black and White*. New York: Oxford University Press, 2005.

Charles, Camille Z., Mary J. Fischer, Margarita A. Mooney, and Douglas S. Massey. *Taming the River: Negotiating the Academic, Financial, and Social Currents in Selective Colleges and Universities.* Princeton, NJ: Princeton University Press, 2009.

Charles, Camille Zubrinsky. *Won't You Be My Neighbor? Race, Class, and Residence in Los Angeles.* New York: Russell Sage Foundation, 2009.

Chito Childs, Erica. "Looking behind the Stereotypes of the 'Angry Black Woman': An Exploration of Black Women's Responses to Interracial Relationships." *Gender & Society* 19, no. 4 (2005): 544.

———. *Navigating Interracial Borders: Black-White Couples and Their Social Worlds.* New Brunswick, NJ: Rutgers University Press, 2005.

Clarke, Averil Y. *Inequalities of Love: College-Educated Black Women and the Barriers to Romance and Family.* Durham, NC: Duke University Press, 2011.

Cohen, Cathy. *Boundaries of Blackness: AIDS and the Breakdown of Black Politics.* Chicago, IL: University of Chicago Press, 1999.

Collins, Patricia Hill. *Black Feminist Thought.* New York: Routledge, 2000.

———. *Black Sexual Politics.* New York: Routledge, 2004.

Contins, Marcia. *Lideranças Negras.* Rio de Janeiro, Brazil: Aeroplano, 2005.

Cooley, Charles Horton. *Human Nature and the Social Order.* New York: Scribners, 1902.

Cornell, Stephen, and Douglas Hartmann. *Ethnicity and Race: Making Identities in a Changing World.* Thousand Oaks, CA: Pine Forge Press, 1998.

Correll, J., B. Park, C. M. Judd, B. Wittenbrink, M. S. Sadler, and T. Keesee. "Across the Thin Blue Line: Police Officers and Racial Bias in the Decision to Shoot." *Journal of Personality and Social Psychology* 92, no. 6 (2007): 1006.

Crenshaw, Kimberlé. "Demarginalizing the Intersection of Race and Sex: A Black Feminist Critique of Antidiscrimination Doctrine, Feminist Theory and Antiracist Politics." *University of Chicago Legal Forum* 189, no. 1 (1989): 139.

———. "Mapping the Margins: Intersectionality, Identity, Politics, and Violence against Women of Color." In *The Public Nature of Private Violence: The Discovery of Domestic Abuse,* edited by M. Fineman and R. Mykitiuk. New York: Routledge, 1994.

Crick, N. R., and D. A. Nelson. "Relational and Physical Victimization within Friendships: Nobody Told Me There'd Be Friends like These." *Journal of Abnormal Child Psychology* 30, no. 6 (2002): 599–607.

Crick, N. R., J. K. Grotpeter, and M. A. Bigbee. "Relationally and Physically Aggressive Children's Intent Attributions and Feelings of Distress for Relational and Instrumental Peer Provocations." *Child Development* 73, no. 4 (2002): 1134–42.

Crocker, J., B. Major, and C. Steele. "Social Stigma." In *The Handbook of Social Psychology,* edited by D. T. Gilbert, S. T. Fiske, and G. Lindzey. Boston, MA: McGraw-Hill, 1998.

DaCosta, Kimberly McClain. *Making Multiracials: State, Family, and Market in the Redrawing of the Color Line.* Stanford, CA: Stanford University Press, 2007.

Daflon, Verônica Toste, and João Feres Júnior. "Ação afirmativa na revista Veja: Estratégias editoriais e o enquadramento do debate público." *Revista Compolítica* 2 (2012): 66–91.

Dalmage, Heather M. *Tripping on the Color Line: Black-White Multiracial Families in a Racially Divided World*. New Brunswick, NJ: Rutgers University Press, 2000.

Daniel, G. Reginald. *Race and Multiraciality in Brazil and the United States: Converging Paths?* University Park: Pennsylvania State University Press, 2006.

Davis, A., B. B. Gardner, and M. R. Gardner. *Deep South*. Chicago, IL: University of Chicago Press, 1941.

Davis, Darién J. *Avoiding the Dark: Race and the Forging of National Culture in Modern Brazil*. Brookfield, VT: Ashgate, 1999.

———. "Racial Parity and National Humor: Exploring Brazilian Samba from Noel Rosa to Carmen Miranda." In *Latin American Popular Culture: An Introduction*, edited by William H. Beezley and Linda A. Curcio-Nagy. Wilmington, DE: Scholarly Resources, 2000.

Davis, Kingsley. "Intermarriage in Caste Societies." *American Anthropologist* 43 (1941): 388–95.

Dawson, Michael. *Black Visions*. Chicago, IL: University of Chicago Press, 2001.

Degler, Carl N. *Neither Black nor White: Slavery and Race Relations in Brazil and the United States*. Madison: University of Wisconsin Press, 1986.

De la Cadena, Marisol. *Indigenous Mestizos: The Politics of Race and Culture in Cuzco, Peru, 1919–1991*. Durham, NC: Duke University Press, 2000.

Delgado, Richard, and Jean Stefancic. *Critical Race Theory: The Cutting Edge*. 2nd ed. Philadelphia, PA: Temple University Press, 2000.

Dennison, Stephanie. "Blonde Bombshell: Xuxa and Notions of Whiteness in Brazil." *Journal of Latin American Cultural Studies* 22 (2013): 287–304.

Desmond, S. M., J. H. Price, C. Hallinan, and D. Smith. "Black and White Adolescents' Perceptions of Their Weight." *Journal of School Health* 59 (1989): 353–58.

Djamba, Y. K., and S. R. Kimuna. "Are Americans Really in Favor of Interracial Marriage? A Closer Look at When They Are Asked about Black-White Marriage for Their Relatives." *Journal of Black Studies* 45, no. 6 (2014): 528–44.

Do Nascimento, Abdias. *Brazil, Mixture or Massacre? Essays in the Genocide of a Black People* (Dover, MA: Majority Press, 1989).

Dorneles de Andrade, Daniella. "On Norms and Bodies: Findings from Field Research on Cosmetic Surgery in Rio De Janeiro, Brazil." *Reproductive Health Matters* 18, no. 35 (2010): 74–83.

Dovidio, John F., Kerry Kawakami, and Samuel Gaertner. "Implicit and Explicit Prejudice and Interracial Interaction." *Journal of Personality and Social Psychology* 82, no. 1 (2002): 62–68.

Drake, John St. Clair, and H. R. Cayton. *Black Metropolis*. New York: Harcourt, Brace, and World, 1945.

Du Bois, William Edward Burghardt. "The Future of Africa in America (April 1942)." In *Against Racism: Unpublished Essays, Papers, Addresses, 1887–1961*, edited by Herbert Aptheker, 181. Amherst: University of Massachusetts Press, 1985.

———. *The Souls of Black Folk: Essays and Sketches*. Chicago, IL: A. C. McClurg and Co., 1903.

Eckard, E. W. "How Many Negroes 'Pass'?" *American Journal of Sociology* 52, no. 6 (1947): 498–500.

Emerson, Michael O., Rachel Tolbert Kimbro, and George Yancey. "Contact Theory Extended: The Effects of Prior Racial Contact on Current Social Ties." *Social Science Quarterly* 83, no. 3 (September 2002): 745–62.

Espino, Rodolfo, and Michael M. Franz. "Latino Phenotypic Discrimination Revisited: The Impact of Skin Color on Occupational Status." *Social Science Quarterly* 83, no. 2 (2002): 612–23.

Feagin, J., and E. O'Brien. *White Men on Race: Power, Privilege, and the Shaping of Cultural Consciousness.* Boston, MA: Beacon Press, 2013.

Feagin, Joe R., and H. Vera. *White Racism: The Basics.* New York: Routledge, 1995.

Feliciano, Cynthia, Belinda Robnett, and Golnaz Komaie. "Gendered Racial Exclusion among White Internet Daters." *Social Science Research* 38 (2009): 39–54.

Ferber, A. L. *White Man Falling: Race, Gender, and White Supremacy.* New York: Rowman and Littlefield, 1998.

Feres Júnior, João, Luiz Augusto Campos, and Veronica Toste Daflon. "Fora De Quadro: A Ação Afirmativa Nas Páginas D'o Globo." *Contemporânea* 2 (2011): 61–83.

Fernandes, Florestan. *The Negro in Brazilian Society.* New York: Columbia University Press, 1969.

Fernandez, Nadine. *Revolutionizing Romance: Interracial Couples in Contemporary Cuba.* New Brunswick, NJ: Rutgers University Press, 2010.

Figueiredo, Angela. *Novas Elites De Cor: Estudo Sobre Os Profissionais Liberais Negros De Salvador.* São Paulo: Annablume, 2002.

Figueroa, Mónica Moreno. "Negociando La Pertenencia: Família Y Mestizaje En México." In *Raza, Etnicidad Y Sexualidades: Ciudadanía Y Multiculturalismo En América Latina,* edited by Peter Wade, Fernando Urrea, and Mara Viveros, 247–79. Bogotá: Universidad Nacional de Colombia, Facultad de Ciencias Humanas, Centro de Estudios Sociales [CES], 2008.

Fleming, Crystal M., Michèle Lamont, and Jessica S. Welburn. "African Americans Respond to Stigmatization: The Meanings and Salience of Confronting, Deflecting Conflict, Educating the Ignorant and 'Managing the Self.'" *Ethnic and Racial Studies* 35 (2012): 400–417.

Fordham, Signithia, and John Ogbu. "Black Students' School Success: Coping with the 'Burden of Acting White.'" *Urban Review* 18 (1986): 176–206.

Frankenberg, Ruth. *The Social Construction of Whiteness: White Women, Race Matters.* Minneapolis: University of Minnesota Press, 1993.

Freyre, Gilberto. *The Mansions and the Shanties: The Making of Modern Brazil* [*Sobrados e Mucambos*]. Translated by Harriet De Onís. Berkeley: University of California Press, 1980.

———. *The Masters and the Slaves: A Study in the Development of Brazilian Civilization.* Berkeley: University of California Press, 1933.

Fry, Peter, and Yvonne Maggie. "Cotas Raciais: Construindo Um País Dividido?" *Econômica: Revista da Pós-Graduação em Economia da UFF* 6, no. 1 (2004): 153–61.

Fry, Peter, Yvonne Maggie, Marcos Chor Maio, Simone Monteiro, and Ricardo Ventura Santos. *Divisões Perigosas: Políticas Raciais No Brasil Contemporâneo*. Rio de Janeiro: Civilização Brasileira, 2007.

Gaither, S. E., J. D. Remedios, J. R. Schultz, K. B. Maddox, and S. R. Sommers. "Examining the Effects of I-Sharing for Future White-Black Interactions." *Social Psychology* 47, no. 3 (2016): 125–35.

Gaither, S. E., and S. R. Sommers. "Living with an Other-Race Roommate Shapes Whites' Behavior in Subsequent Diverse Settings." *Journal of Experimental Social Psychology* 49, no. 2 (2013): 272–76.

Gans, Herbert. "Symbolic Ethnicity: The Future of Ethnic Groups and Cultures in America." *Ethnic and Racial Studies* 2 (1979): 1–20.

Glasser, C. L., B. Robnett, and Cynthia Feliciano. "Internet Daters' Body Type Preferences: Race-Ethnic and Gender Differences." *Sex Roles* 61, no. 14 (2009).

Golash-Boza, Tanya. "A Critical and Comprehensive Sociological Theory of Race and Racism." *Sociology of Race and Ethnicity* 2, no. 2 (2016): 129–41.

———. *Yo Soy Negro: Blackness in Peru*. Gainesville: University Press of Florida, 2012.

Goldani, Ana María. "Racial Inequality in the Lives of Brazilian Women." In *Race in Contemporary Brazil: From Indifference to Inequality*, edited by Rebecca Reichmann. University Park: Pennsylvania State University Press, 1999.

Goldstein, Donna. "'Interracial' Sex and Racial Democracy in Brazil: Twin Concepts?" *American Anthropologist* 101, no. 3 (1999): 563–78.

———. *Laughter Out of Place: Race, Class, Violence, and Sexuality in a Rio Shantytown*. Berkeley: University of California Press, 2003.

Golebiowska, E. A. "The Contours and Etiology of Whites' Attitudes toward Black-White Interracial Marriage." *Journal of Black Studies* 38, no. 2 (2007): 268.

Gordon, Milton Myron. *Assimilation in American Life: The Role of Race, Religion, and National Origins*. New York: Oxford University Press, 1964.

Greene, Margaret E., and Vijayendra Rao. "The Marriage Squeeze and the Rise in Informal Marriage in Brazil." *Social Biology* 42, no. 1–2 (1995): 65–82.

Guimarães, Antônio Sérgio Alfredo. "Racial Democracy." In *Imagining Brazil (Global Encounters)*, edited by Jessé Souza and Valter Sinder, 119–40. Lanham, MD: Lexington, 2005.

———. *Racismo E Anti-Racismo No Brasil*. São Paulo: FUSP (Fundação de Apoio à Universidade de São Paulo), 2005.

Gullickson, Aaron, and Florencia Torche. "Patterns of Racial and Educational Assortative Mating in Brazil." *Demography* 51, no. 3 (2014): 835–56.

Hall, Erika V., Katherine W. Phillips, and Sarah S. Townsend. "A Rose by Another Name? The Consequences of Sub-typing 'African Americans' from 'Blacks.'" *Journal of Experimental Social Psychology* 56 (2015): 183–90.

Hall, J. D. *Revolt against Chivalry: Jessie Daniel Ames and the Women's Campaign against Lynching*. New York: Columbia University Press, 1993.

Hanchard, Michael G. *Orpheus and Power: The Movimento Negro of Rio de Janeiro and São Paulo, Brazil, 1945–1988*. Princeton, NJ: Princeton University Press, 1993.

Harris, M., J. G. Consorte, J. Lang, and B. Byrne. "Who Are the Whites? Imposed Census Categories and the Racial Demography of Brazil." *Social Forces* 72, no. 2 (1993): 451–62.

Hartigan, John. *Racial Situations: Class Predicaments of Whiteness in Detroit*. Princeton, NJ: Princeton University Press, 1999.

Hasenbalg, Carlos. *Discriminação E Desigualdades Raciais No Brasil*. Rio de Janeiro: Graal, 1979.

Hellwig, D. J., ed. *African-American Reflections on Brazil's Racial Paradise*. Philadelphia, PA: Temple University Press, 1992.

Herman, Melissa. "Do You See Me as I Am? How Observers' Backgrounds Affect Their Perceptions of Multiracial Faces." *Social Psychology Quarterly* 73, no. 1 (2010): 58–78.

Herman, Melissa R., and Mary E. Campbell. "I Wouldn't but You Can: Attitudes toward Interracial Marriage." *Social Science Research* 41 (2010): 243–358.

Hernández, Tanya Katerí. *Racial Subordination in Latin America: The Role of the State, Customary Law and the New Civil Rights Response*. New York: Cambridge University Press, 2014.

———. "Sex in the [Foreign] City: Commodification and the Female Sex Tourist." In *Rethinking Commodification: Cases and Readings in Law and Culture*, edited by Joan Williams and Martha Ertman, 222–42. New York: New York University Press, 2005.

———. "Sexual Harassment and Racial Disparity: The Mutual Construction of Gender and Race." *Gender, Race, and Justice* 4 (2001): 183–224.

Hochschild, Jennifer, Vesla Weaver, and Traci Burch. *Transforming the American Racial Order*. Princeton, NJ: Princeton University Press, 2012.

Hordge-Freeman, Elizabeth. *The Color of Love: Racial Features, Stigma, and Socialization in Afro-Brazilian Families*. Austin: University of Texas, 2015.

Htun, Mala. "From 'Racial Democracy' to Affirmative Action: Changing State Policy on Race in Brazil." *Latin American Research Review* 39, no. 1 (February 2004): 60–89.

Hughes, Diane, James Rodriguez, Emilie Smith, Deborah Johnson, Howard Stevenson, and Paul Spicer. "Parents' Ethnic-Racial Socialization Practices: A Review of Research and Directions for Future Study." *Developmental Psychology* 42, no. 5 (2006): 747–70.

Hughey, Matthew W. *White Bound: Nationalists, Antiracists, and the Shared Meanings of Race*. Stanford, CA: Stanford University Press, 2012.

Humes, Karen R., Nicholas A. Jones, and Roberto R. Ramirez. "Overview of Race and Hispanic Origin: 2010." US Census Bureau. March 2011. https://www.census.gov/content/dam/Census/library/publications/2011/dec/c2010br-02.pdf.

Hunt, Darnell M., and Ana-Christina Ramon. *Black Los Angeles: American Dreams and Racial Realities*. New York: New York University Press, 2010.

Hunter, Margaret L. *Race, Gender, and the Politics of Skin Tone*. New York: Routledge, 2005.

Instituto Brasileiro de Geografía e Estadística (IBGE). "Pesquisa Nacional por Amostra de Domicílios (PNAD) 2005." Accessed January 5, 2008. https://ww2.ibge.gov.br/home/estatistica/pesquisas/pesquisa_resultados.php?id_pesquisa=40.

"Interracial and Interethnic Coupled Households Appendix Tables." US Census Bureau. *Households and Families: 2010 Census Brief*, 2012. https://www.census.gov/prod/cen2010/briefs/c2010br-14.pdf.

Jeffries, Michael. "Right to Be Hostile? A Critique of Erica Chito Childs's 'Looking behind the Stereotypes of the "Angry Black Woman."'" *Social Science Research on Race* 3 (2006): 449–61.

Jenkins, Richard. *Social Identity.* New York: Routledge, 2008.

Jimenez, Tomas. "Affiliative Ethnic Identity: A More Elastic Link between Ethnic Ancestry and Culture." *Ethnic and Racial Studies* 33 (2010): 1756–75.

Joseph, Tiffany. *Race on the Move: Brazilian Migrants and the Global Reconstruction of Race.* Stanford, CA: Stanford University Press, 2015.

Judice, Cheryl Y. *Interracial Marriages between Black Women and White Men.* Amherst, NY: Cambria Press, 2008.

Kalmijn, Matthijs. "Trends in Black/White Intermarriage." *Social Forces* 72 (1993): 119.

Kempadoo, Kamala, and Jo Doezema. *Global Sex Workers: Rights, Resist, Redefinition.* New York: Routledge, 1998.

Kennedy, Randall. *Interracial Intimacies: Sex, Marriage, Identity, and Adoption.* 1st ed. New York: Pantheon, 2003.

———. *Sellout: The Politics of Racial Betrayal.* New York: Pantheon, 2008.

Khanna, Nikki. "If You're Half Black, You're Just Black: Reflected Appraisals and the Persistence of the One-Drop Rule." *Sociological Quarterly* 51, no. 1 (2010): 96–121.

———. "The Role of Reflected Appraisals in Racial Identity: The Case of Multiracial Asians." *Social Psychology Quarterly* 67, no. 2 (2004): 115–31.

King, Rosalind, and Jenifer Bratter. "A Path toward Interracial Marriage: Women's First Partners and Husbands across Racial Lines." *Sociological Quarterly* 48 (2007): 343–69.

Klein, Herbert, and Francisco Vidal Luna. *Slavery in Brazil.* New York: Cambridge University Press, 2010.

Kouri, K. M., and M. Lasswell. "Black-White Marriages: Social Change and Intergenerational Mobility." *Marriage and Family Review* 19, no. 3–4 (1993): 241–55.

Lacy, Karyn R. *Blue-Chip Black: Race, Class, and Status in the New Black Middle Class.* Berkeley: University of California Press, 2007.

Lamont, Michèle. *The Dignity of Working Men: Morality and the Boundaries of Race, Class, and Immigration.* Cambridge, MA: Harvard University Press, 2000.

———. *Money, Morals, and Manners: The Culture of the French and American Upper-Middle Class.* Chicago, IL: University of Chicago Press, 1992.

Lamont, Michèle, and Crystal Marie Fleming. "Everyday Antiracism." *Du Bois Review* 2, no. 1 (2005): 29–43.

Lamont, Michèle, and Nissim Mizrachi. "Ordinary People Doing Extraordinary Things: Responses to Stigmatization in Comparative Perspective." *Ethnic and Racial Studies* 35, no. 3 (2011).

Lamont, Michèle, and Jonathan H. Turner. "Culture and Identity." In *Handbook of Sociological Theory*, 171–85. New York: Plenum, 2001.

Lamont, Michèle, and Viraj Molnar. "The Study of Boundaries in the Social Sciences." *Annual Review of Sociology* 28 (2002): 167–95.

Lamont, Michèle, Graziella Moraes Silva, Jessica S. Welburn, Joshua Guetzkow, Nissim Mizrachi, Hanna Herzog, and Elisa Reis. *Getting Respect: Responding to Stigma and Discrimination in the United States, Brazil, and Israel*. Princeton, NJ: Princeton University Press, 2016.

Lee, Jennifer, and Frank D. Bean. "America's Changing Color Lines: Immigration, Race/Ethnicity, and Multiracial Identification." *Annual Review of Sociology* 30, no. 1 (2004): 221–42.

———. *The Diversity Paradox: Immigration and the Color Line in Twenty-First Century America*. New York: Russell Sage Foundation, 2010.

Lesser, Jeffrey. *Negotiating National Identity: Immigrants, Minorities, and the Struggle for Ethnicity in Brazil*. Durham, NC: Duke University Press, 1999.

Lewis, Richard, and George Yancey. "Biracial Marriages in the United States: An Analysis of Variation in Family Member Support." *Sociological Spectrum* 15, no. 4 (1995): 443–62.

Lieberson, Stanley, and Mary Waters. *From Many Strands: Ethnic and Racial Groups in Contemporary America*. New York: Russell Sage Foundation, 1988.

Lipset, Seymour M., and Philip G. Altbach. "Student Politics and Higher Education in the United States." *Comparative Education Review* 10 (1966): 320–49.

Loury, Glenn. "The Anatomy of Racial Equality." Cambridge, MA: Harvard University Press, 2002.

Loveman, Mara. *National Colors: Racial Classification and the State in Latin America*. New York: Oxford University Press, 2014.

Macartney, Suzanne, Alemayehu Bishaw, and Kayla Fontenot. "Poverty Rates for Selected Detailed Race and Hispanic Groups by State and Place: 2007–2011." US Census Bureau. 2013. https://www.census.gov/prod/2013pubs/acsbr11-17.pdf.

Manning, Wendy D., and Pamela J. Smock. "Why Marry? Race and the Transition to Marriage among Cohabitors." *Demography* 32, no. 4 (1995): 509–20.

Marrow, Helen. "To Be or Not to Be (Hispanic or Latino): Brazilian Racial and Ethnic Identity in the United States." *Ethnicities* 3, no. 4 (2003): 427–64.

Marx, Anthony. *Making Race and Nation: A Comparison of the United States, South Africa, and Brazil*. New York: Cambridge University Press, 1998.

Massey, Douglas S., and Nancy A. Denton. *American Apartheid: Segregation and the Making of the Underclass*. Cambridge, MA: Harvard University Press, 1993.

McDermott, Monica. *Working-Class White: The Making and Unmaking of Race Relations*. Berkeley: University of California Press, 2006.

McNeil, Daniel. *Sex and Race in the Black Atlantic: Mulatto Devils and Multiracial Messiahs*. New York: Routledge, 2010.

Mitchell-Walthour, Gladys. "Racism in a Racialized Democracy and Support for Affirmative Action Policy in Salvador and São Paulo, Brazil." In *Re-examining the Black*

Atlantic: Afro-Descendants and Development. Lansing: Michigan State University Press, 2012.

Mizrachi, Nissim, and Hanna Herzog. "Participatory Destigmatization Strategies among Palestinian Citizens, Ethiopian Jews and Mizrahi Jews in Israel." *Ethnic and Racial Studies* 35, no. 3 (2011).

Monk, Ellis. "The Consequences of 'Race and Color' in Brazil." *Social Problems* 63 (2016): 413–30.

Moore, Mignon. *Invisible Families: Gay Identities, Relationships, and Motherhood among Black Women.* Berkeley: University of California Press, 2011.

Mora, G. Cristina. *Making Hispanics: How Activists, Bureaucrats, and Media Constructed a New American.* Chicago, IL: University of Chicago Press, 2014.

Moran, Rachel F. *Interracial Intimacy: The Regulation of Race and Romance.* Chicago, IL: University of Chicago Press, 2001.

Morgan, Marcyliena, and Dionne Bennett. "Getting off of Black Women's Backs: Love Her or Leave Her Alone." *Du Bois Review* 3, no. 2 (2007): 485–502.

Morner, Magnus. *Race Mixture in the History of Latin America.* Boston, MA: Little Brown, 1967.

Moutinho, Laura. *Razão, "Cor" E Desejo.* São Paulo: UNESP, 2004.

Myrdal, Gunnar. *An American Dilemma: The Negro Problem and American Democracy.* New York: Harper Brothers, 1944.

Nagel, Joane. *Race, Ethnicity, and Sexuality: Intimate Intersections, Forbidden Frontiers.* New York: Oxford University Press, 2003.

Nazzari, Muriel. "Concubinage in Colonial Brazil: The Inequalities of Race, Class, and Gender." *Journal of Family History* 21, no. 2 (1996): 107–24.

Nelson, Alondra. *The Social Life of DNA: Race, Reparations, and Reconciliation after the Genome.* Boston, MA: Beacon Press, 2016.

Nemoto, Kumiko. *Racing Romance: Love, Power, and Desire among Asian American / White Couples.* New Brunswick, NJ: Rutgers University Press, 2009.

Nobles, Melissa. *Shades of Citizenship: Race and the Census in Modern Politics.* Stanford, CA: Stanford University Press, 2000.

Nogueira, Oracy. *Tanto Preto Quanto Branco: Estudos de Relações Raciais.* São Paulo: T. A. Queiroz, 1985.

O'Dougherty, Maureen. *Consumption Intensified: The Politics of Middle-Class Daily Life in Brazil.* Durham, NC: Duke University Press, 2002.

Obasogie, Osagie. *Blinded by Sight: Seeing Race through the Eyes of the Blind.* Stanford, CA: Stanford University Press, 2014.

Olzak, Susan. *The Dynamics of Ethnic Competition and Conflict.* Stanford, CA: Stanford University Press, 1992.

Omi, Michael, and Howard Winant. *Racial Formation in the United States: From the 1960s to the 1990s.* 3rd ed. New York: Routledge, 2015.

Osuji, Chinyere K. "An African/Nigerian-American Studying Black-White Couples in Los Angeles and Rio De Janeiro." In *Race and the Politics of Knowledge Production: Diaspora and Black Transnational Scholarship in the United States and Brazil,* edited by Gladys Mitchell-Walthour and Elizabeth Hordge-Freeman, 123–38. New York: Palgrave MacMillan, 2016.

———. "Confronting Whitening in an Era of Black-Consciousness: Racial Ideology and Black-White Marriages in Brazil." *Ethnic and Racial Studies* 36, no. 10 (2013).

———. "Difference or Convergence: Black-White Couples and Race Relations in the US and Brazil." *Qualitative Sociology* 37 (2014): 93–115.

———. "Racial 'Boundary-policing': Perceptions of Black-White Interracial Couples in Los Angeles and Rio de Janeiro." *Du Bois Review* 10 (2013): 179–203.

Paixão, Marcelo, and Luiz M. Carvano. *Relatório Anual Das Desigualdades Raciais No Brasil, 2007–2008.* Rio de Janeiro: Garamond Universitária, 2008.

Paquette, J. A., and M. K. Underwood. "Gender Differences in Young Adolescents' Experiences of Peer Victimization: Social and Physical Aggression." *Merrill Palmer-Quarterly* 45 (1999): 242–66.

Paschel, Tianna S., and Mark Sawyer. "Contesting Politics as Usual: Black Social Movements, Globalization, and Race Policy in Latin America." *Souls* 10, no. 3 (2008): 197–214.

Patterson, Orlando. *The Ordeal of Integration: Progress and Resentment in America's Racial Crisis.* Washington, DC: Civitas/Counterpoint, 1997.

Pearson, Adam R., John F. Dovidio, and Samuel L. Gaertner. "The Nature of Contemporary Prejudice: Insights from Aversive Racism." *Social and Personality Psychology Compass* 3 (2009): 314–38.

Peterson, Richard A., and Roger M. Kern. "Changing Highbrow Taste: From Snob to Omnivore." *American Sociological Review* 61, no. 5 (1996): 900–907.

Petruccelli, José Luis. "Seletividade Por Cor E Escolhas Conjugais No Brasil Dos 90." *Estudos Afro-Asiaticos* 23, no. 1 (2001): 29–54.

Plant, E. A., and B. M. Peruche. "The Consequences of Race for Police Officers' Responses to Criminal Suspects." *Psychological Science* 16, no. 3 (2005): 180–83.

Powdermaker, Hortense. *After Freedom: A Cultural Study in the Deep South.* New York: Viking Press, 1939.

Powell, A. D, and A. S. Kahn. "Racial Differences in Women's Desires to Be Thin." *International Journal of Eating Disorders* 17 (1995): 191–95.

Qian, Zhenchao, and Daniel T. Lichter. "Changing Patterns of Interracial Marriage in a Multiracial Society." *Journal of Marriage and Family* 73, no. 5 (2011): 1065–84.

———. "Measuring Marital Assimilation: Intermarriage among Natives and Immigrants." *Social Science Research* 30, no. 2 (2001): 289–312.

Racusen, Seth. "Fictions of Identity and Brazilian Affirmative Action." *National Black Law Journal* 21, no. 3 (2010).

Radcliffe-Brown, A. R. "On Joking Relationships." *Africa* 13, no. 3 (1940): 195–210.

Rangel, Marcos A. "Marriage, Cohabitation, and Intrahousehold Bargaining: Evidence from Brazilian Couples." Unpublished manuscript, Department of Economics, UCLA, 2003.

Reece, Robert L. "'What Are You Mixed With?': The Effect of Multiracial Identification on Perceived Attractiveness." *Review of Black Political Economy* 43 (2016): 139–47.

Rhodes, G., K. Lee, R. Palermo, M. Weiss, S. Yoshikawa, P. Clissa, T. Williams, et al. "Attractiveness of Own-Race, Other-Race, and Mixed-Race Faces." *Perception* 34, no. 3 (2005): 319–40.

Ribeiro, Carlos Antonio Costa, and Nelson do Valle Silva. "Cor, Educação E Casamento: Tendências Da Seletividade Marital No Brasil, 1960 a 2000." *DADOS* 52, no. 1 (2009): 7–51.

Ribeiro de Souza, Rolf. "As Representações Do Homem Negro E Suas Consequências." *Revista Forúm Identidades* 6 (2009): 97–115.

Rockquemore, Kerry-Ann, and David L. Brunsma. *Beyond Black: Biracial Identity in America*. New York: Rowman and Littlefield, 2007.

Rodriguez, Clara. *Changing Race: Latinos, the Census, and the History of Ethnicity in the United States*. New York: New York University Press, 2000.

Rodríguez-García, Dan. "Intermarriage and Integration Revisited: International Experiences and Cross-Disciplinary Approaches." *Annals of the American Academy of Political and Social Science* 662, no. 1 (2015): 8–36.

Roediger, David. *The Wages of Whiteness: Race and the Making of the American Working Class*. New York: Verso, 1999.

Root, M. P. P. *Love's Revolution: Interracial Marriage*. Philadelphia, PA: Temple University Press, 2001.

Rosenfeld, M. J. "Racial, Educational and Religious Endogamy in the United States: A Comparative Historical Perspective." *Social Forces* 87, no. 1 (2008): 1–31.

Roth, Wendy. *Race Migrations: Latinos and the Cultural Transformation of Race*. Stanford, CA: Stanford University Press, 2012.

Sansone, Livio. *Blackness without Ethnicity: Constructing Race in Brazil*. New York: Palgrave Macmillan, 2003.

Sawyer, Mark. "Don't Even Try to Blame It on Rio." *The Root*, July 3, 2008. http://www.theroot.com/dont-even-try-to-blame-it-on-rio-1790899983.

Schwartz, Christine, and Robert D. Mare. "Trends in Educational Assortative Marriage from 1940 to 2003." *Demography* 43 (2005): 621–46.

Schwartzman, Luisa Farah. "Does Money Whiten? Intergenerational Changes in Racial Classification in Brazil." *American Sociological Review* 72, no. 6 (2007): 940.

Scott, Marvin, and Stanford Lyman. "Accounts." *American Sociological Review* 33 (1968): 46–62.

Sharkey, Patrick. *Stuck in Place: Urban Neighborhoods and the End Process toward Racial Equality*. Chicago, IL: University of Chicago Press, 2013.

Shelton, Nicole J., and Jennifer A. Richeson. "Interracial Interactions: A Relational Approach." *Advances in Experimental Social Psychology* 38 (2006): 121–81.

Sheriff, Robin E. *Dreaming Equality: Color, Race, and Racism in Urban Brazil*. New Brunswick, NJ: Rutgers University Press, 2001.

Silva, Carlos Alberto Figueiredo da, and Jorge França Motta. "Relendo O Significado De RaçA." *Revista Augustus* 14 (2009): 71–84.

Silva, Graziella Morães da. "Ações Afirmativas No Brasil E Na África Do Sul." *Tempo Social, Revista de Sociologia da USP* 18, no. 2 (2006): 132.

Silva, Graziella Morães da, and Elisa P. Reis. "The Multiple Dimensions of Racial Mixture in Rio de Janeiro, Brazil: From Whitening to Brazilian Negritude." *Ethnic and Racial Studies*, 35, no. 3 (2011): 382–99.

——. "Perceptions of Racial Discrimination among Black Professionals in Rio De Janeiro." *Latin American Research Review* 46, no. 2 (2011).

Silva, Graziella Morães da, and Marcelo Paixão. "Mixed and Unequal: New Perspectives on Brazilian Ethnoracial Relations." In *Pigmentocracies: Ethnicity, Race and Color in Latin America*, edited by Edward Telles and PERLA (Project on Ethnicity and Race in Latin America), 172–217. Chapel Hill: University of North Carolina Press, 2014.

Silva, Nelson do Valle, and Carlos Hasenbalg. "Relações Raciais No Brasil Contemporâneo." Rio de Janeiro: Rio Fundo Editora, 1992.

Simpson, Amelia. *Xuxa: The Mega-Marketing of Gender, Race, and Modernity*. Philadelphia, PA: Temple University Press, 1993.

Sims, J. P. "Beautiful Stereotypes: The Relationship between Physical Attractiveness and Mixed-Race Identity." *Identities* 19, no. 1 (2012): 61–80.

Skidmore, Thomas E. "Bi-racial U.S.A. vs. Multi-racial Brazil: Is the Contrast Still Valid?" *Journal of Latin American Studies* 25, no. 2 (1993): 373–86.

——. *Black into White: Race and Nationality in Brazilian Thought*. New York: Oxford University Press, 1974.

Smith, Sandra S., and Mignon R. Moore. "Intraracial Diversity and Relations among African-Americans: Closeness among Black Students at a Predominantly White University." *American Journal of Sociology* 106, no. 1 (2000): 1–39.

Smock, Pamela J. "Cohabitation in the United States: An Appraisal of Research Themes, Findings, and Implications." *Annual Review of Sociology* 26, no. 1 (2000): 1–20.

Song, Miri. "Is Intermarriage a Good Indicator of Integration?" *Journal of Ethnic and Migration Studies* 35, no. 2 (2009): 331–48.

Song, Miri, and Peter Aspinall. "Is Racial Mismatch a Problem for Young 'Mixed Race' People in Britain? The Findings of Qualitative Research." *Ethnicities* 12, no. 6 (2012): 730–53.

Sovik, Liv. "We Are Family: Whiteness in the Brazilian Media." *Journal of Latin American Cultural Studies* 13 (2004): 315–25.

Staley, Austin J. "Racial Democracy in Brazilian Marriage: Toward a Typology of Negro-White Intermarriage in Five Brazilian Communities." *American Catholic Sociological Review* 21, no. 2 (1960): 146–64.

Steinbugler, Amy C. *Beyond Loving: Intimate Racework in Lesbian, Gay, and Straight Interracial Relationships*. New York: Oxford University Press, 2012.

Stepan, Nancy. *The Hour of Eugenics: Race, Gender, and Nation in Latin America*. Ithaca, NY: Cornell University Press, 1991.

Strauss, Anselm. *Mirrors and Masks: The Search for Identity* London: Martin Robertson, 1969.

Sue, Christina A. *Land of the Cosmic Race: Race Mixture, Racism, and Blackness in Mexico*. New York: Oxford University Press, 2013.

Sue, Christina A., and Tanya Golash-Boza. "'It Was Only a Joke': How Racial Humour Fuels Colour-Blind Ideologies in Mexico and Peru." *Ethnic and Racial Studies* 36, no. 10 (2013): 1582–98.

Swidler, Ann. "Culture in Action: Symbols and Strategies." *American Sociological Review* 51, no. 2 (1986): 273–86.

Sykes, Gresham M., and David Matza. "Techniques of Neutralization: A Theory of Delinquency." *American Sociological Review* 22, no. 6 (1957): 664–70.

Tatum, Beverly Daniel. *"Why Are All the Black Kids Sitting Together in the Cafeteria?": And Other Conversations about Race.* New York: Basic, 2003.

Telles, Edward E. *Race in Another America: The Significance of Skin Color in Brazil.* Princeton, NJ: Princeton University Press, 2004.

———. "Who Are the Morenas?" *Social Forces* 73, no. 4 (1995): 1609–11.

Telles, Edward E., and PERLA (Project on Ethnicity and Race in Latin America), eds., *Pigmentocracies: Ethnicity, Race and Color in Latin America.* Chapel Hill: University of North Carolina Press, 2014.

Telles, Edward E., and Christina A. Sue. "Race Mixture: Boundary Crossing in Comparative Perspective." *Annual Review of Sociology* 35 (2009): 129–46.

Telles, Edward E., and René Flores. "Not Just Color: Whiteness, Nation, and Status in Latin America." *Hispanic American Historical Review* 93, no. 3 (2013): 411–50.

Telles, Edward E., and Stanley Bailey. "Racial Ambiguity among the Brazilian Population." *Ethnic and Racial Studies* 25, no. 3 (2002): 415–41.

———. "Understanding Latin American Beliefs about Racial Inequality." *American Journal of Sociology* 118, no. 6 (2013): 1559–95.

Telles, Edward E., and Tianna Paschel. "Who Is Black, White, or Mixed Race? How Skin Color, Status, and Nation Shape Racial Classification in Latin America." *American Journal of Sociology* 120, no. 3 (2014): 864–907.

Tilly, Charles. "Social Boundary Mechanisms." *Philosophy of the Social Sciences* 34, no. 2 (2004): 211.

Tucker, M. Belinda, and Claudia Mitchell-Kernan. "New Trends in Black American Interracial Marriage: The Social Structural Context." *Journal of Marriage and the Family* 52, no. 1 (1990): 209–18.

Twine, France Winddance. *Racism in a Racial Democracy: The Maintenance of White Supremacy in Brazil.* New Brunswick, NJ: Rutgers University Press, 1998.

———. *A White Side of Black Britain: Interracial Intimacy and Racial Literacy.* Durham, NC: Duke University Press, 2010.

Twine, France Winddance, and Amy C. Steinbugler. "The Gap between Whites and Whiteness: Interracial Intimacy and Racial Literacy." *Du Bois Review* 3, no. 2 (2006): 341–63.

Vasquez-Tokos, Jessica. *Marriage Vows, Racial Choices.* New York: Russell Sage Foundation, 2017.

Vianna, Oliveira. *Populações Meridionais Do Brasil.* Brasilia: Senado Federal, 1952.

Vigoya, Mara Viveros. "Más Que Una Cuestión De Piel: Determinantes Sociales Y Orientaciones Subjetivas En Los Encuentros Y Desencuentros Heterosexuales

Interraciales En Bogotá." In *Raza, Etnicidad Y Sexualidades: Ciudadanía Y Multiculturalismo En América Latina*, edited by Peter Wade, Fernando Urrea, and Mara Viveros, 247–79. Bogotá: Universidad Nacional de Colombia, Facultad de Ciencias Humanas, Centro de Estudios Sociales (CES), 2008.

Wade, Peter. *Race and Ethnicity in Latin America*. Chicago, IL: Pluto Press, 1997.

Waters, Mary. *Ethnic Options: Choosing Identities in America*. Berkeley: University of California Press, 1990.

Weiss, Robert S. *Learning from Strangers: The Art and Method of Qualitative Interview Studies*. New York: Free Press, 1995.

Wells-Barnett, Ida B., and Alfreda M. Duster. *Crusade for Justice: The Autobiography of Ida B. Wells*. Chicago, IL: University of Chicago Press, 1970.

Wells-Barnett, Ida B., Frederick Douglass, and Society for the Furtherance of the Brotherhood of Man. "Southern Horrors: Lynch Law in All Its Phases." *New York Age*, 1892.

Wilkins, Amy C. "Stigma and Status: Interracial Intimacy and Intersectional Identities among Black College Men." *Gender & Society 26, no. 2* (2012).

———. *Wannabes, Goths, and Christians: The Boundaries of Sex, Style, and Status.* Chicago, IL: University of Chicago Press, 2008.

Williams, Erica Lorraine. *Sex Tourism in Bahia: Ambiguous Entanglements*. Urbana: University of Illinois Press, 2013.

Williams, Kim M. *Mark One or More: Civil Rights in Multiracial America*. Ann Arbor: University of Michigan Press, 2006.

Wilson, William Julius. *When Work Disappears: World of the New Urban Poor*. New York: Vintage Press, 1997.

Wimmer, Andreas. "Beyond and Below Racial Homophily: Erg Models of a Friendship Network Documented on Facebook." *American Journal of Sociology* 116, no. 2 (2010): 583–642.

———. *Ethnic Boundary Making: Institutions, Power, Networks*. New York: Oxford University Press, 2013.

Wuthnow, Robert J. "Taking Talk Seriously: Religious Discourse as Social Practice." *Journal for the Scientific Study of Religion* 50, no. 1 (2011): 1–21.

Yancey, George. "Who Interracially Dates: An Examination of the Characteristics of Those Who Have Interracially Dated." *Journal of Comparative Family Studies* 33, no. 2 (2002): 179–90.

Yodanis, C., S. R Lauer, and Risako Ota. "Inter-ethnic Romantic Relationships: Enacting Affiliative Ethnic Identities." *Journal of Marriage and Family* 74 (2012): 1–17.

Zamora, Sylvia. "Racial Remittances: The Effect of Migration on Racial Ideologies in Mexico and the United States." *Sociology of Race and Ethnicity* 2, no. 4 (2016): 466–81.

INDEX

Page numbers followed by *t* refer to tables.

ABOUT THE AUTHOR

Chinyere K. Osuji is assistant professor of sociology at Rutgers University at Camden. She received her PhD from UCLA and her master's degree from Harvard University. She was the 2011–13 postdoctoral fellow at the University of Pennsylvania Center for Africana Studies. Chinyere K. Osuji's research has been funded by the National Science Foundation, the US Department of Education US–Brazil Consortium, and the Fulbright Institute of International Education (IIE). Her qualitative research on interracial marriage has won awards from the Population Association of America and the American Sociological Association Section on Racial and Ethnic Minorities. Chinyere K. Osuji was born in the United States to two Igbo (Nigerian) parents and hails from Chicago, Illinois, where she attended Whitney Young Magnet High School.